THE BOOK OF

HEBREWS

CHRIST IS GREATER

Advancing the Ministries of the Gospel
AMG *Publishers*

God's Word to you is our highest calling.

TWENTY-FIRST CENTURY
BIBLICAL COMMENTARY SERIES®

THE BOOK OF

HEBREWS

CHRIST IS GREATER

STEVEN
GER

GENERAL EDITORS

MAL COUCH &
ED HINDSON

The Books of Hebrews: Christ Is Greater
By Steven Ger
Copyright © 2009 by Scofield Ministries
Published by AMG Publishers
6815 Shallowford Road
Chattanooga, TN 37421

TWENTY-FIRST CENTURY BIBLICAL COMMENTARY SERIES is a registered trademark of AMG Publishers.

ISBN–13: 978-161715-496-6

First Published: August 2009
Cover Design by ImageWright, Inc.
Editing and Text Design by Warren Baker
Editorial assistance provided by Weller Editorial Services, Chippewa Lake, MI

Printed in Canada
14 13 12 11 10 09 –T– 8 7 6 5 4 3 2 1

To my great-aunt Hilda Koser:
Missionary to the Jewish people and Bible storyteller extraordinaire, on whose shoulders I stand and in whose footsteps I follow. A great aunt, indeed: my teacher, mentor, model, and second grandmother; the one who, while I was still an infant, used to whisper softly in my ear, "You are God's child"; and the person who first impressed on me the utter indispensability of the epistle to the Hebrews.

Twenty-First Century Biblical Commentary Series®

MAL COUCH, TH.D., AND ED HINDSON, D.PHIL.

The New Testament has guided the Christian church for over two thousand years. This one testament is made up of twenty-seven books, penned by godly men through the inspiration of the Holy Spirit. It tells us of the life of Jesus Christ, His atoning death for our sins, His miraculous resurrection, His ascension back to heaven, and the promise of His second coming. It also tells the story of the birth and growth of the church and the people and principles that shaped it in its earliest days. The New Testament concludes with the book of Revelation pointing ahead to the glorious return of Jesus Christ.

Without the New Testament, the message of the Bible would be incomplete. The Old Testament emphasizes the promise of a coming Messiah. It constantly points us ahead to the One who is coming to be the King of Israel and the Savior of the world. But the Old Testament ends with this event still unfulfilled. All of its ceremonies, pictures, types, and prophecies are left awaiting the arrival of the "Lamb of God who takes away the sin of the world" (John 1:29).

The message of the New Testament represents the timeless truth of God. As each generation seeks to apply that truth to its specific context, an up-to-date commentary needs to be created just for them. The editors and authors of the Twenty-First Century Biblical Commentary Series have endeavored to do just that. This team of scholars represents conservative, evangelical, and dispensational scholarship at its best. The individual authors may differ on minor points of interpretation, but all are convinced that the Old and New Testaments teach a dispensational framework for biblical history. They also hold to a pretribulational and premillennial understanding of biblical prophecy.

The French scholar René Pache reminded each succeeding generation, "If the power of the Holy Spirit is to be made manifest anew among us, it is of primary importance that His message should regain its due place. Then we shall be able to put the enemy to flight by the sword of the Spirit which is the Word of God."

The book of Hebrews is the most unique of all the Epistles. It is unsigned; therefore its author remains a mystery. It is based on a thorough knowledge of the Old Testament; thus it presupposes the reader is familiar with the Hebrew scriptures. It exalts Jesus Christ as Savior in contrast to the inadequacy of the animal sacrifices of ancient Israel. Yet it is addressed to both Jewish and Gentile readers, emphasizing the total sufficiency of Christ's atonement for our sins. Steven Ger's treatment as a Jewish Christian is especially appropriate and insightful for this particular epistle.

John Calvin said of Hebrews, "There is no book in Holy Scripture which speaks so clearly of the priesthood of Christ (and) so splendidly extols the power and worth of that unique sacrifice which he offered by his death." Philip E. Hughes adds, "The author of Hebrews has a superb perspective on Christ's transcendental supremacy, the total efficacy of his sacrifice and the logic of the incarnation." He also observes the author's pastoral concern, earnest warnings, and sympathetic encouragement, stating: "all of which combine to make this writing indeed a tract for the times . . . and for all times."

Contents

Foreword

I am a fourth-generation Jewish believer, nurtured in the faith from birth, whose family first found our Messiah almost a century ago. My great-grandmother Helen Koser was introduced to Jesus in Brooklyn, New York, by Jewish missionaries during the early years of the twentieth century. While an introduction to the gospel is not generally considered a common part of the American Jewish immigrant experience, nonetheless, the American Board of Missions to the Jews did indeed have an extensive outreach in the Brooklyn of that time, of which my family are grateful recipients.

My great-grandmother Helen, having received the Good News, ensured that her eight children were also introduced to the Jewish Messiah. Although all received instruction in the faith, only a few of her children joined their mother in trusting Jesus. One such believing daughter was my grandmother Rose, and another was my great-aunt Hilda, who would become a forty-year career missionary to the Jewish people in Brooklyn. My grandmother, my mother, and eventually myself would be the beneficiaries of her spiritual instruction. She later became a de facto surrogate grandmother following my grandmother Rose's death. In four generations, I was the first male in my family to believe in Jesus, and my aunt always took a special interest in my spiritual nurture and development.

I always had a plethora of what I thought at the time were deep and penetrating questions concerning Judaism, Christianity, and the Bible. My aunt never failed to provide satisfying answers. I distinctly remember one such occasion when, having read through the Bible in its entirety twice in a row, I was interested in finding a shortcut through that circuitous journey in preparation for my next attempt. I therefore asked my aunt to enumerate what she considered to be the indispensable books of the Bible, both the Old and New Testament, without which inclusion our theology and understanding of our faith would be deficient. Her opinion was that perhaps *the* one indispensable

New Testament book was the epistle to the Hebrews! It is only in this book, she reasoned, that the New Testament reveals with great depth and vivid imagery the present work of our Messiah as perfect high priest, his fulfillment of Yom Kippur, the Levitical Day of Atonement, the Melchizedekian priesthood and the necessity of the new covenant, particularly as it is contrasted with the Mosaic covenant.

With time and study, my appreciation of Hebrews has only deepened. The salvific colors and messianic hues painted by Hebrews' anonymous master wordsmith alternately shade, brighten, and intensify in relation to the spiritual maturity of the reader. Not for the faint of heart is this epistle. Hebrews demands attentive, conscientious study but yields rich theological rewards for those who diligently apply themselves. Together with Romans, it is no overstatement to claim that it ranks as the greatest of the epistles.

The challenge that Hebrews poses to the student of the Bible is apparent from the outset; indeed, it "fairly bristles with a number of large and perplexing problems."[1] This enigmatic epistle reveals neither the identity of its author nor its recipients, not the date of its composition nor the location to which it was originally sent, nor even the basic circumstance and occasion for its having been written. In the candid words of William Lane in the introduction to his comprehensive commentary:

> Hebrews is a delight for the person who enjoys puzzles. Its form is unusual, its setting in life is uncertain, and its argument is unfamiliar. . . . Undefined are the identity of the writer, his conceptual background, the character and location of the community addressed, the circumstances and date of composition, the setting in life, the nature of the crisis to which the document is a response, the literary genre, and the purpose and plan of the work. Although these undefined issues continue to be addressed and debated vigorously, no real consensus has been reached.[2]

What separates this particular commentary and, indeed, necessitates its publication, is this author's identity as a Jewish believer in Jesus. It is the singular combination of my ethnic and spiritual background coupled with decades of extensive advanced education in both Christianity and Judaism that qualifies me to contribute yet another submission to the already crowded field of Hebrews commentaries. Nevertheless, commentaries on Hebrews written from the perspective of and with the sensitivities peculiar to a Jewish Christian are in the distinct minority. Hebrews, after all, deals with specifically Jewish issues, questions, concerns and controversies among the believers of the first century. These issues and questions are not often examined through Jewish eyes or explained using Jewish categories. I believe that providing such a basic cultural insight facilitates understanding in the study of this foundational work.

The book of Hebrews, when properly understood and comfortably digested, offers a great deal of both instruction and comfort to the modern church. The author never allows his grand doctrinal themes to overshadow his practical pastoral concerns, and he carefully seasons his theological presentation with generous amounts of faith (4:2; 6:1, 12; 10:22, 38, 39; 11:1–40; 12:2; 13:7), multiple portions of hope (3:6; 6:11, 18; 7:19; 10:23; 11:1) and enthusiastic helpings of love (6:10; 10:24; 13:1).

Hebrews resonates with every believing heart that has ever expressed the desire to "know" Jesus more deeply and intimately. The text offers us a profound glimpse into our Lord's present ministry as the High Priest who intercedes on our behalf. It reveals His acute identification with every believer as well as His personal involvement in every aspect of our lives. In a manner superior to every other New Testament book, Hebrews uniquely reminds us that the motivating purpose behind Jesus' very real incarnation was that he might become "a merciful and faithful high priest," who, because he had been "tempted in that which He has suffered" is now empowered to "come to the aid of those who are tempted" (2:17–18). Hebrews transforms our understanding of Christ, our *Christology*, from abstract theology to intimate relationship.

I submit this volume as my surrogate to accompany you on your sojourn through Hebrews' profound lessons, arguments and exhortations. The following are the modest study notes of this particular "Hebrew of Hebrews"; the views of a twenty-first-century messianic Jew as he ponders this extraordinary epistle to his ethnic and spiritual ancestors. This project is an outgrowth of my family legacy, and I pray that this Jewish Christian perspective may prove of value as you study the book of Hebrews.

Steven Charles Ger
Sojourner Ministries
Garland, Texas

Background of Hebrews

Authorship

It is no exaggeration to claim that the authorship of the book of Hebrews is perhaps the greatest mystery of the Bible. The book itself is unsigned, anonymous. While there can be no doubt that the author's identity was known to its original recipients (13:19), and that he was a member of Timothy's (and Paul's?) circle, the writer's identity became lost quite early in the swirling mists of the church's early history. The writer of a commentary on Hebrews must apply, of necessity, the skills not only of theologian, linguist, and grammarian, but of amateur detective as well. There is not only a text to be understood and explained, but also a mystery to be solved. The clues are collected from both internal evidence (what the text itself says) and external evidence (what has been said about the text).

There are few claims one can make concerning the author with any certainty. What we know is that his command of the Koine Greek language is exquisite,[1] arguably superior to any other New Testament author, with perhaps the exception of Luke. Luke Johnson highlights the breadth of the author's vocabulary: "154 words not found elsewhere in the New Testament, 90 found in only one other New Testament composition, and 10 found nowhere else in Greek literature before Hebrews."[2]

This master wordsmith is unquestionably Jewish; his familiarity with Jewish ritual, custom, tradition, and concerns, and his sheer mastery of Hebrew Scripture prove this point conclusively. The fact that his Old Testament quotations are exclusively drawn from the Septuagint, the second-century BC Greek translation,[3] lead many to believe that the author is a

Hellenistic (Greek) Jew born outside the land of Israel among the Jewish diaspora of the Roman Empire,[4] just as were Paul, Barnabas, and Apollos.

The author is a well-trained master of the rhetorical style of communication common in the first-century Greco-Roman milieu. His argument utilizes all three of Aristotle's so-called artistic proofs of persuasion: *ethos* (an appeal based on reputation and character, usually the speaker's, but in this case, the reputation and character of its subject matter, Jesus), *pathos* (an appeal based on the recipients' emotions, passions, and will), and *logos* (an appeal to reason and the intellect).[5] Unfortunately, a dash of his stylistic glory is lost in the translation. In English it is difficult to appreciate his use of alliteration, assonance, and wordplays, the repetition of particular words throughout successive sentences as well as the addition and subtraction of conjunctions for effect.[6]

This combination of biblical literacy, Greek linguistic fluency, and powerful rhetorical technique, drenched with the inspiration of God's Spirit, created the perfect storm to birth a timeless message for both the ears and eyes of the church throughout the ages. Over the centuries, multiple theories have been offered, both the creative and the pedantic, concerning candidates that either stir the imagination or rouse incredulity over who penned this unique contribution to Holy Scripture[7] (see *Thematic Elements Common to Hebrews and Paul's Epistles* on the next page).

Paul. Authorship of Hebrews has been attributed to the apostle Paul more than to every other authorial possibility combined throughout the history of the church. As to external evidence, by the fourth century and as early as the late second century, many in both the eastern and western branches of the church held that Paul was the author. Indeed, the earliest known manuscript portion that we possess of Hebrews (labeled by scholars as P[46]), dating from approximately AD 200, is in a collection of Paul's letters. Later on, in the Western church, heavyweight ecclesiastical patriarchs Jerome and Augustine favored Pauline authorship, citing the weightiness of traditional Eastern church sentiment. By the turn of the fifth century, church father John Chrysostom went on record for Pauline authorship, even identifying the recipients as Jewish Christians in Judea. Indeed, the antiquity of this tradition is the strongest argument favoring Pauline authorship.

According to fourth-century church historian Eusebius, it was second-century Clement of Alexandria's assertion that Hebrews was originally written in Hebrew by Paul and translated into Greek by his associate, Luke, and purposely left unsigned due to either the negative reputation that Paul had in the Jewish community of the first century or apostolic modesty.[8] Third-century church father Origin, following shortly after Clement of Alexandria in the Eastern church, disagreed with his predecessor's opinion, holding that the document revealed no indication of having been translated from Hebrew, and that it was, contra translation, characterized by a healthy excess of Greek idiom. In addition, Eusebius records contemporary reservations in the West concerning Pauline authorship[9] (nonetheless, the church historian does not exclude Hebrews from his own recorded list of Paul's epistles).[10]

That these reservations concerning Paul's authorship stubbornly refused to evolve into outright rejection was no doubt fueled by the numerous thematic similarities and shared concerns between Paul's writings and the letter to the Hebrews.

Elements Common to Hebrews and Paul's Epistles

Theme	Hebrews	Paul
Christ's preincarnate glory and active role in creation	1:2–3	1 Cor. 8:6; 2 Cor 4:4; Col. 1:15–17
Christ's humiliation	2:14–17	Phil. 2:7
Christ's obedience	5:1–10	Rom. 5:12–21; Phil. 2:8
Distribution of spiritual gifts	2:4	1 Cor. 12:11
The superiority of the new covenant over the Mosaic covenant	Heb. 8:6–13	2 Cor. 3:3–17
Abraham	6:11–18; 11:8, 17	Rom. 4:17–20; Gal. 3:16–18
Sports metaphors	12:1	1 Cor. 9:24
Contrast of spiritual "milk" and "solid food"	5:11–14	1 Cor. 3:1–3

Although many of the book's themes were congruent with those of Paul's epistles, Origen remained unconvinced by these points of contact. He felt that the literary style of Hebrews belonged to an author other than Paul, perhaps an associate or student of the apostle. Numerous subsequent students of the New Testament, through this present age, have drawn the same conclusion. A robust example of this reticence is reformer John Calvin, who briskly summarized, "Paul was not the author . . . the thought of the epistle is not Paul's, the language is not Paul's, and the technique of Old Testament quotation is not Paul's."[12] The most obvious difference between Hebrews and Paul's epistles is that Hebrews is unsigned, whereas every Pauline epistle begins with his name in the first verse.

Specific differences that arise between Hebrews and Paul's epistles are as follows. First, unlike Paul's epistles, Hebrews contains neither personal anecdote nor testimony, nor lays claim to apostolic authority. Second, Paul's epistles are characterized by a vibrant emotionalism that is absent in Hebrews. Third, when quoting Hebrew Scripture, the author uses the Septuagint, the Greek translation. Fourth, commonly expected Pauline themes fail to make an appearance in Hebrews, such as justification by faith, the distinction between Jews and Gentiles, the resurrection of believers, liberty, the flesh, and grace. Conversely, major themes of Hebrews, such as the Day of Atonement, Jesus' high priesthood, and the Levitical rituals are likewise absent in Paul's letters. William Lane explains, "Many of the emphases of Hebrews are alien to those of Paul."[13]

For these reasons, it is difficult to attribute with any confidence the authorship of Hebrews to Paul. Yet once Paul's candidacy is removed from serious consideration, a plethora of secondary and tertiary candidates are thrust forward to fill the resulting void.

Clement of Rome. An alternative to Pauline authorship is that of Clement of Rome. Origen records that by the third century, some in the church had attributed Hebrews to Clement. Indeed, of all the authorial candidates for which we possess writing samples, only Clement shares with the author of Hebrews the stylistic convention of attributing Old Testament quotations directly to the Holy Spirit. However, while Clement may have been familiar with Hebrews and liberally quoted from it in his epistle to the Corinthians,[14] in some instances his teaching seemingly contradicts that of Hebrews (specifically, concerning the establishment of a Christian priestly hierarchy, see 1 Clem. 32:2; 40:5). Furthermore, if Clement was the original author, it is difficult to understand why the early Western church failed to ascribe confident credit to their own Roman bishop. Therefore, his candidacy must be rejected.

Luke. Likewise, Origen also recorded the common attribution in his day of Hebrews to Paul's close associate and biographer, Luke. As noted above, Clement of Alexandria (not to be confused with Clement of Rome) believed that Luke served as Paul's translator based on the superior Greek linguistic style of Hebrews. While the Greek of Hebrews is of comparable (arguably superior) quality to Luke's gospel and Acts, evidence of education is not evidence of authorship. Furthermore, major themes in Hebrews, such as Jesus' Melchizedekian priesthood and God's Sabbath rest, are completely absent, not even alluded to, in Luke's works. Aside from a clever Greek vernacular, the only positive attribute pointing to Luke as author is his close association with

Paul. While an unlikely candidate, nevertheless Luke, as a well-educated Hellenistic Jewish Christian,[15] possessed the education, capacity, and background experience to have written Hebrews.

Barnabas. Alone among the early fathers of the church, Tertullian, at the turn of the third century, confidently assigned the authorship of Hebrews to Barnabas.[16] This candidate certainly possesses the appropriate biographical resume: a Hellenistic Levite of the Jewish diaspora who was well connected to the original Jerusalem church and was a respected colleague of the apostles (who provided his nickname, "Barnabas," Aramaic for "son of exhortation" or, more likely, "son of encouragement"). Of course, he was also a close associate and long-standing partner of Paul and was, indeed, an apostle in his own right (Acts 14:14; 1 Cor. 9:6). As a Levite, his facility with Jewish ritual and imagery would have been extensive.

Some have made a fanciful connection between Barnabas and Hebrews, seeing a coded signature, a veritable tipping of the author's hand of anonymity in the letter's conclusion, when the author (*Barnabas*, the *huios paraklēseōs*, "son of encouragement" or "exhortation," Acts 4:36) urges his readers in 13:22 to "bear with this word of exhortation" (*tou logou tēs paraklēseōs*). While this theory wins points for creativity, it is probably safest to avoid attributing to it much weight. Sometimes a word of exhortation is simply a word of exhortation.

Priscilla and Aquila. Church antiquity reveals not a whiff of the suggestion that Hebrews was the marital team project of Priscilla and Aquila. Nonetheless, this pair is the speculative darling candidacy of contemporary feminists, freethinkers, and progressive theologians, conjuring the possibility that the primary reason the author of Hebrews is unknown is the early church's discomfort with, and suppression of, female (co)authorship. What has placed the wind in the sails of this theory is the geographical association between Priscilla and Aquila with the Pauline/Timotheon locals of Rome (Rom. 16:3), Corinth (Acts 18:1-3), and Ephesus (Acts 18:18-28), and to their instruction of Apollos in the way of faith. Additionally, there are several uses by the author(s) of "we" in the text (although these are far from conclusive indication of plural authorship). Ultimately, however, it is difficult to accept a team authorship or even, as some propose, a predominantly feminine authorship of Hebrews in light of the very clear masculine singular participle used in 11:32. There is simply no satisfactory means to circumnavigate that enormous linguistic roadblock.

Peter. No historical record of any church tradition affirms Petrine authorship of Hebrews. Nonetheless, that has not impeded scholarly attempts to associate "the apostle to the circumcised" (Gal. 2:7) with the book of Hebrews.

Some common points of similarity exist between Hebrews and 1 Peter. For example, there are common metaphors, such as "spiritual milk" (Heb. 5:12; 1 Pet. 2:2), Jesus as Shepherd (Heb. 13:20; 1 Pet. 2:25), Jesus exalted at God's right hand (Heb. 1:13; 1 Pet. 3:22; also a main point in his temple address on the Day of Pentecost, Acts 2:34), the potency of Jesus' blood to eradicate sin once for all (Heb. 9:28; 1 Pet. 2:24; 3:18), and the sprinkling of that blood (Heb. 10:22; 12:24; 1 Pet. 1:2). Furthermore, both books concern themselves with exhortations to steadfastness in light of persecution (Heb. 10:32–35; 1 Pet. 4:12–19; 5:10).

Elements Common to Hebrews and Peter's Epistles

Theme	Hebrews	Peter
"Spiritual milk"	5:12	1 Pet. 2:2
Jesus as Shepherd	13:20	1 Pet. 2:25
Jesus exalted at God's right hand	1:13	1 Pet. 3:22; Acts 2:34
The potency of Jesus' blood to eradicate sin once for all	9:28	1 Pet. 2:24; 3:18
The sprinkling of Jesus' blood	10:22; 12:24	1 Pet. 1:2
Exhortations to steadfastness in light of persecution	10:32–35	1 Pet. 4:12–19; 5:10

Despite these commonalities, there is nothing of further substance to warrant the assignation of Hebrews to Peter. A variant of this theory, and equally uncompelling, is that Peter's amanuensis (secretary), Silas (1 Pet. 5:12; NASB Silvanus), another Jewish believer, recorded, polished, and elaborated on Peter's original dictation, accounting for both the thematic points of similarity between Peter's letters and Hebrews and their marked disparity in rhetorical style.

Jude. Paul Ellingworth makes brief mention of this dark horse candidate Jude, noting passing surface areas of commonality between Hebrews and Jude's epistle, such as angels and particular physical sins, etc.[17] However, the fatal flaw that dooms this theory is the suggestion that the brother of Jesus Himself would claim to have received the gospel indirectly (2:3).

Stephen. The proposal of Stephen as the author of Hebrews stretches credulity. The only possible evidence that might point to Stephen is the similarity between the Old Testament historical themes of Hebrews and those of Stephen's speech recorded by Luke in Acts 7. However, the irrefutable death knell for his candidacy is the fact that by the time Hebrews was written (certainly no earlier than AD 60), Stephen had been dead for at least twenty-five years.

Silas or John Mark. Completely lacking in antiquity of tradition and textual evidence (either internal or external), neither of these men's occasionally proposed authorial candidacies possesses merit aside from their prominent mention in Acts, their close Pauline association, and in Mark's case, his authorship of the gospel bearing his name, and in Silas's case, his participation in the composition of Peter's letters.

Apollos. This candidate hailed from Alexandria, Egypt, the most prominent city in the Roman Empire (behind only Rome itself) as well as the empire's premiere philosophical matrix, the locale of one of three of the empire's universities (the other two being in Athens and Tarsus). With a third of its population comprised of Jews, Alexandria was the de facto center of diaspora Hellenistic Judaism. Indeed, the city had served as the location of the translation of the Hebrew Bible into Greek, birthing the Septuagint in the second century BC.

Scripture certainly testifies to both the certain eloquence of Apollos and his command of Hebrew Scripture. A product of his hometown, he is portrayed in Acts as being an *anēr logios*, "an eloquent man," signifying that he was well trained in the art of rhetoric and exhibited a highly polished eloquence in his communication. In addition, Luke adds that he was thoroughly conversant, *dunatos*, "mighty" in the Scriptures, indicating that, with Apollos, there was just as much "steak" as "sizzle"; the content of his teaching matched his ability to deliver it. In addition, Apollos's association with Paul and company (Acts 18:24–28; 1 Cor. 1:2; 3:4–6; 4:6) and their associated geographic locales of Ephesus and Corinth is well established. Also, to be noted is that Apollos fits the author's self-description of one who had heard the gospel from others (2:3).

Nonetheless, regardless of Apollos's stunning resume, there is neither internal textual evidence with Hebrews itself nor external historical evidence to link Apollos to Hebrews. If Apollos was the author of Hebrews, it is difficult to understand why we have no record of even one person throughout the first fifteen centuries of church history who thought to assign the book to him. It was not until reformer Martin Luther arrived on the scene that Apollos found an advocate to plead his case. Certainly our earliest source, Clement of

Alexandria, whose writings finger Paul as author, would have been quick to proclaim the authorship of a native son of Alexandria if there had existed but a single tradition pointing in that direction. At best, one may state with Ellingworth that Apollos is "perhaps the least unlikely of the conjectures which have been put forward."[18]

Of course, the authorship of one candidate or another cannot be proven conclusively and must remain, at least in this dispensation, an enjoyable exercise in speculation. I will steadfastly and most assuredly avoid succumbing to the temptation of patronizing an epistolary favorite. In other words, the author refuses to back a horse in this literary race. As Johnson eloquently conveys, "The most important thing Hebrews tells us about the author, whoever he was, is that in the first decades of the Christian movement, another remarkable mind and heart besides Paul's was at work in interpreting the significance of the crucified and raised Messiah Jesus."[19]

It is Origen who gets the last word on the subject with his famous quote, almost universally cited in commentaries on Hebrews, "Who wrote the Epistle, God only knows the truth."[20]

Candidates for the Authorship of Hebrews

	Pro	Con
Paul	Antiquity of tradition Limited thematic similarity with epistles Accounts for mention of Timothy (13:23)	Antiquity of uncertainty, doubt and reservation Divergent literary style from epistles Writer claims second-generation believer status (2:3) Lack of self-reference and signature Absence of apostolic claim Exclusion of major Pauline themes Inclusion of non-Pauline themes
Clement of Rome	Author's quotation of Hebrews Attributes authorship of Old Testament to Holy Spirit	Contradictory theology Antiquity's fairly limited acknowledgment
Luke	Author's superior linguistic style Close association with Paul Correspondence with Heb. 2:3 Well-educated Hellenistic Jewish Christian	Exclusion of major Lukan themes Antiquity's fairly limited acknowledgment
Priscilla/ Aquila	Close association with Paul Instruction of Apollos Use of "we" in the text	Use of masculine singular participle (11:32) No church tradition

	Pro	Con
Barnabas	Apostle Levite Hellenistic Jewish Christian Association with the Twelve Close association with Paul	Antiquity's limited acknowledgment Writer claims second-generation believer status (2:3) No mention of Levites in text
Peter	"Apostle to the circumcised" (Gal. 2:7) Surface similarities with 1 Peter	Absent in church tradition No substantive similarity with 1 Peter Rhetorical dissimilarity with 1 Peter
Jude	Surface areas of commonality with Jude	Writer claims second-generation believer status (2:3) No church tradition
Stephen	Similarity of Old Testament themes in Stephen's speech	Stephen died before Hebrews was written No church tradition
Silas	Prominent mention in Acts Close association with Paul	No church tradition No internal or external evidence
Mark	Prominent mention in Acts and author of Mark's gospel Close association with Paul	No church tradition No internal or external evidence
Apollos	From Alexandria, the center of Hellenistic Judaism Eloquence emphasized in Acts (18:24) Association with Paul Was a second-generation believer (2:3)	No internal or external evidence No church tradition, not even Clement of Alexandria

Date of Composition

While the date of Hebrews' composition cannot be affirmed with certainty, nonetheless, there are clear chronological boundaries through which we cannot reasonably pass. In relation to the outer perimeter of compositional possibility, a date later than AD 95 cannot be accepted. As Clement of Rome's First Epistle to the Corinthians (dated AD 95–96 at the latest) contains quotations from and allusions to the book of Hebrews, Hebrews, of necessity, must have been written prior to the composition of Clement's epistle. Furthermore, the plausibility of the first-century bishop of Rome quoting as holy writ that which was "hot off the press" is dubious. Time is required for Hebrews to have gained widespread recognition in the church.

The outer perimeter of compositional possibility retracts further when one considers the career of Timothy, casually mentioned by the author of Hebrews in passing (13:23). Timothy is clearly still in active missionary work at the time of writing. However, church tradition records that from the early 80s through his death in the mid–AD 90s, Timothy was firmly ensconced as the bishop of Ephesus. This fact provides a date no later than AD 82.

Moreover and perhaps decisively, the author's use of the present tense (5:1; 7:5; 8:3–4ff.; 9:6, 9, 22; 10:1–4, 8; 13:10) clearly indicates that the sacrificial system was still fully functional at the time Hebrews was written.[21] Therefore, it was most likely written prior to the destruction of the temple in Jerusalem in AD 70. Most assuredly, if the author of Hebrews penned his letter subsequent to the temple's demolition, it is inconceivable that this master of rhetorical persuasion would fail to mention or allude to the crowning illustration of his argument: that of Israel's incomparable temple reduced to inglorious ruin and rubble. In this context, an argument such as the one made concerning the perpetuation of inadequate Levitical sacrifices (10:1) would neither make sense nor possess force. In addition, if the temple had been razed prior to Hebrews composition, it is implausible to imagine that a verbal imaginer of this proficiency would be content to assert that the Mosaic covenant was merely "ready to disappear" (8:13).[22]

As to the logical starting point of compositional possibility, the author's reference to Timothy (13:23) also provides our earliest possible date. It is not until AD 50 that Timothy leaves Lystra, having been introduced to the Pauline mission (Acts 16:1–5). This date is buttressed by the author's reference to a considerable period of time having elapsed since the gospel had originally been proclaimed by the original apostles and further reference to the recipients of the letter being second-generation believers (2:3). Moreover, some time had passed since these recipients had first believed (enough time that they should be teachers [5:11–12] and had experienced a period of persecution [10:32–34]). These circumstances likely require the passing of several decades since the birth of the church in AD 30–33 and therefore reasonably prohibit a date of composition earlier than AD 60. Based on this data, the composition of Hebrews may be confidently dated between AD 60–69.

For example, if the letter's recipients lived in Rome (one of the two most likely locales, see discussion below, Destination), the date of AD 63–64 would fit quite well. Alternatively, if the letter's recipients were in Judea (the other likely locale, see discussion below, Destination), then a date of AD 65–66 would be preferred. The disastrous Jewish revolt against Roman occupation broke out in AD 66, spawning not just persecution against the church, but a national catastrophe that engulfed believers and unbelievers alike, as conflict escalated into full-scale war the following year.

If the author penned Hebrews at the dawn of conflict, or sometime immediately prior, it would seemingly fit the circumstances alluded to in Hebrews, as well as provide the context for the author's warning to depart "the camp" (13:13) prior to the community experiencing bloodshed (12:4). This corresponds to Jesus' warning for His disciples to flee Judea when warfare broke out against Jerusalem (Matt. 24:15–16; Luke 21:21) since the coming judgment was to be inflicted on the specific generation of Israel which had rejected Him (Luke 11:50–51: Matt. 23:35–36) and would result, in part, in the destruction of the temple (Matt 24:2).[23]

The outbreak of the war with Rome proved to be the event that finally separated Judea's Jewish believers and their fellow Jews. In an act considered traitorous by their fellow Jews, the Jewish believers en masse followed their Master's command to leave the nation and escape the catastrophic war. Traveling east and crossing the Jordan River, they fled to safety in the city of Pella,[24] one of the region's ten major Roman metropolises, collectively known as the Decapolis.

Recipients

General Information. Considering that the epistle's recipients remain unspecified throughout the text, the categorical lack of agreement as to whom this epistle was originally addressed does not surprise. The composition itself provides only clues to the identities of the original recipients and nothing more. The absence of any explicit identifiers places strict limits to our certainty in identification. Having been privy neither to the original author's counsel, it would be imprudent to claim the definitive final word. While it is true that both the available external and internal evidence pointing to the original recipients' identities allows us to advance beyond undomesticated speculation, nonetheless, the best result that may be expected is for the well-trained and educated student of Hebrews to weigh the available evidence and formulate a considered, calculated deduction.

Prior to consideration of areas of disagreement, it would be judicious to first present areas of near universal agreement concerning the recipients' collective identity. In the course of the letter, the author of Hebrews reveals to the readers his possession of specific knowledge of this particular community in several areas. One area of knowledge concerns their faith. These are what can be considered as second-generation believers, in other words, those who had come to faith through the testimony of the apostles, the eyewitnesses who had seen and heard Jesus personally (2:3).[25]

A second area of knowledge is the circumstances surrounding a variety of persecutions suffered on behalf of the community's faith, which, although thus far falling short of martyrdom (12:4), include public slander, abuse, imprisonment, and confiscation of personal property (10:32–35). Additional future persecution looms just over the horizon (13:13–14).

The author's third area of knowledge concerns the recipient community's past ("having ministered") and present ("in still ministering") actions of love toward the greater community of faith (6:9–11), of which they are apparently a subgroup (or possibly, a splinter faction). From this evidence, we can infer that most likely they are a specific house church in a particular city (10:25; 13:17, 24). Also transparently indicated in the text is that the author has a specific relationship and history together with them, expressing his hope to revisit the community (13:19). In addition, their interest in the release of his colleague Timothy is assumed (13:23).

Possible Recipients of the Book of Hebrews

	Pro	Con
Gentile Christians	Exhortation not to fall away from the living God (3:12) Exhortation to faithfulness in marriage (13:4)	In the New Testament, rejecting Jesus means rejecting God Jews not exempt from committing adultery Hebrews' argument of faithfulness in marriage rests on familiarity with the Hebrew Scripture. Return to Judaism was no temptation for Gentiles No church tradition that the letter was addressed to Gentiles Title "To the Hebrews" extends to the second century No Gentile churches
Jewish Non-Christians	Hebrews' argument is redundant to the Jewish believer Concern the warnings teach the believer's loss of salvation	Hebrews' sophisticated and advanced themes were not universally understood Absence of actual messianic prophecy Argument presumes agreement that Jesus is the Messiah Hebrews' warnings concern temporal and physical destiny

	Pro	Con
		Difficult to correlate the community's spiritual concerns relating to threatened persecution with non-Christians
Jewish Christians	Author presumes recognition that Jesus is the Son of God, the Messiah, Apostle and High Priest of "our confession," and "the Lord"	
	Recipients are "holy brethren," "beloved," "partakers of the heavenly calling," "partakers of Christ"	
	Timothy is "our brother"	
	Description of recipients' faith: they have "come to . . . Jesus," as second-generation believers; "we who have believed" exhorted to hold fast to "our confession" and "our hope" and "this hope we have"; admonished not to "throw away your confidence" in "the covenant by which he was sanctified"; endurance through persecution was motivated by faith	
	Recipients are "those who have once been enlightened and have tasted of the heavenly gift and have been made partakers of the Holy Spirit, and have tasted the good word of God and the powers of the age to come"	
	Admonishes lack of spiritual progress, not failure to spiritually begin	

Community Candidates. The areas of disagreement regarding Hebrews' original recipients are profound, even extending to a lack of universal consensus that it was written to Christian believers. Altogether there are three main groups to whom Hebrews may have potentially been written: a church community of Gentile Christians, a community of non-Christian Jews,[26] and a church community of Jewish Christians. The evidence for and likelihood of each alternative will be weighed in turn.

Gentile Christians. Oddly, for a book that has been traditionally designated as having been written "to the Hebrews," there are some who reject that tradition. They see the recipients as being not Jewish at all, but rather Gentile believers in Jesus. Lacking a shred of church tradition or any external evidence to this end, the entire position rests on the passage wherein the author exhorts his recipients not to fall away from the living God (3:12). This "falling away" is understood to indicate a lapse into paganism, certainly a more reasonable temptation for a fresh-faithed Gentile audience than any Jewish (messianic or not) community.[27]

One last piece of internal evidence comes from the grab bag of ethical obligations contained in the final chapter, specifically, the exhortation to faithfulness in marriage (13:4). According to this position, this concern would more likely be addressed to first-century Gentiles than religious Jews (messianic or not). This is a tenuous presumption indeed (John 8:11, anyone?) and not one on which to rest the interpretation of an entire epistle.

Compelling arguments against Gentile Christian recipients are as follows: The entire argument of Hebrews rests on the Hebrew Scripture. While Gentile believers accepted the Old Testament as holy Scripture, it is unlikely that they would continue to exhibit such confidence in God's Word if their commitment to Christianity was impaired, completely undercutting Hebrews' argument.[28]

In addition, it is hard to imagine that a return to Levitical temple Judaism was a temptation for first-century Gentile believers. Yet Hebrews presents no contrast between Christianity and any other religion or religious viewpoint other than Judaism. If Hebrews was addressed to Gentiles, the failure to mention a single contemporary pagan religion is curious.

Jewish (Messianic and Non-Christian) Community in General. The idea of a Gentile Christian audience may be further challenged by examination of the overwhelming evidence in favor of a community of Jewish recipients. The issue of whether this Jewish community was of a Christian persuasion will be treated after first definitively establishing the community's ethnicity.

The first line of evidence is external. F. F. Bruce reminds us of the attributed title's antiquity, affirming that the title "To the Hebrews" extends back to "the last quarter of the second century, if not earlier."[29] The oldest known manuscript copy of Hebrews, the Chester Beatty Papyrus (known as P[46]), dates to the beginning of the third century and possesses the title, "To the Hebrews."[30] Certainly, early church fathers Clement of Alexandria (c. AD 180) and Tertullian of North Africa (c. AD 220) understood that the letter had been written to a Hebrew audience, of which the early churches were predominantly composed.[31] Indeed, it would be an anomaly to have a New Testament epistle addressed to a purely Gentile church. Yet the New Testament has just the opposite occurrence of at least two epistles, James and 1 Peter, that were solely addressed to Jewish believers (James 1:1; 1 Pet. 1:1) According to Eusebius, the Jerusalem church was entirely Jewish throughout the first century and well into the next, until the second Roman revolt in AD 132.[32] It is no stretch of the imagination to posit other first-century homogenous Jewish churches beyond the confines of Jerusalem in cities like Caesarea and throughout Judea.

The entire argument of Hebrews, based on and saturated with Old Testament quotation and replete with Old Testament allusion and frame of reference, can be considered as having been designed for no other audience than a Jewish one. It was assumed by the author that his audience would be familiar with the stipulations of the Torah, fluent in the circumstances surrounding the establishment of the Mosaic covenant as well as conversant with the Levitical priesthood and sacrificial system, the Day of Atonement ritual, and the tabernacle. Furthermore, the author assumed audience familiarity with Israel's history and heroes of faith, awareness of Jewish theology and traditions, and knowledge of the Old Testament along with acceptance of its divine authority.

Bruce provides a prime example.

His insistence that the old covenant had been antiquated is expressed with a moral earnestness and driven home repeatedly in a manner which would be pointless if his readers were not especially disposed to live under that covenant, but which would be very much to the point if they were still trying to live under it, or imagined that, having passed beyond that, they could refer to it.[33]

A detailed knowledge of the Old Testament is indispensable for understanding what the writer of Hebrews is endeavoring to say. He assumes on the part of his audience a deep familiarity with its contents.[34] Vincent forcefully argues: "The whole argument of the Epistle to the Hebrews is *technically* Jewish, and not of a character to appeal to Gentile readers."[35]

Non-Christian Jews. Having firmly established the Jewish ethnic and cultural background of Hebrews' recipients, it remains to be ascertained whether their faith persuasion was as interested seekers or confirmed Christian believers. The opinion that the book of Hebrews was an evangelistic effort originally addressed to a nonmessianic Jewish community is well explained by Kenneth Wuest, who maintains that Hebrews' argument is redundant to the Jewish believer, who has evidenced, by his faith, that he already accepts the letter's major premise.[36]

It is, however, an unwarranted *leap of faith* to assume that every community of Jewish Christians, by virtue of their authentic faith in Christ, automatically possessed a commensurate and accurate theological understanding of Christ's superior high priesthood, superior sacrifice and the supremacy of the new covenant. To assume the blanket acceptance of these major, rather sophisticated doctrines, developed here as nowhere else in the New Testament, is somewhat unrealistic.

Furthermore, it seems curious that in what is purported to be an evangelistic tract directed to the Jewish people for the purpose of demonstrating that Jesus is the Messiah, and one that is otherwise saturated with the Old Testament, there is, nonetheless, within its contents a complete absence of actual messianic prophecy. It is certain that it was not for the author's lack of familiarity with God's word. One may only wonder as to the spectacular fashion in which this skilled rhetorician and theologian might have presented the Scripture's major messianic prophecies.

If the recipients of Hebrews are non-Christian Jews, what entity is persecuting the community, and for what reason? As to the persecutors, there are only two possible alternatives, Jewish Christians or pagan Gentiles. There is no evidence in the text or historically that the early Christians persecuted the Jews. The current of persecution only flowed one way between these two parties in the first century. This then leaves the persecution of Jews by Gentiles. In the Roman Empire, Judaism was a *religio licita* (an officially licensed religion), and being Jewish was no crime.[37] While outbreaks of Roman persecution against the Jews had precedent in this era,[38] it was uncommon.

Jewish Christian. The overwhelming preponderance of internal evidence as to their (Jewish) Christian faith must now be considered. The first line of evidence relates to the treatment of Jesus in the text. The author presumes the recipient community's recognition, without qualification of any kind, that Jesus is the Son of God (1:2, 5, 8; 3:6; 4:14; 5:5, 8; 6:6; 10:29) and that Jesus is the Messiah, the Christ (3:6, 14; 5:5; 6:1; 9:11, 14, 24, 28; 10:10; 11:26; 13:8, 21). The author confidently assumes that his audience will concur with his affirmation that Jesus is the Apostle and High Priest of "our confession" (3:1), and that Jesus is recognized by the recipient community, without qualification, as "the Lord" (2:3).

The second line of evidence relates to how the author portrays the recipient audience. He refers to them as "holy brethren" (3:1, 12) and "beloved" (6:9); he notes that they have become "partakers of the heavenly calling" (3:1) and "partakers of Christ" (3:14); and refers to Timothy as "our brother" (13:23). In the absence of any conditions, qualifications, or the slightest whiff of irony, it is difficult to accept the recipients as anything other than Jewish Christians.

The third line of evidence relates to the author's description of the recipient audience's faith and beliefs. His readers have "come . . . to Jesus" (12:22–24) as second-generation believers (2:3). The community members, "we who have believed" (4:3), are exhorted to hold fast to "our confession" (4:14) and "our hope" (10:23) and "this hope we have" (6:19). The community is admonished not to "throw away your confidence" (10:35) in "the covenant by which he was sanctified" (10:29). Furthermore, the author recognizes that the motivation for the community's endurance through adversity and multiple series of persecutions was their eschatological expectation based on a commitment to their messianic faith (10:32–34).[39]

When all the evidence is taken into account, the sole position that can successfully reconcile all internal and external facts is that Jewish Christians were the original recipients of the letter to the Hebrews.

Hellenistic Jews. The identity of these Jewish Christians must be further modified by identifying them as Hellenistic Jews. Hellenistic Jews were generally those Jews living outside of Judea, in the diaspora (dispersion), some five million strong (roughly three-fifths of the Jewish people's total population)[40] in communities strewn throughout the Roman Empire (Acts 2:9–11). While maintaining their Jewish distinctives, they were nonetheless thoroughly immersed in the Greco-Roman culture of which they were a part. They spoke Greek and worshiped in separate Greek-speaking synagogues in contrast to the conventional synagogues in Judea that conducted their services in Hebrew. Indeed, such was the pervasive influence of the surrounding culture that many of the Hellenistic Jews, experiencing an elevated level of Greek cultural absorption after having lived so long outside of Israel, could no longer speak Hebrew, the language of Judean worship, or Aramaic, the Judean common vernacular. Consequently, the version of the Hebrew Scripture (the Old Testament) used by the Hellenistic Jews was a Greek translation, the Septuagint, compiled in second-century BC Alexandria (the Egyptian city considered to be the Hellenistic Jewish center of the diaspora). It is the exclusive use of the Septuagint in Hebrews that allows us to conclude, with some security, that the author's intended recipients were Hellenistic Jewish Christians.

Linguistically, in order to thrive in the Roman world, both Jewish groups, Judeans and Hellenists, would have had to demonstrate fluency in the Greek language, although the Hellenists would have been more proficient than the Aramaic speakers as Greek was their mother tongue. Therefore, while likely, it cannot be irrefutably concluded that Hebrews' use of the Septuagint thereby completely excludes native Aramaic speaking Judeans from consideration. After all, every New Testament book was originally written in Greek (with the possible exception of Matthew),[42] and Luke's preference for the Septuagint in

Acts may or may not indicate that the Septuagint was the translation of the Hebrew Bible utilized by the apostles.[43]

Destination

Just as commentators cannot agree on author, date, and recipients, neither can they agree on the letter's intended destination. Speculation runs the gamut from one corner of the Roman Empire to another, from Alexandria in the south to Antioch in the north to Jerusalem in the east to Spain in the west, and in between these compass points, a veritable travelogue of possible communities. The presumption that the letter of Hebrews was authored, if not by Paul himself, then by a associate in his circle, has found scholars assigning the letter's destination "to almost every place visited or supposed to have been visited by him"[44] or his colleagues.

One clue that presents itself is the author's pointed declaration that the believers "do not possess a permanent city" (13:14). In order for the author's metaphorical point to hit its intended mark, this illustration would seem to demand the recipient community's placement not just in a general urban setting, but their residence in one of the great cosmopolitan centers of the Roman Empire. Of course, the Empire had no shortage of impressive cities. However, what is required is a great Roman metropolitan area with four major qualifications: first, a sufficient population to sustain multiple house churches (13:17; 24); second, a sufficient general Hellenistic Jewish population for at least one of the house churches to be comprised exclusively of Hellenistic Jewish believers (10:25); third, persecution befalling Jewish Christians in the first century's seventh decade (Hebrews' impending persecution, 12:4); and fourth, persecution befalling Jewish Christians in the first century's fifth or sixth decade (Hebrews' previous persecution, 10:32–34).

Although multiple locales actually fulfill these criteria, two cities, Rome and Jerusalem (along with the surrounding region of Judea), best meet these four preliminary qualifications and are the most likely destinations for the letter to the Hebrews.

Rome. The Eternal City as Hebrews' destination possesses a great deal of currency in modern commentaries. It has become the de facto city of choice for many, for the following reasons. First, referencing the salutation from the author's companions to the recipients ("those from Italy greet you," 13:24). Second, the first known example of the epistle of Hebrews being quoted was by Clement, from Rome, in his Corinthian epistle (AD 95). Those holding to Rome assume that since Hebrews was already in Clement's possession at this early date, Rome, therefore, had been the letter's original destination. Third, there is an attractive correlation between the history of the Roman church and the two seasons of persecution alluded to in the text of Hebrews, one season that occurred in the past (10:32–35) and one that looms imminently (12:4).

Yet the case for Rome provides two possible areas of concern. First, some hold that the geographic distance between Rome and Jerusalem somehow undermines the possibility that the vacillating Jewish believers would feel the kind of sufficiently compelling attraction toward returning to the Levitical temple sacrificial system that is indicated by Hebrews' subject matter.[45] Second, Hebrews 2:3–4 indicates the establishment of the church in question by eyewitnesses of Jesus. Furthermore, the fact that their faith was confirmed by signs and wonders indicates that at least one of the eyewitnesses was an apostle or apostolic associate.[46] However, Paul seems to indicate that the Roman church had not been established by an apostle (Rom. 15:20). It is reasonable to assume that the Roman church may have been established following the return of the new Jewish believers who had been saved in Jerusalem at Pentecost (Acts 2:10ff.) in AD 33.

Jerusalem and Judea. Although the case for Rome is certainly a compelling one, it is the capital and center of the Jewish world, Jerusalem, along with the surrounding region of Judea that is the most appealing candidate for Hebrews' original destination. If, indeed, as we have demonstrated, the letter was written to Jewish Christians who are tempted to renounce their Christianity and return to Judaism, a destination of Israel makes certain sense.

It may be argued that the title that was assigned to the letter, "To the Hebrews," is in itself a testament to the early church's memory of the epistle's original destination in Israel, namely, Jerusalem. Certainly something must account for the fact that Hebrews, unlike every other New Testament letter with a given addressee, is not directed to a specific individual or group of individuals in a particular geographic location. By the turn of the fifth century, church father John Chrysostom of Antioch presented his position regarding Hebrews, going on record for Pauline authorship and at the same time identifying the recipients of the letter as Jewish Christians living in Judea.[47]

The text of Hebrews' abundant reference to the Levitical system of worship would be of particular relevance to the population of greater Judea and, specifically, Jerusalem because of the geographic immediacy of the temple. While the nation of Judea was itself, of course, not a city, as seemingly necessitated in the text (13:14), such was the power and emotional pull of Jerusalem over the Jewish imagination that a setting anywhere within proximity of Jerusalem would fulfill the author's metaphor.

Nonetheless, some fail to see the inevitability of a Jerusalem or Judean destination, basing their conclusion on the author of Hebrews' scrupulous avoidance of the common New Testament Greek term for the temple, *hieron* (used 45 times in the Gospels and 24 times in Acts), and his preference for the term normatively used for the tabernacle, *skēnē*. In fact, in Hebrews, all references to Israel's Levitical sacrificial system are placed in the context of ancient tabernacle practice and not that of the first-century contemporary temple. However, the author's purposeful choice of vocabulary to describe the Levitical system finds its exclusive basis in Old Testament covenantal terminology, and he jettisons any other expressions, including those commonly used of contemporary temple practice, that might muddy his argument's penetrating clarity. If anything, this strengthens the candidacy of Jerusalem and Judea.

None of the objections generally raised affects the superior quality of Jerusalem and Judea's candidacy. However, the following claim, concerning the issue of persecution will conclude the matter. As with Rome, there is an attractive correlation between the history of the church in Jerusalem and Judea and the two seasons of persecution alluded to in the text of Hebrews, one season that occurred in the past (10:32–35) and one that imminently looms (12:4).

The persecution previously experienced by the recipients of Hebrews regarding public slander, abuse, imprisonment, and confiscation of personal property (10:32–35) can be connected to the incidents described in Acts (8:1; 12:1ff.; 22:19; 26:11). The impending persecution that is alluded to in Hebrews (12:4) and the severity of the author's five warnings should be connected with the events of the first Jewish revolt against Rome (AD 66–73).

If the author penned Hebrews at the dawn of conflict or sometime immediately prior to the dawn, it would seemingly fit the circumstances alluded to in Hebrews as well as provide the context for the author's warning to depart "the camp" (13:13) prior to the community experiencing bloodshed (12:4). This corresponds to Jesus' warning for His disciples to flee Judea when warfare broke out against Jerusalem (Matt. 24:15–16; Luke 21:21) since the coming judgment was to be inflicted upon the specific generation of Israel that had rejected Him (Luke 11:50–51: Matt. 23:35–36) and would result, in part, in the destruction of the temple (Matt. 24:2). This divine judgment had been central to the witness of John the Baptist, who repeatedly warned his audience of "the wrath to come" which would imminently descend on Israel (Matt. 3:7). This judgment was also the centerpiece of Peter's evangelistic proclamation to the Jewish masses assembled in the temple on Pentecost morning as he warned them to save themselves from the excruciating and cataclysmic judgment forthcoming upon this particular generation of the nation of Israel that had rejected the Messiah (Acts 2:40).[48]

The outbreak of the war with Rome proved to be the event that finally separated Judea's Jewish believers and their fellow Jews. In an act considered traitorous by their fellow Jews, the Jewish believers en masse followed their Master's command to leave the nation and escape the catastrophic war. Traveling east and crossing the Jordan River, they fled to safety in the city of Pella,[49] one of the region's ten major Roman metropolises (collectively known as the Decapolis).

Outline of Hebrews

I. Theological Declaration of the Supremacy of the Messiah in Both Person and Priesthood (1:1–10:18)
  A. The Superiority of the Messiah as Divine Revelation (1:1–3)
  B. The Superiority of the Messiah to Angels (1:4–2:18)
    1. While Angels Are God's Servants, Jesus Is God's Son (1:4–14)
    2. First Resultant Warning of Danger: Concerning Drifting from Messianic Faith (2:1–4)
    3. Jesus' Temporary Inferiority to Angels Contrasted with His Current Exaltation (2:5–9)
    4. The Superiority of the Messiah's Purpose to That of Angels (2:10–18)
      a. Messiah's Purpose Was to Bring Many Sons to Glory (2:10–13)
      b. Messiah's Purpose Was to Overcome the Devil (2:14)
      c. Messiah's Purpose Was to Liberate the Believer from Slavery (2:15)
      d. Messiah's Purpose Was to Render Aid to Humanity (2:16–18)
  C. The Superiority of the Messiah to Moses (3:1–6)
    1. Superior to Moses in Person and Purpose (3:1–4)
    2. Superior to Moses in Position (3:5–6)
  D. Second Resultant Warning of Danger: Concerning Disobedience and Doubt (3:7–4:13)
    1. Admonition to Faithfulness (3:7–19)
    2. God's Rest for the Faithful (4:1–10)
    3. Exhortation to Enter into God's Rest (4:11–13)
  E. The Superiority of the Messiah to Aaron (4:14–10:18)
    1. The Superiority of Messiah's Position (4:14–16)
    2. The Superiority of Messiah's Priesthood (5:1–10)
      a. The Offices of Priesthood (5:1–4)
      b. The Superiority of the Messiah's Qualifications (5:5–10)
    3. Third Resultant Warning of Danger: Concerning Spiritual Stagnation (5:11–6:20)

  2. Fourth Resultant Warning of Danger: Concerning the Inferior Lifestyle of Faithlessness (10:26–31)
  3. Encouragement to Persevere in a Faithful Lifestyle (10:32–39)
B. The Evidence of the Lifestyle of Faith (11:1–40)
  1. The Outcome of Faith (11:1–3)
  2. Paragons of Faith (11:4–40)
    a. Paragons of Faith: Prior to the Patriarchs (11:4–7)
    b. Paragons of Faith: The Patriarchs (11:8–22)
    c. Paragons of Faith: The Exodus Generation (11:23–31)
    d. Paragons of Faith: Israel's National History (11:32–34)
    e. Paragons of Faith: Amid Trials (11:35–38)
    f. The Promised Goal of Faith (11:39–40)
C. The Enduring Lifestyle of Faith (12:1–29)
  1. The Model and Measure of Endurance (12:1–4)
  2. The Relationship between Discipline and Endurance (12:5–11)
  3. The Obligations Regarding Faith (12:12–29)
    a. Encouragement to Live Sanctified Lives (12:12–17)
    b. The Superiority of the Believer's Status (12:18–24)
    c. Fifth Resultant Warning of Danger: Concerning Spiritual Insensitivity (12:25–29)
D. Concluding Exhortations (13:1–25)
  1. Exhortation to Discharge Community Obligations (13:1–6)
  2. Exhortation to Discharge Religious Obligations (13:7–17)
  3. Exhortation to Discharge Personal Obligations (13:18–25)

Section I

Theological Declaration of the Supremacy of the Messiah

Hebrews 1:1–10:18

CHAPTER 1

Superiority of the Messiah as Divine Revelation
Hebrews 1:1–3

Preview:

The author of Hebrews begins his presentation with a straightforward, no-holds-barred announcement of his letter's subject, which is a theological declaration of the supremacy of the Messiah. The first three verses of chapter 1 serve as the author's opening salvo in his attestation to Jesus' definitive supremacy, which is revealed in both His person and His priesthood. While this opening statement provides only the briefest of introductions to the idea of Jesus' priesthood (a subject that will be developed at length further along in the epistle), it nonetheless sets forth an unparalleled series of seven assertions that extol His incomparable person. The initial focus is on Jesus' identity as God's final and finest revelation.

The book of Hebrews begins with a forceful expression of literary skill and compositional artistry. Utilizing the manifest rhetorical dexterity of a theological impresario, the author immediately commands our attention and directs our focus toward the individual in the center of his spotlight: the Son of God. Although familiarity with the original Greek language allows appreciation of the author's use of alliteration, assonance, parallelism, and sense of rhythm (e.g., five of the initial twelve Greek words start with p, etc.), it is not necessary. His accomplishment in composing this veritable "hymn" is apparent enough through the ideas expressed in our own English translation.

There is not one superfluous word in the opening verses' dense thicket of messianic doctrine. The compactness of the author's prose is stunningly contrasted with the expansiveness of his thought. Without pausing to provide customary epistolary greetings or even a preliminary Greek equivalent of "shalom," the author launches full force into his introductory premise, that of the superiority of the Messiah as divine revelation. While over the past fifteen centuries God had progressively revealed Himself to Israel through the agency of a series of prophets whom He employed and deployed in various ways, in this new, current era, He has revealed Himself with decisive finality in His Son. The Son is unveiled as "God's revelation 2.0," an upgrade in divine disclosure that in every way is qualitatively advanced, improved, and superior to that which it replaced (see God's Superior Revelation on p. 30).

The author assumes the recipients' acceptance of his presuppositional premise that God exists and that He has actively communicated with His people throughout their history. The Jewish people considered the Old Testament, the Hebrew Scripture, the Law (Torah), Prophets (Nevi'im), and Writings (Ketuvim, all three divisions abbreviated together as "the Tanakh") to be the word of God expressed through the prophets, the authors of Scripture (with the exception of the Sadducees, who rejected the divine authority of all but the Torah).[1]

God revealed Himself to Israel through two related means. The first, *polumerōs*, "in many portions," refers to the series of prophets who had successively communicated God's word over a roughly fifteen-century period as recorded in various books of the Old Testament. The use of the term "the fathers," indicates Israel's ancestors. The context dictates that our understanding of "the fathers" should not be limited to the three Hebrew patriarchs Abraham, Isaac, and Jacob. Nonetheless, the use of "the fathers" indicates that these "portions" are intended to be understood as the content specifically communicated through Israel's prophets and not every message of every individual throughout history to whom God prophetically spoke (Adam, Enoch, Noah, et al.)

These prophetic "portions" were distributed progressively, in fits and starts and in varying measures, throughout Israel's history. He chose not to overwhelm His people by unloading everything at once, but rather slowly unveiled His identity, purposes, and plans for Israel and the world over a period of centuries, allowing time for absorption and digestion of divinely disclosed truth. Yet Jewish tradition holds that this divine revelation ceased in the fifth century BC with the death of Malachi, the final prophet and author of the final Old Testament book.[2]

The concept of revelatory "portions" or "parts" is a natural means by which Jewish people still conceive of the Old Testament. In both conventional synagogue and messianic congregation, the Scripture is divided into week-ly portions, called in Hebrew, *parashahs*, that are read aloud in the public wor-ship service. It is to the theological study and linguistic mastery of these indi-vidual "portions" of Hebrew Scripture that all thirteen-year-old initiates, whether Bar Mitzvah boys or Bat Mitzvah girls, devote themselves. Interestingly, the sections of Scripture allocated as *parashahs*[3] are not all apportioned evenly. Indeed, every congregant in attendance at these cere-monies appreciates the extra effort that the young man or woman must exert who, through circumstance of birthdate, happens to draw one of the rare extra-long weekly *parashahs* as his or her text to recite.

Related to God's prophetic revelation of Himself "in many portions" is His revelation, *polutropōs*, "in many ways or means." Our infinitely creative God has chosen to communicate with his prophetic messengers through types, covenants, a legal code, a burning bush, angels, pillars of fire and cloud, a quaking, fiery mountain, dreams, visions, signs and wonders, "still, small voices," and in other ways. The cumulative effect of the "many portions and many ways" was to provide an indispensable and requisite primer to prepare Israel for the pinnacle of divine revelation (see Gal. 3:24–25).

A new time calls for new tactics. "In these last days" or "in these final days" is a specific Jewish idiom for the messianic age, the time for the fulfill-ment of God's yet unfulfilled promises (1 Pet. 1:20; Jude 18; LXX Num. 24:14; Deut. 4:30; Isa. 2:2; Jer. 23:20; Dan. 10:14; Mic. 4:1). The Greek word here for "last" is *eschatos*, from which is derived the term *eschatology*, the study of the final (days or things). This messianic age stands in contrast to *palaios*, "times past" or "long ago." If the author had meant to simply indicate a neutral, "the old days," it is far more likely that he would have used the term *archaios* (from which we get our word *archaic*). However, the loaded term he chose means "old in point of use, worn out, ready to be displaced by something new."[4] A new and improved era, a new age or dispensation, has dawned through the revelation of the Messiah.

The term *messiah* or *Christ* is not yet employed, nor is the name Jesus. This transformational revelatory figure is simply referred to here as *huios*, "Son." There is no grammatical article provided; God has not spoken in "the Son" in a parallel fashion to how he previously spoke in "the prophets" (article included). God's Son is not merely the instrument through which God's mes-sage is communicated, as were the prophets. Uniquely, He Himself is also the message. God's final revelation is the person of the Son.

In sum, God's revelation to us through His Son is superior to that received in Israel's past through the prophets in three ways. First, while His previous revelation was fragmentary, addressed through many prophets, the new mode of revelation is through one individual. Second, while His previous revelation was through diverse means and various ways, the new revelation is through one means and one way only. Finally, while prior revelation was progressive and disclosed over centuries, the Son is God's final and conclusive revelation of Himself.

God's Superior Revelation

In the Past	In These Last Days
Addressed to the fathers	Addressed to us
Through many prophets	Through one Son
Through diverse means	Through one means
In various ways	In one way
Revelation was progressive	Revelation is final

The author proceeds to define what he means through his designation of the Messiah as God's Son. In doing so, he provides not a definition of Jesus' sonship per se but, rather, a seven-point demonstration of the Son's relationship to His Father.

The first of the author's seven "fast facts" demonstrating Jesus' sonship is that Jesus has been appointed the heir of all things. The law of primogenitor, which assumes the firstborn son's greater inheritance, would have been the cultural norm in the ancient world of the Bible (Deut. 21:17). Therefore, as God's "firstborn" (1:6; 12:23), Jesus' inheritance, by any measure, would have been expected to be quite considerable. In the first of several dozen Old Testament passages that will be quoted, referenced, alluded to, and used as an illustration throughout the text, the author reveals just how considerable the Son's inheritance is through the employment of a central messianic text, Psalm 2:7–8.

As biblically literate Jews (as all Jews were in the first century), the original recipients of Hebrews could be relied on to supply the original context of the author's Old Testament quotations, allusions, etc., without having everything spelled out for them. Certainly, if the author needed to provide elaborate contextual backgrounds for every use of the Old Testament, the scroll containing his epistle would have needed supersizing (this is precisely why chapter 8's extensive quotation of Jeremiah 31:31–34 is so unprecedented; we will discuss that passage at length when we reach chapter 8). However, unlike first-century Jewish believers, few twenty-first-century believers' brains function as biblical concordances; therefore, for the purposes of this commentary, certain Old Testament passages will be summarized and discussed as they arise in Hebrews' argument.

Psalm 2 is the first of several messianic psalms written by both king and prophet David. The psalm opens with a description of an impudent and conspiratorial worldwide opposition ("The kings of the earth take their stand and the rulers take counsel together") to both God and to "His Anointed" (Heb., *meshiach*), the Messiah (Ps. 2:1-3). This is followed by a depiction of the Lord's wrath being unleashed on all those who contest the Jewish King whom He has personally installed ("My King") to rule Israel from Jerusalem, "upon Zion, My holy mountain" (Ps. 2:4-6).

The author of Hebrews' focus on the psalm begins at the point when David's poetry shifts from third person narrative to the first person voice of the Messiah (Ps. 2:7-9). The text affirms that the Messiah is the Lord's Son, endowed with the very authority of God Almighty Himself ("Thou art my Son, Today I have begotten Thee"). This authority not only extends over Israel, but over all nations of the earth ("Ask of Me, and I will surely give the nations as Thine inheritance, and the very ends of the earth as Thy possession"). The phrase "son of God" appears in the Hebrew Scripture to denote the unique qualities of and relationship between God and Israel (Hos. 11:1) and God and the Davidic king of Israel in the context of the Davidic covenant (2 Sam. 7:11-16; 1 Chron. 17:10b-14). In this psalm the phrase denotes the relationship between God and the promised Messiah (Ps. 2:7).

Unless one attributes to David a vast hyperbolic perpetration concerning his descriptions and imagery, one must undoubtedly conclude that the scope of what David described here extends far beyond the immediate prospects of any contemporary Old Testament Israelite king and into the far reaches of an eschatological future. The author of Hebrews uses this psalm to further his argument, first here in Heb. 1:2 and a few verses later in 1:5. Since neither David nor his royal descendants ever possessed the worldwide authority attributed to this psalm's king (Ps. 2:8), it therefore must refer to the ultimate Son of God, the Messiah.

This is confirmed by the psalm's distinctive conclusion. The passage then shifts back to the third person with a warning of the unqualified severity of the Son of God's judgment and wrath ("lest He become angry, and you perish in the way, for His wrath may soon be kindled") to be directed toward all those who do not worship the Lord by showing due reverence toward His Son ("Worship the LORD with reverence and rejoice with trembling. Do homage to the Son"). Humankind's rapport with the Lord is determined through their stance regarding His Son, the messianic king ("How blessed are all who take refuge in Him!") (Ps. 2:10-12).

Without question, this psalm has traditionally been recognized as messianic. As the revered eleventh-century rabbi Rashi acknowledged, "Our rabbis relate it as relating to King Messiah."[5] Various ancient Jewish sources have viewed Psalm 2 as "full of Messianic references"[6] and endowed it with messianic import. For example, commenting on 2:7–8, the Talmud records this messianic scenario based on the two-messiah theory then in vogue:

> Our Rabbis taught, The Holy One, blessed be He, will say to the Messiah, the son of David (May he reveal himself speedily in our days!), "Ask of me anything, and I will give it to thee," as it is said, *I will tell of the decree* etc. *this day have I begotten thee, ask of me and I will give the nations for thy inheritance.* But when he will see that the Messiah the son of Joseph is slain, he will say to Him, "Lord of the Universe, I ask of Thee only the gift of life." "As to life," He would answer him, "Your father David has already prophesied this concerning you," as it is said, *He asked life of thee, thou gavest it him [even length of days for ever and ever].*[7]

The author of Hebrews' extraordinary claim is that the Son's inheritance is not limited to Israel and the nations, as promised in Psalm 2, but that He is, rather, the heir of the entire cosmos. This aligns with the traditional Jewish belief that the world was created "for the sake of the Messiah."[8]

This leads to the second "fast fact" that demonstrates Jesus' sonship. Jesus was God's instrument of creation. This corresponds with other New Testament teaching, specifically both John's "all things came into being by Him, and apart from Him nothing came into being that has come into being" (John 1:3) and Paul's "all things have been created by Him and for Him" (Col. 1:16). In divine partnership, Father and Son together created the Son's inheritance. The concept of God using a personified agent in creation is a common Jewish theme found in Proverbs, where the agency is Wisdom (8:22–31, see also the apocryphal Wisdom of Solomon 9:9), in John, where the agency is the Word (John 1:1–3), and in the Mishnah (the central record of Jewish oral tradition) where God's agency is a personified Torah (Avot 3:14).

The term *aiōnas*, generally translated "universe" or "worlds," finds its primary meaning in the concept of "ages." Therefore, the Son's creation is in no way limited to dimensions of space, but extends to dimensions of time. As Lord of all time and space, the Son is responsible for every star, planet, astronomical body, age, era, dispensation, black hole, white hole, and worm hole: the entire glorious space-time continuum—every aspect of Carl Sagan's and Stephen Hawking's wildest imaginings combined and then some.

The third "fast fact" is that the Son is the radiance of God's glory and God's express image. In other words, Jesus is God in fundamental and elemental reality. For His creation, God has provided Jesus, the ideal expression of His reality, both visible and tangible. The difficulty in understanding the concept of Jesus actively radiating God's glory (not to be misunderstood as mere passive reflection) or being *apaugasma*, the "brightness," or "effulgence" of God's glory, is alleviated when understood in "light" of the Jewish conception of God's Shekinah glory, His visible, luminous manifestation.[9] Alongside John in his gospel ("the true light which . . . dwelt among us, and we beheld His glory," John 1:9–14), the author of Hebrews explicitly identifies Jesus as the Shekinah glory of God.

The fourth "fast fact" is that the Son is the exact representation of God's nature. Jesus is God in both fundamental and elemental reality. God has revealed to His creation Jesus, the ideal expression of His reality, both visible and tangible. The word used here, *charaktēr*, occurs nowhere else in the New Testament and was used "of an engraver, one who mints coins, a graving tool, a die, a stamp, a branding iron, a mark engraved, an impress, a stamp on coins and seals."[10] The Son, therefore, is an exact reproduction of the Father (John 1:14–18; 14:8–9; Col. 1:15).

This is a doctrine readily understood in the digital age in which we live. For many of us who came of age in the technologically darker ages, that is, the twentieth century, the idea of duplication implicitly carried the connotation of a reduction in quality. For example, to make a cassette copy of a record or CD (from one's own music collection, of course, not from the massively appealing collection of your neighbor across the hall) always entailed a generational loss of quality. The cassette copy, although serviceable, never sounded quite as good as the original. Likewise, the copied recording onto videotape of a television program or film always lacked the viewing quality of the original broadcast. However, those unfortunate analog days are behind us. Today, for example, every single copy sold of Sojourner Ministries' DVD *The Unleavened Messiah: A Portrait of Christ in the Passover*, being digital, looks and sounds exactly the same. Any copy made at any time is absolutely indistinguishable from the original DVD master. Just so, we may think of Jesus as "the digital Messiah," a perfect copy of His Father, alike in every way.

The word *hupostasis*, "that which makes it what it is,"[11] is correctly translated "nature," "substance," or "essence" and is the root of the infamous phrase known to all historians of early church controversies, the "hypostatic union": the doctrine, formally ratified at the Council of Chalcedon in AD 451, that recognizes Jesus' possession of both human and divine "natures" or "essences." Sometimes certain believers find themselves a bit uncomfortable discussing either the ratification method of doctrines at historic church councils, or perhaps certain nuances of the doctrines themselves, or the occasional use of hairsplitting language, or perhaps they question the necessity for such doctrinal ratification. If such individuals are among my readers, please relax. The hypostatic union is an essential doctrine that simply collects the facts concerning Jesus' equal possession of humanity and deity scattered throughout the book of Hebrews (and elsewhere in both Old and New Testaments) and presents them in a structured, synthetic manner.

The fifth "fast fact" is that Jesus actively maintains all things by the word of His power; that is, He maintains, or governs, His creation through the exercise of His own intrinsic authority. Several commentators are quick to point out that the present active participle *pherōn*, usually translated "upholds" or "sustains," is best understood as conveying the Son's "active maintenance." Unlike the Greek god Atlas, famous for bearing the world on his shoulders, Jesus has the whole world in His hands as He actively engages in governing each of creation's intricate processes (see also Col. 1:17).

The sixth "fast fact" is that Jesus has made purification of sins. This is the author's initial introduction of the theme that will later consume a significant portion of his argument, that of Jesus' high priesthood. Using language reminiscent of the Torah's discussion[12] of Yom Kippur, the Day of Atonement (Exod. 30:10; Lev. 16:30), the author indicates that through this purification of sins, Jesus has become the fulfillment of this Jewish Holy Day. His accomplishment far exceeded the Levitical priests' provision of covering for sin; Jesus successfully realized a definitive removal of sin's internal defilement. The use of the aorist tense with the participle *poieō*, "having made," means that the act of making purification for sins was one final and effective action with continuing results. No further action is required on anyone's part. Christ has removed the monumental impediment between God and man. Nor will any action need future renewal or refreshment. In addition, the use of the middle voice with the same participle underscores that the Son's accomplishment was achieved by Himself, through Himself, and by means of His own sacrificial effort.

The final "fast fact" is that the Son sits at God's right hand. This is sequentially related to the Son's purification of sins. There could be no divine exaltation without a divine passion. Likewise, Jesus' exaltation at His Father's side was the necessary consequence of His passion and of its effectiveness. In contrast to the Levitical priests who, lacking the ability to make final purification of sin, were required to continually serve before the altar (10:11), Jesus' priestly work was finished, and He was invited by His Father to take a seat.

The seat Jesus was invited to take was a royal throne at "the Majesty's" right hand. For Jesus to enjoy this intensity of divine favor through this enthronement denotes the Father's unprecedented conferral of dignity and authority on the Son. Lane notes that Psalm 110:1 is "the only biblical text that speaks of someone enthroned beside God."[13] In antiquity, the concept of enthronement at a ruler's right hand was a singular honor that conveyed the highest level of regal favor and shared authority. In the Old Testament we see this illustrated in Solomon's invitation to his mother, Bathsheba, making her his equal (1 Kings 2:19). Furthermore, in the ancient world, kings would likewise customarily invite visiting royalty to sit at their right hand. Consequently, it is quite reasonable to conclude that God's invitation for the Messiah to sit at His right hand indicates coequality.[14]

The language employed in this phrase is regal and ceremonial, having its origins in Psalm 110:1, the most frequently cited messianic prophecy in the New Testament (from the most frequently cited psalm), even used by Jesus Himself to perplex the Pharisees (Matt. 22:44–45; Mark 12:35–37; Luke 20:42; see also Acts 2:34–35): "The LORD says to my Lord: 'Sit at My right hand, until I make Thine enemies a footstool for Thine feet'" (Ps. 110:1). There are three individuals designated in this verse.

The initial pair of individuals are both called "Lord," and there is the author, David. In the English translation it is more difficult to perceive the messianic dynamic of the psalm than in the original Hebrew, primarily because David, in reference to these two individuals, used two different words, both of which are translated in English as "lord." The same difficulty applies to the Greek translation, which also makes reference to the two individuals through use of the same word, *kurios*, twice.

The first "Lord" is the name YHWH and refers to the covenant-making God of Abraham, Isaac, and Jacob. The second "Lord" is the Hebrew *Adonai*. This second "lord," Adonai, is the individual whom David called "my Lord." If the first "Lord" refers to God and the second "Lord" is David's lord, then, obviously, neither of these "lordly" individuals could have been David. Indeed, it was universally accepted that David had neither been resurrected nor had he ascended into heaven. However, if God is the first Lord, and David is the "my" of "my Lord," the question remains as to the identity of David's Lord. Certainly, while he lived, David had no mortal lord. As the undisputed sovereign of all Israel, his only Lord was God Himself.

Of course, this is one of David's prophetic psalms, and the New Testament reveals the fulfillment of this prophecy through Jesus' exaltation. Our Messiah is currently sitting as an equal to God at His right hand until such time as Jesus' enemies are made His "footstool." Indeed, this passage has a long pedigree in both Jewish tradition and rabbinic literature of being interpreted in reference to the Messiah (albeit, never with reference to Jesus). For example, Psalm 110:1 is cited in the Midrash: "R. Yudan said in the name of R. Hama: In the time-to-come, when the Holy One, blessed be He, seats the lord Messiah at His right hand. . . ."[15] In addition to interpreting this passage as portraying the Messiah at God's right hand, some rabbis also pictured Abraham sitting on His left.[16]

Christ's Superiority in Hebrews 1:2–3

1. Christ Jesus has been appointed heir of all things.

2. Christ Jesus was God's instrument of creation.

3. Christ Jesus is the radiance of God's glory.

4. Christ Jesus is the express image of God.

5. Christ Jesus maintains all things by His authority.

6. Christ Jesus has made purification of sins.

7. Christ Jesus has sat down at God's right hand.

Conclusion

As presented in the opening lines of Hebrews, God's revelation of His Son both captivates and staggers the imagination. The enumerated characteristics of Hebrews 1:1–3 are applied to a single, contemporaneous Jewish man from Galilee whose life was tragically abbreviated by a violent and ignoble end. In pondering the sheer enormity of the author's claims concerning Jesus, His identity and His relationship to God, one cannot help but wonder why anyone would believe such outrageous claims. There is only one satisfactory answer to this enigma. The sole reason why anyone, and specifically, a first-century, religious, highly educated Jew such as the author, would or could believe these claims is a steadfast conviction concerning the accuracy of each assertion.

Study Questions

1. What primary means has God chosen through history to reveal Himself to Israel? Are there advantages to one method over another? What are they?

2. Based on just this section of Hebrews, what titles would you assign Jesus? How should you personally respond to Him in light of those titles?

3. List the three most compelling facts, in your opinion, concerning the superiority of the Son. What about those three facts make them most personally meaningful?

CHAPTER 2

Angels Are the Servants of God; Jesus Is the Son of God
Hebrews 1:4–14

Preview:

Although it is not apparent in the English translation, the fourth verse of chapter 1 is actually the conclusion of the massive and complex sentence that the author initiated in verse 1. Although it continues and builds on the majestic thoughts previously expressed, it nevertheless serves as a contextual hinge, marking the beginning of a new section and a new, although related, line of thought. In the opening verses, the author demonstrated the superiority of the Son as God's means of divine revelation in comparison with the Old Testament prophets. He will now continue expounding the theme concerning the superior revelation of the Son in relation to the angels. While angels are demonstrably awesome creatures, they cannot compare to God's Son.

Angels. Angels are the infinitely numerous (Heb. 12:22; Rev. 5:11) supernatural and celestial agents, or messengers, of God. In the context of Hebrews, the referenced angels are to be distinguished from the fallen angels (Rev. 12:9), or demons, led by Satan, the devil (2:14). The Bible speaks of angels as immortal (Luke 20:36) created beings (Ps. 148:2) who are spiritual in nature (Heb. 1:14), although they can exercise corporeality when the situation merits (Gen. 18:3; et al.). Angels possess a range in status, with some ruling over nations as "chief princes" (Dan. 10:13) and others assigned to individuals (Acts 12:15; Heb. 1:14). The names of only two angels are revealed in Scripture: Michael, the archangel over the nation of Israel (Dan. 10:21; 12:1,

Jud. 9; Rev. 12:7) and Gabriel, God's special messenger (Dan. 9:21; Luke 1:26). There are various classifications of angels. Some for example, bear distinctive features like cherubim (Gen. 3:24; Exod. 25:18–22; 26:31; 2 Chron. 3:7) and seraphim (Isa. 6:2–6), while others possess a more human (although intimidating, Matt. 28:3; Acts 10:4) appearance. In sum, Scripture reveals that angels exist to worship God as well as to carry out His plan and program for His creation, serving both individually and corporately (Matt. 26:53).

Although angels rate hundreds of references throughout the pages of the Old and New Testaments, the available facts are surprisingly limited and present a tantalizingly restricted picture. In reaction to what they considered the paucity of details provided in the Hebrew Scripture, the rabbis filled in the theological gaps through the creative development of a sophisticated angelic hierarchy that had become quite theologically elaborate by the Second Temple era.[1] While this amplified emphasis did not lead to the Jewish worship of angels (as some may have erroneously conjectured based on this section of Hebrews), nevertheless, these supernatural beings rose to a prominent theological position in first-century Judaism.

In wrestling with the reason behind the necessity of the author's inclusion of this segment, an interesting speculation is the proposal that the recipients may have experienced some confusion over whether Jesus should be more accurately classified as an elevated angelic being rather than as the singular concept of God-man. Certainly, there is precedent to be found in the Jewish conception of a man transformed into an angelic Messiah. According to Patai, "The earliest Biblical figure who in later literature was endowed with a superhuman Messianic character is Enoch. . . . This brief enigmatic statement (Gen. 5:24) sufficed to turn Enoch into a superhuman figure: after his translation he became Metatron, the chief of all angels, and according to the (first century BC) book of Enoch (71:14–17) . . . he became the Messiah."[2]

However, a likelier contextual (as opposed to speculative) reason for Hebrews' inclusion of the section on angels relates to their role as mediators of the Mosaic Law, the Torah. By the Second Temple era, this agency of mediation was the most important acknowledged fact concerning angels, even though that role had not been previously disclosed in the text of the Old Testament. That this tradition held common Jewish acceptance is revealed not only through New Testament references by Stephen in his Sanhedrin defense (Acts 7:38–39, 53) and by Paul in his letter to the Galatian church (Gal. 3:19), but also by references in Josephus's *Antiquities*[3] and the first-century BC pseudepigraphal book of *Jubilees* (1:26–2:1).[4]

For the author of Hebrews, the transmission of the Torah through angelic mediation is unquestioningly accepted (2:2). In Hebrews' first chapter, it is the authority of angels as divine revelatory mediators that is being contrasted with that of the Son's identity as God's final revelation.[5] The superiority of Jesus as God's ultimate revelation will provide a crucial component to the author's contention that the Mosaic covenant had been replaced by God's superior new covenant.

The word *kreittōn*, translated "better," appears in Hebrews thirteen of the nineteen times it is utilized in the entire New Testament, clearly indicating the importance of this concept to the author. He takes as his assignment the task of demonstrating the Messiah's superiority over every prominent person and theological concept in first-century Judaism. Interestingly, this claim of Messiah's supremacy finds a captivating parallel in later Jewish Midrash, which would likewise claim that the Messiah would be "greater than the patriarchs . . . higher than Abraham . . . lifted up above Moses . . . and loftier than the ministering angels."[6]

Use of "Better" in Hebrews

Hebrews 1:4	Jesus has become "much better than the angels"
Hebrews 6:9	"better things concerning you"
Hebrews 7:7	"lesser is blessed by the greater"
Hebrews 7:19	"a better hope"
Hebrews 7:22; 8:6	"a better covenant"
Hebrews 8:6	"better promises"
Hebrews 9:23	"better sacrifices"
Hebrews 10:34	"a better possession"
Hebrews 11:16	"a better country"
Hebrews 11:35	"a better resurrection"
Hebrews 11:40	"God had provided something better"
Hebrews 12:24	"better than the blood of Abel"

Hebrews 1:4's phrase "He has inherited" proves critical in understanding what is meant by the same verse's "more excellent name." This name should be thought of as a possession revealing Jesus' character, position, and identity, merited through His immediately preceding work of making "purification of sins" through death and resurrection (1:3). Therefore, we need not specu-

late on the identity of the particular "name" that Jesus has inherited. While it may relate to His divinely granted secret, enigmatic name referenced elsewhere in the New Testament (Phil. 2:9; Rev. 19:12), contextually, it far more likely concerns the divine ratification of His identity as God's "Son" (1:5) upon His exaltation.[7] It is on this concept of divine ratification of sonship that the author immediately begins to build.

Beginning in 1:5, Jesus' superiority over angels is demonstrated using a series of seven Old Testament passages for support. The first use of the Old Testament is a direct quotation of Psalm 2:7, previously alluded to in Hebrews 1:2. Although the Old Testament collectively called angels "sons of God" (Gen. 6:2; Job 1:6; 2:1; 38:7; Pss. 29:1; 89:6), no individual angel was ever referred to by the Lord as *huios mou*, "My Son." This is a title reserved exclusively for the messianic line of David and finds decisive expression as the divine endorsement of Israel's Messiah. The second quotation, from either 2 Samuel 7:14 or its parallel, 1 Chronicles 17:14, provides an emphatic literary counterweight that balances Psalm 2:7's structure of first line referencing the Son with second line referencing the Father, reversing it with 2 Samuel 7:14's (or 1 Chron. 17:14's) first line referencing Father and second line referencing Son.

Davidic Covenant. With the quotation of 2 Samuel 7:14 and 1 Chron. 7:14, the author securely connects Jesus with the promised Davidic covenant. These verses are taken from their larger contexts in 2 Samuel 7:8–16 and 1 Chronicles 17:7–14, two parallel, corresponding passages that establish the Davidic covenant.[8] This indissoluble covenant housed the unconditional set of divine promises that David received of a perpetual dynasty, an unshakable kingdom, and an eternal throne. David was promised that one of his descendants, somehow an ultimate son of both David and God, would forever rule over Israel (2 Sam.7:12–13; Pss. 89:3–4; 132:11).

The importance of the Davidic covenant to a correct interpretation of Hebrews cannot be overemphasized, and we will expend some energy together in the obligatory performance of covenantal deconstruction. This covenant undergirds the book's entire argument concerning Jesus' identity as God's Son and humanity's Messiah. Furthermore, it is not only critical to Hebrews but to the interpretation of both Old and New Testaments. The Davidic covenant, the main fount of biblical messianic expectation, is "the source of the messianic hope as it developed in the message of prophets and psalmists."[9] Specifically, it is impossible to comprehend the basis of the Hebrew Scripture's numerous messianic prophecies (Isa. 9:6–7; 11:1–16; Jer. 23:5–8; 30:1–11; 33:14–17; Ezek. 34:23–26; 34:24–27; Hos. 3:5; Amos 9:11–12; et al.) absent the foundational expectations relayed in the Davidic covenant.

Indeed, "this enduring promise to David has placed messianism at the heart of both Judaism and Christianity.[10] Bergin explains:

> The significance of the eternal covenant between the Lord and David for the New Testament writers cannot be overemphasized. . . . The hopes that were raised by the Lord's words—that God would place a seed of David on an eternal throne and establish a kingdom that would never perish— were ones that no Israelite or Judahite monarch satisfied, or even could have satisfied. But they were ones that the first-century Christians under-stood Jesus to fulfill. The Lord's words recorded here arguably play the single most significant role of any Scripture found in the Old Testament in shaping the Christian understanding of Jesus.[11]

The Davidic covenant as it is presented in 2 Samuel 7:8–16 and 1 Chronicles 17:7–14 consists of eight related components. First, while the immediate introductory context concerned David's desire to build a temple for the Lord, the Lord, however, articulated a clever reversal. Rather than David building a house for the Lord (in the sense of a temple), God Himself pro-nounced that He would build a house (in the sense of a royal dynasty) for David (2 Sam. 7:11).

Second, upon David's death, the son yet to be born, who would serve as his successor and heir, would reign securely (2 Sam. 7:12–16). As Scripture unfolds, it is revealed that this is fulfilled through the rule of David's son Solomon (1 Chron. 22:8–10).

Third, this immediate heir of David would be the one permitted to build a temple for the Lord (2 Sam. 7:13). Solomon did indeed build the temple, both fulfilling this prophecy (1 Kings 6:1–38: 2 Chron. 3:1–5:14) and in ful-fillment of Moses' expressed prophetic expectation of a central, permanent location of Israelite worship (Deut. 12:11–12, 21; 14:23–24; 16:2, 6, 11; 26:2).

Fourth, the throne of this son's kingdom is established forever. The royal dynasty is portrayed not merely as possessing an enduring nature, but an eter-nal one. Furthermore, only the Davidic dynasty would possess the exclusive, divinely authorized authority to rule over the nation of Israel. This theme of the eternality of the Davidic throne, mentioned in 2 Samuel 7:13, 16, is fur-ther developed in the parallel 1 Chronicles passage.

Fifth, as God had long ago promised to his servant Abraham (Gen. 12:2), He likewise promised that He would make great (i.e., renowned, respected) the name of His servant David (2 Sam. 7:9). This was already being accom-plished in David's lifetime, and even now, some three millennia afterwards, he is still both beloved and revered.

Sixth, God pronounced that at some unspecified future time, Israel, plant-ed securely in their land, would experience an unprecedented era of permanent tranquility, peace, security, and justice (Amos 9:11–15; et al.) that had, as its basis, the Davidic covenant (2 Sam. 7:10). This coming millennial kingdom is the oft-mentioned, fervently anticipated hope of the Hebrew prophets who wrote in the centuries-wide wake of this covenant.

Seventh, there is an unconditional divine commitment to this covenant expressed in the promise never to remove the Lord's covenant love/mercy (Heb., *chesed*) from the dynasty as it had previously been removed from David's royal predecessor, Saul, whose dynasty was subsequently cut off. Although divine discipline would be meted out for individual kings' sin, David's dynasty would never be abolished and would continue in perpetuity (2 Sam.7:15–16). Certainly Solomon, who did indeed sin according to the biblical record, required and received the Lord's discipline (1 Kings 11:14, 24–26). Nonetheless, the Davidic dynasty continued, although Solomon's kingdom split almost immediately subsequent to his death (1 Kings 11:31–38). Revealingly, the 1 Chronicles passage, which so closely parallels much of the 2 Samuel passage, omits any mention of the possibility of the future Davidic heir sinning. That is because 1 Chronicles looks beyond the 2 Samuel passage's immediate and imperfect Davidic successor, Solomon, and looks toward a future, perfect, ultimate son of David.

The final, vital component of the Davidic covenant, enumerated solely in the 1 Chronicles account, is the promise of a unique future descendant, an undying son ("established forever," v. 14), who through his immortality would permanently guarantee the seven prior promises. While the 2 Samuel passage empathizes the Davidic dynasty, kingdom and throne, 1 Chronicles emphasizes an eternal king.

Hebrews is just one example of multiple New Testament passages fairly saturated with reference to Jesus being the once and future royal fulfillment and living embodiment of the Davidic covenant. The very opening statement of Matthew's gospel identifies Jesus as "Son of David" (Matt. 1:1). The annunciation, the angel Gabriel's announcement informing Mary, David's direct descendant through his son Nathan (Luke3:23–31), that she would give birth to the Messiah, the long-anticipated Davidic heir, references the Davidic covenant in the angel's very specific, unmistakable, and unambiguous regal covenantal terminology (Luke 1:32–33), concluding that this son of David would also be the Son of God (Luke 1:35). Here we see that the role of angels concerning the Davidic covenant is merely to announce the agency of the covenant's fulfillment.

In first-century Israel, the title "son of David" conveyed a potent political punch. It was widely understood to refer to an idealized political revolutionary who would cast off the shackles of Roman oppression, judge the wicked, and purge evil from the midst of Israel. Israel enthusiastically anticipated that the dynasty of David would be restored and the kingdom of Israel made glorious. This expectation, based on the Hebrew prophets (Isa. 11:1–16; Jer. 23:5–8), is widely espoused throughout first-century Jewish literature, including the Dead Sea Scrolls.[12]

Jesus conducted His ministry amid this whirlwind of amplified Davidic anticipation. In fact, one of the foremost messianic titles ascribed to Jesus in the New Testament is "Son of David." This designates Jesus as the recipient of all the promises God had made to David concerning the future and eternal government of one of his descendants. It specifies Jesus to be a royal, majestic Messiah who is entitled by birthright to rule and reign over all Israel (Matt. 2:2; 9:27; 20:31; Mark 10:48; Luke 23:38; John 7:42; 18:36; Acts 1:6–7).

The "Son of David" concept is specifically linked to Jesus by both Peter (Acts 2:30–31) and Paul (Acts 13:23). It was an important theological component in the presentations of both apostles and, according to their teaching, is primarily applicable to Jesus' future function as King of the earth, when He reigns from His father David's throne in Jerusalem. In Acts 2:30–31 Peter argued that the Holy Spirit showed David that an eternal throne and an unending dynasty required an immortal descendant. To fulfill the Davidic covenant, this Son of David would need to be resurrected. In Acts 13:23 Paul argued that Jesus, the promised Son of David, is the ultimate Davidic King, the prophesied Branch and Root of Jesse (Isa.11:1, 10), Savior of Israel.

Through the establishment of the Davidic covenant, God had prepared Israel for the Messiah's coming. In fact, the fifteenth of the eighteen benedictions contained in the *Amidah*, a corporate prayer regularly recited in the synagogue service, explicitly prays for the coming of this Messiah, reading, "Speedily cause the Branch of your servant David to flourish. Exalt his horn by your salvation, because we hope for your salvation all the day. Blessed are you, O Lord, who causes the horn of salvation to flourish."

Some mistakenly view the Davidic kingdom that Jesus will bring at His second advent as being for the church and not for Israel, a spiritual kingdom and not a literal, national one. In fact, they view this spiritual kingdom as being already here, among the church, as Jesus reigns in our hearts and lives. Because His "eternal Davidic throne" is merely spiritual in nature, what the church is currently experiencing is the entire and only kingdom that we can hope to expect until the day when Jesus returns and takes us back with Him to heaven.

However, the New Testament church would have wondered what other sort of kingdom could be in view if not the physical kingdom promised to Israel throughout the Old Testament. They would have had no conception of the church being a "spiritual" kingdom or any sort of kingdom at all. The concept of a "spiritual Davidic kingdom" is an ingenious notion born in European ivory spires, a great distance removed in both chronologic time and geographic space from first-century Jerusalem, the apostolic witness, or any Jewish Christian with a basic education in the promises God made throughout the Hebrew Scriptures.[13]

There is no question that both testaments of the Scripture together present and confirm the reality of the future restoration of Israel as a nation and the reestablishment of an actual, physical, political Davidic kingdom. The coming messianic age will be characterized by the physical, actual rule and reign of the Messiah, Jesus. His throne will be that of His ancestor, King David, and as the kings of Israel did in ancient days, Jesus will rule from Jerusalem. In what is the next-to-last recorded statement of the risen Lord Jesus in the concluding verses of the entire Bible, the Messiah Himself revealed His own literal understanding of the Davidic covenant when He claimed, "I, Jesus, have sent My angel to testify to you these things for the churches. I am the root and the offspring of David, the bright morning star" (Rev. 22:16).

The third quotation, from Psalm 97:7 (or conversely, a parallel phrase from Deut. 32:43[14]), reveals that the angels pale in comparison to Jesus not only through His embodiment of the Davidic covenant, but also because He, as God's "firstborn" Son, is to receive their worship (1:6). The word *prōtotokos*, "firstborn" (12:23), also used of Jesus by Paul (Rom. 8:29; Col. 1:15, 18), is an Old Testament messianic title (Ps. 89:27) "expressing priority in rank"[15] and "sovereignty over all creation."[16] Jesus is, after all, both creation's creator and heir (1:2).

Although eternally worthy of angelic worship as preexistent and as God from all eternity, Jesus will, according to the text, receive this specific worship at His second advent. There is some ambiguity in the grammatical construction. This leads some to reasonably translate 1:6's *palin* as "again" in reference to the author's additional quotation,[17] instead of in reference to the immediately adjacent verb, *eisagō*, "to bring" (again), which is the preferable choice. When faced with ambiguous grammar, surrounding context should prove determinative. Therefore, in light of the preceding quotation concerning the Davidic king, we should view the angelic worship of the Son as occurring at the second advent. In addition, it appears that the normative use of *palin* when paired with a verb means "again" or "a second time" (5:12; 6:1–2).[18] Furthermore, the term *oikoumenē*, "world," was used of "the inhabited earth," that is, "the entire Roman empire."[19] This correlates with the author's other use of the same term in reference to the messianic kingdom, "the world to come" (2:5).

The fourth quotation is from Psalm 104:4, which emphasizes the changeable nature of angels, who as God's servants (*leitourgos*, the same word used for the service of Levitical priests, from which we derive the English "liturgy") serving at His whim can become elemental forces of wind or fire as He requires (1:7). David Stern provides support for this understanding in Jewish thought, noting "the angel of Judges 13 is described as having said to Manoah, Samson's father, "God changes us hour by hour; . . . sometimes he makes us fire, and sometimes wind."[20] The mutable nature of angels stands in contrast to the unchanging, immutable nature of the Son.

Hebrews' fifth quotation is of Psalm 45:6-7, once again in reference to the intrinsic superiority of the Messiah over angels (1:8-9). In its original context, Psalm 45 is a royal wedding song, and its public recitation was likely designed to be incorporated in the matrimonial festivities. However, nestled snuggly within the psalm is an audacious assertion concerning the divine nature of the king, startling in its very matter-of-factness. The king himself is recognized as God (Heb., *elohim*): "Thy throne, O God, is forever and ever" (45:6). Furthermore, in the following verse, 45:7, the divine king ("O God") of 45:6 is clearly distinguished from God Himself ("Therefore God, Thy God, has anointed Thee with the oil of joy above Thy fellows").

It is this extraordinary passage in Psalm 45 that the author of Hebrews selects to embellish his argument, which should not surprise the astute reader of Hebrews even at this early place in the text. The revelatory light of the New Testament regarding the messianic incarnation dissolves any ambiguity or hint of hyperbole in the psalm's assignation of divinity to the king. It is indisputable that Psalm 45 was interpreted through a messianic lens by the ancient Jewish rabbis, although they are reticent to take the psalm's words at face value and ascribe deity to King Messiah.[21]

Hebrews 1:8-9 (along with Rom. 9:5; Titus 3:4; 2 Pet. 1:1; and a handful of passages in John's gospel) is one of those portions of the New Testament where the casual reader is shocked by the reminder that its authors were rarely coy and sometimes marvelously forthright in not only asserting Jesus' deity, but in actually calling Him "God." Reading this passage in light of the foundation previously laid through the author's opening statements (1:3), we are rhetorically forced to agree that "as God, the divine Davidic Son shares all the attributes of his divine Father."[22] The king's throne symbolized his authority."[23] The means by which this king's throne can endure forever is through "the *eternal duration* of the Davidic Son himself."[24] Luke Johnson's opinion is that "nowhere outside John is the intention to designate the 'son' as (God) so obvious and deliberate."[25]

The use of this psalm allows the author to quietly foreshadow a later theme. The Son, here identified as the king who has "loved righteousness," will later be associated by the author with Melchizedek, translated from Hebrews as "the righteous king." There is some ambiguity concerning the identity of the messianic king's *metochoi*, "companions," "partners," "associates," "coparticipants," or "colleagues." In the context of Hebrews' comparison of the Son with angels, at first glance it would seem natural to identify such supernatural beings as the Son's companions. Yet, contextually, angels are not presented in Hebrews as Christ's "partners" as much as they are His servants. Furthermore, the author's use of the same Greek term elsewhere in Hebrews is exclusively in reference to believers (3:1, 14; 6:4; 12:8). Therefore, the companions of 1:9 are probably best understood in similar fashion, not as angels but as the Son's brethren (2:11). The only other use of the term in the New Testament is in reference to Peter's business partners (Luke 5:7).

Hebrews 1:10–12 contains the author's sixth Old Testament quotation, from yet another psalm (Ps. 102:25–27). This passage builds on the previous quotation's assignation of the Son's deity. In its original context, the psalm begins as a lament (Ps. 102:1–11) but concludes with a section of prophetic praise describing conditions during the messianic kingdom (Ps. 102:12–28). At that time the Lord will "have compassion on Zion, for the appointed time has come" (Ps. 102:13). Zion will be "built up," and the Lord will appear "in His glory" (Ps. 102:16). The nations and their kings will join Israel in worship of the Lord (Ps. 102:15, 22). Notably, the psalm identifies itself as a prophetic message to a future "generation to come, that a people yet to be created may praise the LORD" (Ps. 102:18).

The author of Hebrews apparently concurred with ancient Jewish interpretation that recognized this psalm as referencing the messianic age.[26] He quotes Psalm 102:25–27, reinforcing His previous declaration (1:2) that the Son was the divine, eternal instrument of the entirety of His creation. Having made that point quite well already, the emphasis here is on comparing the temporary, finite nature of creation with the infinite, immortal nature of the Son.

Hebrews' use of this psalm reveals that the clock of creation is running down; time is running out for the earth as we know it. The countdown's commencement is not due to the Lord's impatience or because He has set an arbitrary deadline or has an urgent appointment. If time were the fundamental issue, the Greek word *archaios*, "old in point of lapsed time"[27] (from which we derive the English *archaic*) would have been used in 1:11. Instead, the term utilized is *palaioō*, "to become ancient or worn out." Based on this passage, it appears that the earth, indeed the entire universe, has a definite shelf life.

There is a high probability that readers of a certain age can join me in personally testifying to the veracity of this passage based on personal experience. I can even pinpoint the exact year in my life when the accurate measure of my existence was altered from *archaios* (the normative advancement of consecutive years, from my birth through age thirty-nine) to *palaioō* (the process of "wearing out" that began circa age forty that will eventually, at some far-distant moment, culminate with my "becoming ancient")! All of creation has a built-in shelf life by divine design. Our contemporary headlines are consumed with the international hand wringing over the earth's shifting atmospheric conditions. Hebrews reminds us that even heroic efforts to perpetually preserve the earth are futile; the attempt to regulate our collective carbon footprint on behalf of Mother Earth is a losing battle with no long-term prospects of success. That is very bad news for those individuals who have dedicated their lives to saving the planet but unusually good news for those of us who have dedicated our lives to the Son of God.

In stark contrast to the increasing obsolescence of creation with each passing day, the Creator is eternal. He remains the same (1:11–12) "yesterday, and today . . . and forever" (13:8). From His yesterdays in eternity past, He has planned not only our "todays" but also our "forevers": the eventual transformation and replacement of the entire created order following His reign over the messianic kingdom (Heb. 12:26–27; 2 Pet. 3:10-13; also Isa. 66:22; Rev. 6:14; 21:1).

The language of the psalm paints a wonderfully vibrant portrait. Just as old clothing is rolled up (*helissō*, "to roll up," "to coil") and disposed of by its owner, the entire time-space continuum, the earth, the heavens, even history as we know it, will likewise be "rolled up," tossed away, and replaced with something beyond our imagination (1:11–12). For me, this means that every time I take an old worn-out undershirt, so ratty (I call them "holey") that it cannot even be given away or used as a rag, bunch it up into a ball, and dramatically toss it with a swish into the "round file," I am reminded of creation's divinely designed future.

In 1:13–14 the author uses two ways to rhetorically indicate the conclusion of this present facet of his argument. First, the same question previously asked in 1:5 at the commencement of the series of Old Testament quotations is repeated, "But to which of the angels. . . ." Second, the seventh and final quotation is given from the previously alluded to Psalm 110:1, "Sit at My right hand, until I make Thine enemies a footstool for Thy feet." This combination of repeated question and quotation not only provides rhetorical balance to the open and close of Hebrews' first chapter, but it conclusively reinforces the superiority of the Son over angels. While the angels, the *leitourgika pneumata*, "religiously ministering spirits," are still hard at work on behalf of those who will inherit salvation, the Son is pictured as seated and at rest, awaiting His future reign following the Father's final conquest of the Son's enemies.

Use of Old Testament Passages in Hebrews 1

Hebrews	Old Testament	Subject
1:2	Ps. 2:8	The Son as heir of creation
1:3	Ps. 110:1	The divine authority of the Son
1:5	Ps. 2:7	The sonship of the Messiah
1:5	2 Sam. 7:14/1 Chron. 17:13	The sonship of the Messiah
1:6	Ps. 97:7	Worship of the Son by angels
1:7	Ps. 104:4	The position of angels
1:8–9	Ps. 45:6–7	Deity of the Son
1:10–12	Ps. 102:25–27	Deity of the Son
1:13	Ps. 110:1	The divine authority of the Son

Conclusion

Through the use of quotations from six psalms and a Davidic covenant passage, the author of Hebrews has used the testimony of God Himself to establish the superiority of Jesus over angels. He has a superior name, a superior position, and superior authority. While they are God's servants, He is God's Son. While they are supernatural beings, He is deity. In the following section, the author will provide the first of five "so what?" passages where, through warnings, he will encourage his readers to avoid impending danger through applying his theological argument to their lives.

Study Questions

1. What role do angels play in the advancement of the author's argument?

2. List three ways in which the Son is superior to angels.

3. Why do you think that angels are so popular in twenty-first-century society? Does that popularity impact how people view Jesus, and if so, how?

4. What role, if any, did angels play in relation to the Mosaic covenant?

5. What is the connection between Jesus and the Davidic covenant?

6. What impact, if any, does 1:10–12 have on your personal priorities for the immediate future? For the long term?

CHAPTER 3

Superiority of the Messiah to Angels
2:1-18

Preview:

Having successfully established the superiority of Jesus over angels regarding name, position, and authority in the previous passage, the author of Hebrews allows a momentary rhetorical pause in his presentation. This brief interruption reveals a pastoral concern that his recipients clearly understand the gravity of what is at stake for the recipient community of Jewish believers and the potential devastation that threatens upon an inadequate response to his letter. He encourages his readers to avoid the impending danger through the diligent application of his theological argument to their lives. Indeed, their very lives are at stake. This section commences with the first of five such suspensions he will allow through the letter for the sake of underscoring, through increasingly stern warnings, the necessity of application.

First Resultant Warning of Danger: Concerning Drifting from Messianic Faith (2:1-4)

In a first-century Greek rhetorical equivalent to shouting, "Ahoy mate, there be danger ahead!" the author takes up a decidedly nautical theme to warn his readers of the severity of the impending danger that awaits the community if they continue along on the course they have charted for themselves. The specific risk is that of their community's ship of state being blown off course, graphically stressed through the term *pararreō*, "to drift away," "to flow by," or "to be washed away." The recipients' "holding fast," *prosechein*, to the Messiah and to their confession of faith in Him was as essential as a boat being securely fastened to its anchor amid a turbulent current. As a practiced rhetorician, the author writes here in the first person plural, firmly associating himself with the recipient community. It is essential for every believer, not just of the first-century variety but rather in every age, to follow the author's grave admonition to hold tight to "what we have heard," that is, the gospel, with all diligence.

Use of Old Testament Passages in Hebrews 2

Hebrews	Old Testament	Subject
2:6–8	Ps. 8:5–7	The divine authority of the Son
2:12	Ps. 22:22	The purpose of the Son
2:13	Isa. 8:17–18	The purpose of the Son
2:13	Isa. 12:2	The purpose of the Son
2:16	Isa. 41:8–9	Messiah as Son of Abraham

Once the necessity of remaining anchored in the faith is established, the author presents his concern of potential judgment by using the Jewish rhetorical technique of *qal vachomer*, the "light and heavy." This is an argument that compares a truth with lesser significance to that with greater significance (recognizable by the telltale "How much more so?" comparison, as in 9:13–14; 10:28–29; 12:25). The thrust of 2:2–3 is that since "transgression and disobedience" to the Mosaic Law resulted in severe penalty (*endikon misthapodosian*, "a fair wage" or "a just reward"), the consequences of such neglect regarding the superior new covenant would be that much more calamitous. The author will shortly develop this argument using the specific illustration of Israel's disobedience in the wilderness sojourn (3:6ff.).

As discussed in the previous chapter, although the role of angels in mediating the Mosaic covenant had not been previously disclosed in the text of the Old Testament, it was nonetheless the most important acknowledged fact concerning angels by the Second Temple era. This tradition held unquestioning Jewish acceptance and is revealed not only through New Testament references by Stephen in his Sanhedrin defense (Acts 7:38–39, 53) and by Paul in his letter to the Galatian church (Gal. 3:19), but also by reference in Josephus' *Antiquities*[1] and the first-century BC pseudepigraphal book of *Jubilees* (1:26–2:1).[2] The argument of 2:2–3 is built on the new covenant's inherent superiority to the Mosaic covenant by virtue of the superiority of the mediation of the Messiah over that of angels.

The rhetorician poses a weighty rhetorical question to his audience. The Mosaic Law contained very specific penalties concerning transgression of its 613 commandments, such as the offering of various sacrifices, degrees of restitution, excommunication, and the like, culminating in the death penalty for deliberate, purposeful "high-handed" sins (Num. 15:30). If an Israelite was guilty of such gross disobedience, punishment was automatic with no possible appeal.

The author's impassioned plea to his recipients is to avoid developing an attitude of indifference (*ameleō*, "to neglect" or "to be careless with") the Messiah's great work of salvation (*sōtēria*, "deliverance," "preservation," "salvation") through the superior new covenant. The potential penalty for such disobedience would be no less automatic and no less severe. There is no available means of escape (*ekpheugō*, "to flee away from") from divinely meted discipline.

The Warnings. Of course, determining the exact nature of the inferred divine discipline is the infamous stumbling stone that has tripped up interpreters and expositors of Hebrews throughout Christendom. It is a remarkable fact that today we are no closer to a consensus on Hebrews' warning passages than in "the days of the early church."[3] Interpretive disagreement is found between both the generally anticipated sectarian stances of Catholic versus Eastern Orthodox versus Protestant and the theologically polar positions of Calvinist versus Wesleyan or Reformed versus Arminian. Indeed, the interpretive disagreement cuts across the entirety of Christendom, dividing even theologically harmonious groups, such as premillennial dispensationalists (about as theologically homogenous an evangelical subset as one may find).

Ultimately, two basic views are maintained concerning the warning passages, although there are multiple nuanced interpretive variations and modifications that are derived from the two seminal positions. The first basic interpretive position, generally held by those tending toward the direction of Arminianism, is that the warning passages concern the "very real danger of apostasy that true believers can commit, and if they do so it is an unpardonable sin from which there is no possibility of repentance, but only of eternal judgment."[4] In short, once apostate, a genuine believer may, through loss of faith, permanently forfeit his or her salvation with no opportunity for appeal. Simply, if believers abandon Christ, He will likewise follow suit and permanently abandon them in turn, with no further possibility of reconciliation. "It becomes quite clear that the author has in mind an eternal sense of destruction."[5]

This approach originates from an attempt to grapple with the apparent plain meaning of the final four of the five passages in question. Yet this first position must be rejected on the basis that a believer's transitory state of rebellion possesses insufficient power to nullify the eternal, completed work of our Messiah. Christ's efforts were sufficiently powerful to initially save us from the depths of our slavery to sin and reconcile us to God (Rom. 5:10ff.; 6:6–11). As the blood of Christ has no shelf life, the potency of His work is undiminished upon our redemption. It is impossible for the traveler to turn back or turn aside once the journey along the pathway of eternal life has begun. There is no switch to reset, rewind, or erase the finished work of Jesus (see New Testament Passages on Assurance of Salvation below). This position overvalues the *qal vachomer* ("lesser and greater") contrast, imagining that since the punishment for disobedience to the lesser covenant resulted in physical death that disobedience to the far greater covenant would logically result in that which transcends the physical realm, eternal damnation. The text in no way warrants this level of escalation.

The second basic interpretation, set forth in this commentary and usually held by those generally tending toward the direction of Calvinism, is a bit more complex in makeup in that it is more presupposition than position per se. It maintains that in light of the strong, clear passages in the text of Hebrews (as well as the remainder of the New Testament, again, see New Testament Passages on Assurance of Salvation below), whatever it may be that the warning passages are referencing, under no condition are they to be understood as assertions that believers can forfeit their salvation. It is the fact that this second position finds its raison d'être not so much in what the warning passages teach but rather in that which they do not that explains the quantity of variations it has necessarily spawned in order to adequately address the question as to just what it is that the warnings reference.

New Testament Passages on Assurance of Salvation	
John 1:12	*"But as many as received Him, to them He gave the right to become children of God."*
John 6:37–40	*"All that the Father gives Me shall come to Me, and the one who comes to Me I will certainly not cast out. . . . of all that He has given Me I lose nothing . . . everyone who beholds the Son and believes in Him may have eternal life; and I Myself will raise him up."*
John 10:28–29	*"They shall never perish; and no one shall snatch them out of My hand. . . . no one is able to snatch them out of the Father's hand."*
John 14:16	*"He will give you another Helper, that He may be with you forever."*

Rom 4:21	*"Fully assured that what [God] had promised, He was able also to perform."*
Rom. 5:10	*If while we were enemies, we were reconciled to God through the death of His Son, much more, having been reconciled, we shall be saved by His life."*
Rom. 8:1	*"There is therefore now no condemnation for those who are in Christ Jesus."*
Rom. 8:29–30	*"For whom He foreknew, He also predestined to become conformed to the image of His Son . . . whom He called, these He also justified; and whom he justified, these He also glorified."*
Rom. 8:34–35	*"Christ Jesus . . . who also intercedes for us. Who shall separate us from the love of Christ."*
Rom. 8:38–39	*"Neither death, nor life, nor angels, nor principalities, nor things present, nor things to come, nor powers, nor height, nor depth, nor any other created thing, shall be able to separate us from the love of God."*
Rom. 11:29	*"The gifts and the calling of God are irrevocable."*
1 Cor. 1:8	*"Who shall also confirm you to the end, blameless."*
1 Cor. 5:5	*"Deliver such a one to Satan for the destruction of his flesh, so that his spirit may be saved in the day of the Lord Jesus."*
2 Cor. 1:21–22	*God, who also sealed us and gave us the Spirit . . . as a pledge."*
2 Cor. 5:17	*"If any man is in Christ, he is a new creature."*
Gal. 3:3	*"Having begun by the Spirit, are you now being perfected by the flesh?"*
Eph. 1:5	*"He predestined us to adoption as sons through Jesus Christ to Himself, according to the kind intention of His will."*
Eph. 1:13–14	*"Having also believed, you were sealed in Him with the Holy Spirit of promise, who is given as a pledge of our inheritance."*
Eph. 2:4–6	*"God, because of His great love . . . raised us up with [Christ], and seated us with Him in the heavenly places."*
Eph. 2:8–9	*"For by grace you have been saved through faith; and that not of yourselves, it is the gift of God; not as a result of works."*
Eph. 4:30	*"The Holy Spirit of God, by whom you were sealed for the day of redemption."*
Phil. 1:6	*"He who began a good work in you will perfect it until the day of Christ Jesus."*
Heb. 5:9	*"He became to all those who obey Him the source of eternal salvation."*

Heb. 6:19	"This hope we have as an anchor of the soul, a hope both sure and steadfast."
Heb. 7:25	"He is able also to save forever those who draw near to God through Him, since He always lives to make intercession for them."
Heb. 9:12	"He entered the holy place once for all, having obtained eternal redemption."
Heb. 9:15	"Those who have been called may receive the promise of the eternal inheritance."
Heb. 10:14	"For by one offering He has perfected for all time those who are sanctified."
Heb. 13:20	"The blood of the eternal covenant."
1 Pet. 1:3	"According to His great mercy has caused us to be born again to a living hope."
1 Pet. 1:4–5	"An inheritance . . . reserved in heaven for you, who are protected by the power of God through faith for a salvation ready to be revealed."
1 Pet. 3:18	"Christ also died for sins once for all . . . in order that He might bring us to God."

The first of these subset positions is that the warnings concern the danger of eternal judgment not for believers (who possess unshakable assurance of salvation) but rather for those who, while having joined themselves to the community of faith and even made outward profession of belief, demonstrate the superficiality of their faith through its abandonment under pressure.[6] In short, although they outwardly appear Christian, nonetheless, their belief never progressed beyond an initial abstract, cerebral assent to the facts of Christianity to develop into a genuine, personal faith of the heart. The basis for this interpretation is two conditional statements (3:6, 14) that indicate that confident perseverance and endurance will eventually verify their faith.[7]

However, acceptance of this view seems to guarantee that practically, one cannot truly gauge the genuineness of one's own faith until life's final moment. In addition, as has been previously discussed in the introductory section on Recipients (see especially Possible Recipients of the Book of Hebrews starting on p. 12), the author, unconditionally and without qualification or irony, portrays the recipient audience as genuine believers, not false confessors (2:3; 3:1, 12, 14; 4:3, 14; 6:9; 10:23, 29, 32–35; 12:22–24;13:23). It is both a strenuous challenge and a tenuous endeavor to construe this passage in reference to a nominally Christian community. Furthermore, the text contains the author's admonition regarding the community's lack of spiritual progress (2:1; 5:11–6:3) as well as his assumption that they possesses the potential to develop rapidly into mature believers (6:1). His concern is for the stunting of the community's spiritual progress, not that they had failed to launch themselves off the spiritual starting line (5:11–14).

A second, yet equally unsatisfactory subset position is that the warnings are indeed addressed to true believers and do in fact conceptually concern eternal punishment. Nonetheless, the warnings are completely hypothetical in nature and presented by the author for rhetorically provocative, hyperbolic effect.[8] This position, while imaginative, nonetheless seems somewhat forced and a bit shallow.

A third subset position is that the warnings concern eternal punishment, yet they are addressed to recipients who are characterized as either a mixed group of both believers and unbelievers or, alternatively, a group that is composed in its entirety of unbelievers. However, the Christian identity of the Hebrews recipients has been previously established both in the introductory discussion on Recipients (again, see Possible Recipients of the Book of Hebrews beginning on p. 12) and in the discussion of the first subset position, immediately above.

The fourth subset position is that the warnings concern not eternal punishment but rather a loss of rewards: the disqualification of disobedient believers from enjoyment of future honored service in the millennial age. This interpretive position is the most attractive of the above alternatives and shares a certain contextual perspective with the position set forth in this commentary. The strengths of the "rewards" position are as follows. First, it recognizes that the recipients are indeed true believers. Second, it incorporates the New Testament's (including Hebrews) doctrine of the believers' assurance of salvation. Third, in perhaps the seemingly severest of Hebrews' warning passages (6:7–8), it is not the field that is destroyed by burning but the worthless vegetation. Thus, the believer's apostasy would be punished but the consequence would fall far short of loss of salvation. Fourth, there is significant correlation between the historical punishment cited as illustration, that is, the judgment on Israel's wilderness generation and their subsequent loss of reward, and the present threat of which the author warns the recipients. Finally, Paul's expressed concern regarding the avoidance of disqualification (1 Cor. 9:27) as well as his teaching on each believer receiving commensurate reward or loss, depending on whether the quality of his work endures the assessment of divine fire (1 Cor. 3:11–15, note that it is the subpar work that is burned up, not the believer).[9] However, the inherent failure of this position is a deficient view of the calamitous physical judgment that awaits the Jewish Christian apostasy of this generation. The idea of loss of reward or glory in the millennial kingdom is a great step in the correct direction, yet insufficiently correlates to the severity of discipline indicated in the next to last warning passage (10:26–31).

As previously discussed in detail in the introductory material regarding both Recipients and Purpose, the position of this commentary is that the "warning passages" are time-bound and relate only to one specific generation of Jewish Christians concerning the impending judgment that was to be inflicted on the specific generation of Israel that had rejected Jesus and attributed the source of His miraculous work to Satan (Matt 23:35–36; Luke 11:50–51; Acts 2:40). For the apostasy spoken of here, the believer's abandonment of the Messiah and return to Judaism's obsolete Levitical system, the punishment was certain and inescapable. Divine discipline would be meted out to those Jewish believers who chose to realign themselves with Judaism.

This view is the only one of the interpretive positions that addresses each of the warning passages' elements that make a consistent systematic analysis so challenging. While each alternative view has at least one strong aspect to commend it (and many have several aspects), they all find themselves with a "fatal flaw," an element that does not fit the system and must be explained away with varying levels of success. However, first of all, this view maintains fidelity to the multiple Scriptures that teach assurance of salvation. Second, this view affirms that with the exception of the unpardonable sin committed by the Jewish leadership of the first century, forgiveness is always God's response to repentance. Third, this view recognizes the genuineness of the recipient community's Christian faith. Fourth, this view exercises measured restraint in understanding the typological correspondence between the recipients of Hebrews and their ancestors that does not surpass what is indicated by the text. Fifth, this view approaches the passages from a consistently Jewish perspective that pays appropriate attention to the Old Testament context that serves as the foundation of the argument of Hebrews.

The repercussions and ramifications of this interpretive position against the framework of the text will be explored in the remaining four warning passages as they appear in context throughout the commentary.

The gospel to which the community was to strongly attend is described as having initially been delivered by Jesus through his teaching and ministry. His message of great (*tēlikautēs*) salvation (*sōtēria*) began at the inauguration of His ministry when He announced repentance for the sake of the coming kingdom of God/heaven, the Hebrew *olam haba*, the messianic age (Matt 3:2; Mark 1:15), referenced by the author of Hebrews as "the world to come" (2:5), "the age to come" (6:5), and "an unshakable kingdom" (12:28), of which Christians currently experience but a foretaste (6:5).

The significance of His being called here *tou kuriou*, "the Lord," a word that is commonly used in the Septuagint to translate the covenant name of God,

YHWH, must not be overlooked. The new covenant message of the gospel was delivered not merely through supernatural agents, but via a divine one.

Warnings of Danger in Hebrews

Hebrews	Warning	Eternal Security
2:1–4	Drifting from messianic faith	No impact on this doctrine
3:7–4:13	Disobedience and doubt	No impact on this doctrine
5:11–6:20	Spiritual stagnation	No impact on this doctrine
10:26–31	The inferior lifestyle of faithlessness	No impact on this doctrine
12:25–29	Spiritual insensitivity	No impact on this doctrine

Those who heard. Following Jesus' death, resurrection, and ascension, His singular message of salvation was disseminated through "those who heard," the apostles. The term *apostolos* is primarily used throughout the New Testament in a specialized sense to mean "commissioned one," with the commissioning having been done by Christ. Thus, an apostle is a commissioned representative of Christ who is empowered by His delegated authority. The New Testament teaches two extremely restricted classifications of the apostolic office. The first category was the more restrictive. This is the primary category of apostle, and membership was limited to the Twelve who were personally selected by Jesus to be His representatives, act as authoritative witnesses of His ministry, and provide the founding leadership for His church.[10]

The second classification of apostle was more inclusive but possessed requirements that were no less stringent. The New Testament does not supply a complete list of this group of apostles, but it includes James (the brother of Jesus), Barnabas, and Paul. Paul's first letter to the Corinthians reveals that the essential requirement for this level of apostleship is to have actually seen the resurrected Lord Jesus (1 Cor. 9:1). We can infer from Paul that while the capacity of this category of apostle is seemingly not restricted to twelve, it is limited to a set number (some five hundred; 1 Cor. 15:5–8) of individuals to whom Christ personally appeared. Moreover, Paul is clear that in addition to the unprecedented fashion by which he has witnessed the resurrected Christ (Acts 9:3–8), he was the very last (and least) one of this group to do so (1 Cor. 15:8–9). Paul was adamant that, by definition, there can never be any other apostles after him.

Paul gives one final delimiter concerning this category of apostle: the ability to perform "the signs of a true apostle," that is, signs, wonders, and miracles (2 Cor. 12:12). Like identifying "calling cards," these signs were the divine validation, the credentials of those with genuine apostolic authority. In addition to serving as commissioned witnesses of the Lord Jesus' resurrection, the apostles also provided the leadership of the community of faith, overseeing its growth and radical expansion outward from Jerusalem. Additionally, Paul refers to apostleship as being one of the gifts of the Holy Spirit (1 Cor. 12:28; Eph. 4:11).

The author quite expressly excludes himself from the category of apostolic eyewitness. He, along with the addressed Hebrews' faith community, was a second-generation beneficiary of the apostolic witness (although one likely to later become an intimate in Paul's circle, see discussion on Authorship in the introductory material).

The apostolic message of God's final revelation (1:1) was confirmed and authenticated through God's accompanying testimony of "signs and wonders," "by various miracles," and "by gifts of the Holy Spirit." These supernatural manifestations were distributed "according to His own will." It is of extreme importance to note that the miracles that characterized the early church's characteristic miracles exclusively took place through and solely by means of the apostles (Acts 2:1–43; 3:1–11; 5:1–12, 15–16; 9:32–41; 13:6–11; 14:3, 8–10; 15:12; 16:16–18; 19:11–12; 20:7–12; 28:3–5, 8–9) or their close associates (Acts 6:8; 8:6). Miracles, signs, and wonders were an essential component of apostleship and served as one means to authenticate their authority. Every supernatural manifestation recorded in the New Testament's brief record of early church history, the book of Acts, was carried out through an apostle or a close apostolic associate, without exception.

The evidence provided in Acts is corroborated by the grammatical and contextual linkage in 2:3–4 between the eyewitnesses (the apostles, "those who heard") and the supernatural confirmation of their message to the audience ("us," the author and the letter's recipients). There is enormous significance to be found in the fact that the word *ebebaiōthē*, "was confirmed" or "secured," is in aorist passive indicative form. What the author is saying is that sometime in the past, the gospel had been confirmed in their midst through signs and wonders. However, this was no longer the community's present experience. By the midpoint of the seventh decade of the first century, this church was no longer witness to the great manifestations of God's power they had experienced at some previous point.

From this can be derived two conclusions. First, it confirms the obvious assumption that the community no longer had direct apostolic contact (by this time the majority of apostles from either classification were dead). Second, it confirms that even if signs and wonders had commonly manifested themselves beyond the apostles and their circle in the earliest church history, by this point that was no longer the case. Otherwise, the meticulous persuader missed an opportunity to exhort his audience to heed the apostolic testimony still being confirmed in the midst through signs and wonders.[11]

Jesus' Temporary Inferiority to Angels Contrasted with His Current Exaltation (2:5–9)

Having drawn an emphatic application to the theological argument of 1:1–14, the author now resumes his line of reasoning concerning the Messiah's superiority to angels, this time in relation to future rule. Hebrews 2:5 is an important verse relative to a premillennial understanding of prophecy. The phrase "the world to come" translates *tēn oikoumenēn tēn mellousan*, literally, "the inhabited world about to be." The author avoids figurative language of a "heavenly" or "spiritual" future world and instead references the graphic concept of Old Testament expectation. A corporal messianic king will rule a corporal messianic kingdom. The word *hupotassō*, "to subject," is a military term used of arranging soldiers in order under the commanding general.[12]

Psalm 8:5–7 is now employed by the author to advance his argument, casually introduced with the nonspecific, "one has testified somewhere." Since for the author of Hebrews the Holy Spirit is the ultimate author behind the author (3:7; 9:8; 10:15), apparently a citation of the human agency was occasionally dispensable.[13] However, the author's ignorance of David's identity should not be presumed. This is, after all, a particularly potent psalm with powerful messianic imagery.

The enigmatic title "son of man," in Greek *huios anthropou* and in Aramaic *bar enash*, was Jesus' preferred messianic self-designation. His use of this term for Himself is studded throughout the Gospels. Jesus used this phrase as an allusion to the vision of the Hebrew prophet Daniel of a divinely exalted figure, "one like a son of man," coming with "the clouds of heaven" (Dan. 7:13–14). This mysterious figure receives authority over God's kingdom from the "Ancient of Days," God Himself. As frequently as Jesus employed this term, He is the only one in the entire New Testament who does so with the exception of Stephen (Acts 7:56) and the author of Hebrews in this passage.

However, "son of man" was not universally used this way in Scripture. Although Jesus did not wish merely to indicate that he was a human being, a "regular Joe," in the original context of Psalm 8 the phrase is used as an alternate means to indicate humankind, those in possession of the character of humanity. The psalm is concerned with man's original divine design for dominion over creation. The author of Hebrews, however, sees messianic prophecy at play and goes beyond the original context and uses the loaded messianic phrase "son of man" to advance his argument.

Although during His earthly incarnation the Messiah was made temporarily inferior ("for a little while") in status to the angels through emptying Himself of divine glory (Phil. 2:6–8), His current, permanent exaltation definitively demonstrates His superiority. Although we do not yet see all things in subjection to His authority as promised, we will most assuredly do so in the future age to come. The great paradox of this passage is that the creator and heir of the universe (1:1–3), who, as Lord of all, possesses every right to exercise His authority and dominion at present, is willing to temporarily defer the exercise of that dominion and the accompanying glory until the millennial age (Dan 7:27).[14]

It is fitting that at this juncture, for the first time in the text, the author finally explicitly mentions the name of Jesus in 2:9. His exaltation, that is, His being "crowned [Gk., *stephanoō*, 'to crown,' as in a Greco-Roman political or athletic triumph] with glory and honor" was made possible only through the intensity of the suffering He endured to the death. Achievement of this level of honor entailed more than conquest of mere enemies or competitors; it demanded the conquest of death itself. He has tasted (*geusētai*, "to fully partake of," "to come to know," "to taste," "to appropriate") death on our behalf by means of "the grace of God."

The Superiority of the Messiah's Purpose to That of Angels (2:10–18)

The author's argument continues with the affirmation that the purposes of the Messiah were superior to that of angels. In order to "bring many sons to glory," the Messiah necessarily had to die. No messianic death would mean no salvation for humanity. Furthermore, the Messiah would overcome the devil and liberate believers from slavery. Finally, he would render to humanity a prime quantity of messianic aid.

Messiah's purpose was to bring many sons to glory (2:10–13). God the Father is the subject of 2:10, identified as "Him for whom are all things, and through whom are all things." This was a phrase that the Stoics used to reference their supreme deity of deities, "but the idea fit Jewish thought about God and divine Wisdom and was widely used by Diaspora Jewish writers, including Paul (1 Cor 8:6)."[15] God is, indeed, both the ultimate first cause and final reason for the existence of universal matter.

The author maintains that using the process of suffering to perfect His Son was somehow "fitting" (*eprepen*, "becoming," seemly," "inherently appropriate"). As Kenneth Wuest powerfully comments:

> It was an inner fitness in God's dealings. The fact that God the Father decreed that it must be through the blood of Christ's Cross that the Captain of our salvation would become the Saviour of sinners, did not find its origin in a divine fiat, but in the very constitution of the nature of God. A holy God cannot look upon sin with any degree of allowance. A righteous God cannot but require that the demands of the violated law be satisfied. And a loving God cannot but provide the very payment of the penalty which His law demands. Thus, the writer shows the sweet reasonableness of the Cross. And because only God can satisfy the demands of God, so only the Messiah who is one of the Persons of the Godhead, could in the great plan of salvation, provide the sacrifice. God the Father provides the salvation, God the Son procures it, and God the Holy Spirit applies it.[16]

The term *teleiōsai* is translated here as "to perfect," and rather than indicating corrective need to address imperfection in Jesus, moral or otherwise, the word actually signifies the completion or consummation of a goal or the termination of a process once the accomplishment is attained. The goal that He has achieved at such great cost is our salvation. This directly links Jesus to His qualifications for His role as our great High Priest. "The Greek words for perfecting are used in a similar way in the LXX in connection with ordaining or consecrating priests (Exod. 29:9, 29, 33; Lev. 8:33; 21:10), and the link with high priestly service appears in each of the contexts in Hebrews in which Jesus is said to have been perfected (Heb. 2:10; 5:9; 7:28)."[17]

Our Messiah is designated as the *archēgon*, "the champion," "the leader," the very source and author of our salvation. This is a rare messianic title that is used by the author of Hebrews in 2:10 and 12:2 and only an additional two times in the New Testament in Acts (3:15; 5:31).[18] Jesus is presented here almost as a dramatic protagonist, a heroic captain who has blazed a new trail through the wilderness for his men to follow. However, although the path leads to glory, it is a journey along the way of suffering. Once we have decided to follow Jesus, we must understand that this is the path He has pioneered on our behalf.

Jesus is not only our accomplished champion, but also our sanctifier, the One who consecrates us, who makes us *hagiazō*, "holy." Furthermore, He is our Brother as well. We belong to His family. We share with Jesus the same Father. His familial love and acceptance of us are completely devoid of condescension. While I myself am an only child, I have nonetheless observed the youthful pattern of older brothers or sisters being occasionally embarrassed or chagrined by their younger siblings, sometimes not so much because of words or behavior but by their very existence. However, we may confidently rest assured that our older Brother is not ashamed of us. This fact would have enormous significance to a community of Jewish believers being pressured by the circumstance of persecution to abandon their hold on faith in Christ alone.

The author illustrates this point through quick quotation of three Old Testament passages—Psalm 22:22; Isaiah 8:17; and 8:18—linked together in a daisy chain of Scripture. The third quotation is notable in that the family metaphor moves from our relationship to Jesus as His brothers to our relationship as His children. This singular idea of Jesus being our parent and we His children is found only here in the New Testament but is rooted in Isaiah 53:10, which states that the Lord's Suffering Servant would see His offspring. It is nice to pause at this point where one can take a momentary break from the meticulously arranged theological argument and simply ponder the image of Jesus as our father, and God (the Father) as our grandfather.

Messiah's purpose was to overcome the devil (2:14). Hebrews echoes John's affirmation that the purpose of Jesus' incarnation was "that he might destroy the works of the devil" (1 John 3:8) through His (Jesus') death. Satan is a tyrant with divinely permitted dominion over the realm of physical death. To destroy (*katargeō*, "to render inoperative") the *kratos*, "dominion," or "power" of Satan, here referenced as "the devil," it was paradoxically necessary for the Messiah to experience death Himself. That, of course, required Him to "partake of" the full human condition.

Thanks to our Messiah's faithful commitment, believers may have no fear of Satan's dominion over death, for eternal life has been granted. Nonetheless, Satan can still exercise dominion over the death of the believer's physical body in the case of excommunication (1 Cor. 5:1–5), wherein the material body may be destroyed, but as with all believers, the immaterial soul is eternally preserved to be in God's presence.

The rabbinic legends record an account of Satan bewailing his future humiliation at the hands of the messianic champion. "When Satan saw the Messiah, he trembled and fell upon his face and said: 'Surely this is the Messiah who in the future will cast me . . . into Gehenna (hell).'"[19]

Messiah's purpose was to liberate the believer from slavery (2:15). This verse is the true source of biblical liberation theology. In the ancient world, no people understood slavery like God's chosen people. Nevertheless, Pharaoh's power had nothing on that of the devil. Humanity's enslavement to Satan through fear of death has been shattered once and for all through Jesus' own death and resurrection. The assurance of our eternal life through our Messiah efficiently breaks the enslaving bondage of fear. Our chains are gone.

Messiah's purpose was to render aid to humanity (2:16–18). The Messiah was to be the Savior of humanity, not the Savior of the angels. The only way He could do that was to become human Himself. In 2:16, the author's use of the Greek phrase *spermatos Abraam*, "descendant of Abraham," points toward the fact that for the Messiah to provide salvation for humankind, he could not incarnate as just any human anywhere in the world. His incarnation would necessarily be as a Jewish man in the chosen people's promised nation of Israel. We should not, therefore, understand "descendant of Abraham" in the general sense that all believers, Jewish and Gentile alike, are the spiritual children of Abraham (Rom. 4:16), but in the basic, physical sense of the phrase as it is likewise used by God in addressing His servant, the nation of Israel through the prophet Isaiah (41:8). To save humanity, Jesus would have to be Jewish. It was, after all, a basic component of the Abrahamic covenant that Abraham's seed would ultimately be the means of universal blessing (Gen. 12:3; Gal. 3:16).

The purpose of Jesus' Jewish ethnicity is continued in 2:17–18. It is spoken of as an obligation (*ōpheilō*, "what is owed"). The prerequisite for the successful completion of the messianic mission was to become a Jewish man. Through identification and solidarity, His humanity enabled Him to become two things, both merciful and faithful. His mercy indicates His ability to sympathize with humanity, not only the ability to feel compassion but to extend actual relief to the suffering. His faithfulness indicates his unwavering fidelity and trustworthiness. Yet it is His identity as a Jewish man that entitles Him to become a High Priest, a sufficient representative, first for Jews and then for Gentiles.

Although the author had previously introduced the concept of Jesus' priesthood in subtle fashion (1:3; 2:9–11), this is his first explicit use of the term *High Priest* (Gk., *archeireus*; Heb., *cohan gadol*).[20] The overarching purpose of Jesus' high priesthood was to make propitiation for the sins of the people, to reconcile humanity to a holy God through satisfying His righteous requirements concerning their sin. This High Priest does not hold Himself aloof from the community, but has fully identified with them. Since Jesus passed the ultimate test through His suffering, there is no temptation, no pressure, and no trial so great to which Jesus cannot apply His unique brand of messianic first aid (*boētheō*, "to run to the aid of one who cries for help").

Conclusion

In Hebrews 2 we see the conclusion of the author's comparison between the Messiah and angels and demonstration of Jesus' definitive superiority with regard to both status and purpose. We have also been introduced to the subject of Jesus as our High Priest. The author has thus far gently opened the faucet to allow the flow of a gentle trickle on the subject of Jesus' priesthood, but he is preparing for a torrential theological stream that will accompany his full turn of the knob in upcoming chapters.

Study Questions

1. Summarize the basic views and their variations concerning the interpretation of the warning passages. Which view do you find most compelling? What is the most compelling support for your position?

2. How would you recognize if a fellow believer was beginning to "drift away"? What counsel would you offer? Would you recognize the signs in your own life? What steps would you take to address the issue?

3. Have you ever ignored "so great a salvation"? What corrective steps did you take?

4. What importance does the title "son of man" possess?

5. Summarize the purposes of the Messiah and their significance.

CHAPTER 4

Superiority of the Messiah to Moses
Hebrews 3:1–6

Preview:

Having established the supremacy of Jesus over angels, the supernatural mediators of the Mosaic covenant, the author of Hebrews turns his attention to the
"lawgiver" himself, the covenantal namesake. Moses is the towering personality
of the Hebrew Scriptures. His massive shadow falls over not only the five books
he authored, the Pentateuch, but over the entirety of the Old Testament. There are
772 occurrences of the name of Moses in the Old Testament, a number of mentions surpassed only by David. Moses, the prince of Egypt, shepherd, prophet,
mediator, and sea parter is at the core of Judaism in his identity as both proto-
prophet and lawgiver par excellence. He is also at the center of Christianity in
his role as typological progenitor of the Messiah, Jesus, the prophet like unto
Moses (Deut. 18:15–18). In the New Testament, his name appears more times
than any other Old Testament figure (surpassing David by twenty mentions).

In the world of first-century Judaism (and throughout ensuing Jewish history),
Moses was held in quasi-supernatural esteem. The Talmud, the Jewish oral law,
contains the Jewish belief expressed by various rabbinic sages "that there was a
cosmic relationship, or rather equivalency, between Moses and the Messiah."[1]
For example, in a discussion concerning the express purpose of creation, while
one rabbi opined that that the world was created for the sake of the Messiah,
another was of the opinion that that honor belongs to Moses.[2] While somewhat
less grandiose in his messianic conceptions, the greatly influential twelfth-centu-
ry rabbi Maimonides nevertheless elevated Moses over the long-awaited (in his
expectation) Messiah, writing that the Messiah would be greater than all
prophets with the exception of Moses and that "the Messiah, indeed, ranks after
Moses in eminence and distinction."[3]

In this succinct portion of Hebrews, the author adroitly demonstrates Jesus' superiority to Moses in person, purpose, and position.

Use of Old Testament Passages in Hebrews 3

Hebrews	Old Testament	Subject
3:2–5	Num. 12:7	The position of Moses
3:7–11	Ps. 95:7–11	Israel's wilderness rebellion
3:8	Exod. 17:7	Israel's wilderness rebellion
3:11	Num. 14:22–23 *	Israel's wilderness rebellion
3:15	Ps. 95:7–8	Admonition to faithfulness
3:16–18	Num. 14:1–35	Israel's wilderness rebellion

Superior to Moses in Person and Purpose (3:1–4)

Moses. Deuteronomy 18:15–18 contains the significant prophecy of the prophet like unto Moses. It is seen that the Messiah would also be the greatest of the Jewish prophets, Moses' successor. As a result of the Israelites having deferred any further direct communication with God (Exod. 20:18–19), Moses promised that the Lord would elevate a prophet like himself from among the people of Israel. The passage goes on to stress that obedience to the prophet like Moses would be so crucial, of such utmost importance to God, that those who neither recognize this prophet nor obey him will suffer the severest penalty. God's harshest judgment will fall on those who willingly disregard this singular prophet. Jesus' fulfillment of this prophecy was an established association that had been made by the Jewish people throughout Jesus' ministry (John 1:21, 25, 45; 5:46; 6:14; 7:40) and was powerfully contended for in the early days of the church (Acts 3:22–26; 7:37).

The nascent church viewed the Messiah's identification with Moses as a key thread in the messianic fabric. Jesus' ministry shared certain unique features with Moses. First, the quality that made Moses distinct from all other Jewish prophets was his intimate relationship with the Lord, speaking together with Him "face to face" (Deut. 34:10) and "mouth to mouth" (Num. 12:8). As the exact representation of God's nature (1:3), the Son of God exhibited similar, although superior, intimacy with the One He called "My Father."

Second, Moses' relationship with the Jewish people was unique for a prophet in that he played two primary roles. He was both Israel's deliverer (Exod. 3:10), bringing the nation forth from the shackles of Egypt, and an intercessor between Israel and God (Exod. 20:19). However, just as Jesus' intimate relationship with God reflects and surpasses that of Moses, so, too, the deliverance Jesus wrested for His people from the slavery of sin reflects and surpasses the ministry of Moses. Regarding his superior intercessory function, Jesus represented God to the people of Israel with an authority greater than even that of Moses as he descended from Sinai cradling two stone tablets in his arms. Moses was a magnificent intercessor, but his humanity created built-in limitations. Our exalted Messiah knows no such restrictions in His continual ministry in the heavenlies.

Third, Moses had the honor to present the old covenant, but Jesus, as the quintessence, the fulfillment, the personification, and the application of every regulation, statute, and commandment recorded by Moses, presented the new covenant. He is the living, breathing, resurrected embodiment of God's Word (John 1:1).

The recipient Hebrews community is addressed with a double reference to the authenticity of their messianic faith. They are "holy brethren," sacred through their status as *metachoi*, "partakers," or "partners" of a heavenly calling. They are resolutely cautioned to "consider" Jesus, to carefully consider and study the One whom they have confessed as Messiah. The word translated "confession," *homologia*, conveys the idea of a binding obligation, a public expression of commitment and profession of allegiance, and likely references the act of baptism (4:14; 10:23). Decisions arrived at concerning the community's continued allegiance to Christianity or their reversion to Levitical Judaism would prove determinative regarding their immediate destiny.

Jesus also receives a double designation. He is both the Apostle and High Priest of the believers' confession. Both titles are used to better illustrate the connection between Jesus and Moses. While Moses was never officially Israel's high priest, he did perform the priestly installation of his brother, Aaron, and preside over the inauguration of the Levitical priesthood (Lev. 8:1–36). Furthermore, he was a Levite, he provided the blueprints for and supervised the construction of the tabernacle, he occasionally performed priestly functions (Exod. 24:4–8), and he is actually referred to one time in the Old Testament as a priest (Ps. 99:6). Jewish philosopher Philo's *Life of Moses* provides precedent from first-century literature for the notion of Moses' priesthood.[4]

Priesthood. The Levitical priests were the classification of Israelites who both belonged to the tribe of Levi and were descendants of the original high priest, Aaron. They were the servants of the Lord who were commissioned for ministry to the chosen people. Their primary responsibility was to administrate the many and varied tabernacle/temple sacrifices that comprised the core of Israel's daily worship. They served as God's physical representatives to his holy nation, teaching the responsibilities of God's Torah to the people, making intercessory prayer on their behalf, examining the ill, adjudicating matters of law, and arbitrating matters related to the practical lifestyle of holiness demanded by God. Just as God demanded that sacrifices offered to Him be without blemish, so too did major physical imperfections disqualify priests from serving in the holy sanctuary.

In first century, New Testament era Jerusalem, many priests lived in proximity to the temple and comprised the city's wealthy aristocracy. Thousands of additional priests, of somewhat humbler means than their Jerusalem brethren, resided throughout various other cities of Israel.

Due to the elevated number of priests coupled with a limited roster of priestly temple duties, a rotational schedule was followed by all priests throughout the year. Josephus estimates that the population of the first-century priesthood was over twenty thousand.[5] Therefore, the priests were divided into twenty-four divisions, with each priest serving for one week twice each year (1 Chron. 24:7–19). Accordingly, on any given week, hundreds of priests might be serving in the temple.

In addition to this semiannual rotation, every priest served in the temple during the three weeks of the great annual pilgrimage festivals: Passover, Pentecost and Tabernacles. Consequently, each priest spent approximately five weeks every year in temple service. As a means of support during the remainder of the year, most priests engaged in either a trade or the teaching of Torah.

While on the topic of priests, a word about the Levites is in order. Levites, like priests, derived from the tribe of Levi, without, however, the specificity of being direct descendants of Aaron. Levite males, like priests, also served in the temple, but in a supportive capacity. They functioned as temple musicians, maintenance workers, and temple guards. There were even more Levites than priests, so most of them served in the temple only briefly during the course of a year, if at all, supporting themselves as craftsmen or scribes.[6]

High Priest. Every responsibility and requirement for priesthood also pertained to this priest of priests. In addition, once a year the high priest bore the awesome responsibility of making atonement for the sins of the nation of Israel. As president of the Sanhedrin and the leading religious figure, he was the most powerful man in first-century, New Testament era Israel next to the king and the Roman procurator. According to the Levitical legislation, the high priest inherited this critical position for a lifetime appointment. In the first century, however, the high priest was appointed by Rome. Serving at the pleasure of Rome, the high priest's function had become more political than theological. Not only did he serve as intermediary between Israel and God, but he also was to represent Rome's interests toward Israel.

To ensure political survival, the high priest had to become a wily politician, possessing both exceptional political skills and diplomatic ability in managing his dual constituencies of Israel and Rome. Under Roman rule, the position had become a revolving door. High priests were frequently appointed and routinely demoted according to the whims and moods of the procurators. Josephus records twenty-eight appointments in the century between 37 BC and AD 70.[7]

The singular designation of Jesus as *ton apostolon* is, at first glance, a head scratcher, that is, until one focuses on the author's painstaking connection of Jesus with Moses. As previously discussed in the treatment of the opening verses of chapter 2, an apostle was a commissioned individual sent forth to proclaim a particular message. Moses was, in effect, God's apostle, commissioned to present a specific message to Pharaoh (Exod. 3:1–6ff.). Just so, Jesus was also divinely commissioned to present a specific message, like Moses, of liberation.

Both Jesus and Moses faithfully discharged their divine commissions. The "house" in which Moses proved faithful was the nation of Israel. This is a direct allusion to God's affirmation that "My servant Moses . . . is faithful in all My household" (Num. 12:7). No mention is made or indicated of Moses' failures in ministry. His faithfulness was marred only by his possession of flawed humanity.

On the other hand, the author argues, Jesus has been counted worthy of more glory than Moses. It is difficult to appreciate just how powerfully radical a statement that would have been to first-century Jewish ears. The author provides perspective, explaining that the builder of the house is necessarily greater than the house he builds. While Moses belonged to the house of Israel, the chosen family of faith, that household had been built by the Messiah. His faithfulness proved flawless.

Superior to Moses in Position (3:5–6)

The comparison of Jesus to Moses continued, with Moses portrayed as a faithful household servant. As God's prophet to the nation of Israel, Moses' role was preparatory, to provide "testimony of the things which were to be spoken later." This he accomplished through the successful mediation of the covenantal relationship between God and His chosen people. Every component of the legislation contained in the Torah, the Mosaic covenant, was designed to prepare the nation for the coming of the Messiah, designed to foster Israel's recognition of their inherent sin and subsequent need for messianic atonement, for the nation to comprehend that the only acceptable means of true ultimate reconciliation between humankind and God was the holy blood of the Messiah.

As honorable as was the position of servant, there can be no contest when even the most faithful household servant is compared to the son of the house.[8] Our Messiah is God's faithful Son. As a son will always possess more influence, clout, and prestige than a servant, so, too, Moses' exalted position in the Jewish conception must defer to that of Jesus.

In context, Jesus' house, "whose house we are," should be specifically understood as referring to first of all Jewish believers, the remnant of Israel (Rom. 11:5), the Israel of God (Gal. 6:16). This was the composition of the early church and certainly the recipients of Hebrews. However, by the midpoint of the first century, Jesus had added on a few additional rooms to incorporate all members of nations in the holy family of faith. Christ's building program continues to this day as the church continues its exponential expansion program.

The Superiority of the Messiah to Moses

Moses	Jesus
Intimate relationship with God	Exact representation of God
Prototypical prophet	Definitive Prophet
Deliverer from slavery to Pharaoh	Deliverer from slavery to sin
Occasional intercessor	Continual intercessor
Temporary priest	Everlasting High Priest
Old covenant mediator	New covenant mediator
Presenter of Torah	Embodiment of Torah
Servant of God	Son of God
Resident of God's household	Builder of God's household

The conditional clause "if we hold fast our confidence and the boast of our hope firm until the end" is intended by the author as a reminder that every believer needs to administer an occasional reality check on his or her faith. It assuredly does not indicate that believers are saved only through continued confidence until our final living moments. Nor does it mean that we can never be genuinely certain of our salvation until we draw our last breath. Salvation is by means of God's grace, not by the measure of the depth of our confidence, although we can be categorically confident regarding that truth.

Conclusion

Comparisons of Moses to the Messiah are nothing particularly novel in Jewish tradition. As noted above, there are several examples in rabbinic writing of the elevation of Moses over the Messiah. We shall close with two examples, one ancient and one modern, of Jewish expectation that, like the author of Hebrews, anticipate the supremacy of the Messiah over Moses. The first example is from the Midrash Tanhuma, a collection of Jewish homilies from Talmudic times. "This is King Messiah. . . . He is greater than the Fathers . . . loftier than Abraham. . . . He shall be more elevated than Moses . . . and higher than the ministering angels."[9]

The second example concerns the messianic expectations of an ultraorthodox Jewish sect based in Brooklyn, New York, the Chabad-Lubavitch. Until the death in 1994 of their leader, Menachem Mendel Schneerson, almost all Chabad-Lubavitch were confident that he was the Messiah. The debilitating stroke he suffered in 1992 that removed his ability to speak did nothing to quell their enthusiasm—they merely quoted the suffering servant passage of Isaiah 53! Although many have moderated their messianic fervor since the 1990s, today countless true believers still insist either that Schneerson will soon be resurrected or that he never really died and that he is in hiding during this early period of the world's redemption and will reveal himself as the glorious Messiah. In addition, beliefs circulate that this messiah is not only greater than Moses and the angels but that he is divine, "the Essence and Being of God,"[10] the "master of the Universe,"[11] "omniscient, omnipotent, without limits and incapable of sin because he is pure divinity."[12]

The theological ideas expressed in both these examples are impeccable and align with those of the author of Hebrews. How very sad it is that those represented by the first quotation were unaware or unwilling to accept that Jesus was their exalted Messiah. How utterly tragic it is that those represented by the second quotation have backed the wrong messianic candidate.

Study Questions

1. List four points of correspondence between Moses and Jesus and in what way the superiority of Jesus is demonstrated in them.

2. Briefly describe the role of a Levitical priest.

3. Explain the difference, if any, between a priest and a Levite.

CHAPTER 5

Concerning Disobedience and Doubt
Hebrews 3:7–4:13

Preview:

This section contains the author of Hebrews' second warning. Building on his immediately previous theological discussion of Moses, the author capitalizes on the opportunity to utilize Israel's historical wilderness experience of rebellion as an analogical example of the peril that may result from the recipient community's continuance along their present, potentially destructive, spiritual path. He introduces the intriguing (and interpretively contentious) concept of "God's rest" to his argument. The discussion is constructed through the selective quotation of and allusion to several Old Testament texts that represent a broad swath of Israel's history: Genesis 2:2; Exodus 17:7; Joshua 22:4; and of central importance, Numbers 14:1–35 and Psalm 95:7–11. In his appeal to the recipient community, the author purposefully emphasizes the typological correspondence between the contemporary community and their ancestors regarding their level of spiritual commitment and potential for catastrophic judgment if their faith is found negligent.

Admonition to Faithfulness (3:7–19)

Immediately prior to employing a remarkably substantial quotation from Psalm 95:7–11, the author links the passage to his previous encouragement for the recipients to hold fast to their faith confessions (3:6). Using the particle *dio*, "therefore," he elevates the intensity of the discussion with a follow-up admonition for them to avoid "hardening their hearts." The basis of the author's admonition is the typological correspondence he will demonstrate that existed between the recipient community of Jewish Christians whom he is addressing and their infamous ancestors, the rebellious Exodus generation who failed to enter the Land of Promise through their rebellion.

Unlike the vague introduction of the quotation from Psalm 8 in 2:6, the words of David in Psalm 95:7–11 are introduced as the handiwork of the Holy Spirit ("as the Holy Spirit says"). Attributing the words of Scripture to authorship of the Holy Spirit was not an uncommon Jewish convention, a similar formula being recorded in no less seminal a work than the Mishnah, the core collection of the Second Temple era Jewish oral laws and traditions.[1] Notable is the fact that the verb *legō*, "to speak," is used in the present active form *legei* ("he is speaking"), indicating not merely an instance of what the Holy Spirit had said at a historical point of time long past, but what He is still asserting in the present moment.

The text of Psalm 95 would have been quite familiar as the passage was incorporated into the regular Jewish worship service held on the Sabbath.[2] The contextual background of the psalm would have been even more familiar to everyone in the community, as it is based on events that were pivotal to Israel's history as recorded in the Torah, specifically Numbers 14:1–35, the passage that contains the account of the Exodus generation's determinative wilderness rebellion.

Numbers 14. By this point in the Numbers' text, the Israelites had received the lion's share of Torah at Sinai, had constructed the tabernacle as their portable center of worship, and had successfully inaugurated the Levitical priesthood, all that in addition to having survived their first year of freedom in the desert. While Israel camped along the border of the Land of Promise at an oasis known as Kadesh-Barnea and stood poised for conquest, twelve spies were dispatched to cross the border and investigate from within the land's interior (Num. 13:1–24).

Upon returning from their mission forty days later, the spies presented two conflicting reports to the encamped nation. Representing the minority, Joshua and Caleb presented a report characterized by a faith-based optimism. However, the pessimistic majority report, presenting the opinion of the ten remaining spies, convinced their fellow Israelites that the military and numerical supremacy of the land's inhabitants would constrain any successful campaign of conquest on which the nation might embark (Num. 13:25–33). This immediately led to a popular movement to abandon Israel's quest for the Promised Land in favor of returning to Egypt and their former status as slaves (Num. 14:1–4). It is hard to believe this degree of disobedience could erupt from those who had progressed so far from their former lifestyle of hopelessness and who had been eyewitness to so much of God's manifest power through multiple miracles, signs, and wonders. The revolt against Moses' leadership was of such vicious intensity that Moses and his brother, Aaron, along with the two optimistic spies, would have lost their lives were it not for God's intervention (Num. 14:1-10).

In essence, the nation was ultimately rebelling against the leadership of God Himself, yet again exhibiting a stunning failure of faith. So aroused was God's anger that He threatened to destroy the nation through plague and to start over from scratch with a nation born of Moses' descendants. Only Moses' passionate intercession on Israel's behalf constrained the threatened outpouring of God's wrath (Num. 14:11-19).

Although God pardoned the nation for their great sin, nonetheless, they would not go unpunished for their rebellion. Having been a liberated nation for only just over a year, Israel had already succeeded, on a remarkable ten separate occasions, in provoking the Lord through their faithless, rebellious tendencies. The most recent action, however, was the proverbial straw that broke the camel's back. This was a revolt that catapulted the nation past the point of no return. The divine judgment was that an entire generation, every adult over the age of twenty (with the exception of Joshua and Caleb) would live their remaining lives wandering in the desert, denied both entrance to and possession of the Promised Land. Israel's young people were not held responsible and would receive the promised blessings now forfeited by their parents (Num. 14:20-35).

This judgment was experienced by Israel for the next thirty-eight years, until the final members of the Exodus generation had died (with the exception of Moses, Joshua, and Caleb). Natural causes (i.e., old age) would not account for the passing of the entirety of the generation, as those who had been only twenty years of age at the rebellion would have died prematurely at the still youthful age of fifty-eight. While He had forgiven the nation of rebels and refrained from slaughtering them outright, a component of the Lord's judgment included the hastening of their death (Deut. 2:14-15). This was particularly the case for the ten spies whose lack of trust served as the rebellion's catalyst. They died by plague soon afterward (Num. 14:37).

It is essential to remember that the account does not end at this juncture. Following the announcement of God's judgment, the nation mourned, recognizing and repenting of their sin. In order to demonstrate their renewed faith, the following morning an unauthorized military invasion force was dispatched, or rather, dispatched themselves, and as was to be anticipated in light of God's decision, met with disaster (Num. 14:39-45).

What is instructive to glean from this account is that while Israel had been characterized by near systemic outbreaks of doubt, they were, nonetheless, a nation of genuine believers. Harsh judgment befell them upon their having acted one time too many with such self-defeating inconsistency. Moses highlights Israel's faith and their redemption repeatedly in the text of Exodus (4:30–31; 12:27–28; 14:30–31; 15:2, 13, 16; 19:8).

Furthermore, God Himself announced His salvation to the nation at the Red Sea (Exod. 14:13). In fact, the whole point of the Exodus was for God to redeem His own people. Until the death, burial, and resurrection of Christ, the Passover/Exodus event was the greatest act of redemption the world had ever seen. It strains credulity to imagine just why the Israelites would stain their doorposts with the blood of unblemished lambs if they were without faith. Indeed, the author of Hebrews himself affirms the genuineness of the Exodus generation's faith in the great "hall of faith" passage (11:29, 39). Even more incredible is the suggestion that God would enter into the Mosaic covenant, which was never means of salvation (Heb. 10:4), with a nation of reprobates.[3] Israel is a covenant nation, and while Israel as a corporate whole has proven consistently faithless throughout its history (see Stephen's speech in Acts, especially 7:51), God has ever been a paragon of covenant fidelity. If God's intention was a thorough rejection of that specific generation of His chosen people, then they would not have lasted another forty seconds, let alone an additional forty years.

Even so, the newly liberated Exodus generation rapidly fell into a self-destructive pattern of doubt. Having personally experienced, as eyewitnesses, their God's unprecedented series of spectacular signs and wonders, they genuinely believed in Him, and how! Nevertheless, they ultimately failed to spiritually progress in their faith by allowing doubts to crop up and fester concerning God's ability to care for them. As Randall C. Gleason, whose discussion of this section in particular and of the warnings in general is the most reasonable and cogent I have read thus far, has expressed, "The sin of the Exodus generation was a growing lack of trust in God's life-sustaining presence (Exod. 17:7) to provide for their needs (Num. 11:4–6, 18–23; 14:7–9)."[4]

That this must be so is evidenced through God's pardon of their transgression (Num. 14:19–20), even as with His next breath, as it were, He pronounced His modified judgment on them (Num. 14:21ff.). The nation's subsequent repentance and confession of sin, while it did nothing to assuage their just experience of divine punishment for their sin, nonetheless reveals a people whose hearts were beating for God. Rather than renouncing their faith, Israel proceeded to build and develop a society that, at least for their children's generation, could be characterized as a holy nation and kingdom of priests (Exod. 19:6). Moreover, God, in turn, neither destroyed Israel nor redeposited them into the cesspool of Egypt. Instead, He preserved and strengthened the nation, His child, even as an entire generation passed away.

This, then, is the essential point of correspondence between the Exodus generation and the recipients of Hebrews. The discipline meted out to the Exodus generation was premature physical death in order to deprive them of the blessing of entering the Land of Promise. While they suffered loss and over time their corpses fell in the wilderness (Num. 14:29), their spiritual lives were preserved. Israel's sin caused the forfeit of their lives, not their salvation. Salvation, once divinely granted, is never ours to forfeit. Even Moses and Aaron shared the fate of the Exodus generation as a result of their own rebellion (Num. 20:12) and thus suffered the deprivation of not entering the land. Nonetheless, having suffered loss of physical blessing, as believers they would never be deprived of God's eternal salvation.

The recipients of Hebrews, while genuine believers, were beginning to manifest the self-destructive patterns of their ancestors in their doubt and failure to trust in God's sufficient provision to see them through their present experience of persecution. In Psalm 95 David had used Israel's historical wilderness rebellion to call a contemporary generation of Jews to continued faithfulness in his own day. The author of Hebrews, recognizing a typological relationship, followed David's precedent. The relevance of the call of God to his people has no time constraints.[5] This will serve as our cue to return to the specifics of our text in Hebrews.

The quotation from Psalm 95 opens with what will prove in this section not only to be a key word but a central concept as well. The word is *sēmeron,* translated here as "today," which in English is slightly too restricted for one to completely appreciate the emphasis the author will place on it. To increase our accuracy of comprehension, "today" must also include the sense of "this particular day" or "this particular time," that is, a conveyed sense of special "now-ness."

The psalm's exhortation that directly relates to the now-ness of "today," is that if the believing community does indeed possess the capacity to hear the voice of God, it is essential that they do not "harden their hearts" in response. This exhortation is a direct reference to the fact that God had specifically charged the Exodus generation with an obstinate refusal to hear His voice (Num. 14:22) along with a provocative pattern of rebellion. The words "rebellion" and "testing" are the equivalent words that translate the Hebrew names found in the original psalm for the two archetypical locations of Israel's rebellion, Meribah and Massah (Exod. 17:7).

Hebrews 3:9 contains reference to "forty years." Timing is everything, regarding not only comedy, but also all effective communication. The letter was most likely composed and received at the midpoint of the first century's seventh decade. The forty-year anniversary of Jesus' ministry was rapidly approaching,[6] and with it the conclusion of a generational span. It is quite possible that the author's presumed underlying subtext is the impending contemporary judgment in correspondence with the historical forty years in the wilderness.[7]

As the quotation of Psalm 95:7–11 concludes in Hebrews 3:11, we are briefly introduced to an additional central concept to this section of Hebrews, that of God's "rest," into which, as a result of the intensity of God's anger (*orgē*, "wrath"), the Exodus generation would be prevented from entering. The author develops the idea of "rest" in the section that immediately follows.

An admonition is levied in Heb. 3:12 by the author of Hebrews to his recipients. Addressed as *adelphoi*, "brothers," they are warned (*blepete*, "see," "carefully observe or notice") as to whether any individual in the faith community had developed a *ponēra*, "evil" heart. The word for evil is absent in all five books of Moses in the Septuagint with the exception of Numbers 14, where it is used twice in reference to the rebellious congregation (vv. 27, 35). That which makes the heart "evil" is unbelief. Unbelief is the practical result of allowing a pattern of failure to trust. Before long, a lack of trust coupled with a healthy dose of irrational fear and incubated in a cauldron of external pressure will develop what began as doubt into the stubborn refusal to believe, which, in turn, will eventually manifest itself in outright disobedience toward God, a highly self-destructive pattern to exhibit. It is labeled here as *apostēnai*, "standing off," "falling away," "deserting," "departing" (from which we derive our word *apostasy*) from the living God. This is not a wholesale abandonment of the faith, but rather, a failure of personal faith; it is not so much a rejection of God but a rebellion against Him. This process is labeled by the author not just as sin, but as "the" sin. The use of the article with *hamartia* singles this out as the same sort of infamous sin committed by the children of Israel in the desert.

The suggested antidote is the mutual encouragement (*parakaleō*, a meaning-rich word that, along with encouragement, also encompasses the idea of exhortation, correction, help, and counsel) of community members toward one another. The direct result of this enriched atmosphere of encouragement, exhortation, and so on would be a faith community devoid of being hardened by the deceitfulness of their own self-sabotaging disobedience.

The question of how often such encouragement should be extended is answered with the phrase "as long as it is called 'Today.'" This admonition was appropriate in what was the long ago "today" of David's contemporary age and will always be appropriate in every ensuing era for as long as mortal existence can be measured by means of time. Although our present "today" inevitably becomes tomorrow's "yesterday," each new day yields a fresh "today" during which to respond favorably to God. Therefore, there is a timelessness about Hebrews' concept of "today" as an unending stream of "todays" ultimately transcends time to become the perpetual "now."

This idea of the perpetual "today" is famously illustrated in an ancient rabbinical legend from the Talmud. According to Jewish tradition, the prophet Elijah, having never died, meanders rather casually through the corridors of Jewish history (and is always available whenever a rabbi needs his presence to spin a good yarn). He sends a rabbi to interview the Messiah, who is still incognito, having not yet made his appearance on the world stage. The rabbi wants to know when the Messiah plans on coming. The Messiah answers the rabbi's question with one word, "Today." The rabbi returns to Elijah, who asks him how the interview went. The rabbi is disappointed, because the Messiah had falsely told him that his coming would be "today," and since they had spoken, the day had already passed. Elijah answers that the rabbi misunderstood. What the Messiah had said was, "Today, if you hear his voice. . . ."[8] In other words, each day the Messiah stands ready to appear, if only Israel will heed David's admonition in Psalm 95:7.

Once again the author provides a conditional statement that indicates that community's confident perseverance and endurance will eventually verify their faith. Each believer should perform a habitual "reality check" to ensure that their attitudes, behavior, and faith are sufficiently aligned with having become partakers (*metachoi*, the same word used of believers in 3:1) of Christ.

Yet what the author is driving at here goes far beyond the measurement of subjective internal feelings. For whatever reason, many popular versions of Hebrews choose to translate the word *hupostasis* in 3:14 as "confidence" or "assurance." However, as previously discussed when the word was used of the relationship between the Father and Christ only two chapters earlier in 1:3, *hupostasis* literally means "that which makes it what it is"[9] and is correctly translated "nature," "substance," or "essence," for it is nonsense to assert that Christ is "the exact representation of God's assurance." It is usually best to attempt a degree of consistency in translating the same word used by a single author within the span of a brief letter.

The word in question appears only one additional time in the text of Hebrews, in 11:1. Here *hupostasis* is usually translated "substance" or "essence" ("Now faith is the substance/essence of things hoped for"). However, some translate *hupostasis* in 11:1 as assurance, in order to maintain consistency with their choice in 3:14. Yet, while 3:14 and 11:1 may correspond with each other, interpretive consistency with the meaning of *hupostasis* in 1:3 is sacrificed. As the word is used only five times in the New Testament, three of which are by the author of Hebrews, I believe we should be cautious with the amount of linguistic elasticity we allow.

Therefore, *hupostasis* should not be limited to vague translations of "assurance" or "confidence," but should rather be understood as the more substantive, "objective reality that gives a firm guarantee and basis for confidence or assurance."[10] This is confirmed by the author's choice of the modifying adjective *bebaian*, a business and legal contractual term that means "firm or binding guarantee." In short, Hebrews does not exhort believers to cling to distant memories of previous feelings of assurance, nor to attempt generating a state of self-induced confidence. We must hold fast to the objective and unchanging reality that is the very basis and guarantee of our faith, our Messiah.

The author again quotes Psalm 95:7, summarizing his argument thus far and reinforcing the urgency of his recipient audience not hardening their hearts and following the rebellious example of their ancestors. What cannot be overstated and must be appreciated is the rarity of a New Testament author's use of not just snippets of words and phrases, but lengthy quotations from the Old Testament. The scrolls on which these letters were originally written do not extend to unlimited length.[11] By devoting such a substantial portion of his letter's literary real estate to the inclusion of Old Testament block passages, and to then insert repetitions of blocks previously included, the author reveals both his priorities and emphases. This can be considered the attention-getting equivalent of the author shouting his message or sending an email composed of all caps, saying, "TODAY, IF YOU HEAR HIS VOICE, DO NOT HARDEN YOUR HEARTS AS THEY DID IN THE REBELLION!!!!!"

"Each generation has the awesome responsibility of standing before the claim of God expressed in His word. 'Today' signals a fresh moment of biography and history, which is always conditioned by the response of obedience or disobedience, of faith or unbelief."[12]

The author follows this exhortation by developing an inductive chain of inquiry. He asks three progressively escalating questions in Hebrews 3:16–18: Who provoked God? With whom was God angry for forty years? To whom did He swear that entrance into His rest would be forbidden? The author subsequently proceeds to answer his own questions. Those who provoked God included all those who had been miraculously delivered out of Egypt, including Moses (Num. 14:13, 19, 22; Ps. 95:7–8). Those with whom God was angry for forty years were those who sinned, whose corpses fell in the wilderness (Num. 14:10, 33, 43; Ps. 95:10). Those to whom He forbade entrance into His rest were those who were disobedient (Num. 14:30, 33, 43; Ps. 95:11). Rebellion aroused divine wrath, yielding divine discipline.

The "bodies" of evidence led to the author's conclusion in 3:19 that this contemporary generation of Jewish believers must avoid following in the unbelieving footsteps of their ancestors if they hoped to enter God's *katapausis*, "rest."

Use of Old Testament Passages in Hebrews 4

Reference	Old Testament	Subject
4:3	Ps. 95:11	God's rest denied to the faithless
4:4	Gen. 2:2	God's rest following creation
4:5	Ps. 95:11	God's rest denied to the faithless
4:7	Ps. 95:7–8	Israel's wilderness rebellion
4:8	Josh. 22:4	Israel's conquest of the Land
4:10	Gen. 2:2	God's rest following creation

God's Rest for the Faithful (4:1-10)

The author links this section to the previous illustration of God's discipline through *oun*, "therefore." Once again associating himself with the recipient community, he exhorts them to exert a proper measure of apprehension (*phobēthōmen*, "let us fear," not exactly an insubstantial term) concerning the *epaggelias*, "promise," "pledge" of entrance into God's rest that remains for them. "The promise had not been revoked. The formulation of v. 1 takes account of Num 14:31, where the rejected promise is extended to the children of the desert generation."[13] It is not that the believers must either receive rest or receive wrath. It is that entering into God's rest relationship will mitigate any propensity to exercise self-destructive doubt and the potential of receiving His discipline.

God's rest. Absent an understanding of this, the core concept in this section, interpretation of this chapter becomes a minefield, laden with theological explosives hidden under almost every verse. The interpretation of this concept has been almost as diverse as that of the warning passages, and indeed, the interpretation of the latter generally has determinative bearing on that of the former. Prior to presenting the various views, it will be helpful to collect and summarize the facts about God's rest that can be gleaned from the text.

First, as to vocabulary, the noun *katapausis*, "rest," is employed eight times (3:11, 18; 4:1, 3 [2x], 5, 10, 11), and its related verb, *katapauō*, "to rest," an additional three times (4:4, 8, 10). A third word, *sabbatismos*, "sabbath celebration," is used once (4:9), which is its sole appearance in the New Testament (and earliest recognized appearance in ancient Greek literature). These three words are all employed by the author in the service of a single concept.

Second, it is God's rest because three times in this section the author records that God calls it "My rest" (3:11; 4:3, 5). This is God's prototypical rest that He has continuously enjoyed since having ceased from His creative labor in creation (Gen. 2:2). It serves as the basis for the proffered rest that is available for believers.

Third, God's rest was in some portion realized by Israel's enjoyment of their land; however, the nation's presence in the land did not exhaust the entire meaning of God's rest (Heb. 4:7–8). Fourth, God's rest is still available through believers' continued faith and is both something to be entered into at present and something to anticipate in the future (4:1–11). Fifth, it is possible to forfeit entrance into God's rest through covenantal infidelity and lack of faith (Heb. 4:2). The precedent of the Exodus generation being denied entrance indicates that unbelief could similarly prevent this current generation of believers from entering rest (3:19).

There are four major interpretations of what is meant by entrance into God's rest. The first view is that of enjoyment of the land. The concept of *katapausis*, "rest," in the context of the promise to the Exodus generation, had the local connotation of entrance into Canaan, where Israel would experience relief from turmoil and security from their enemies (cf. Deut. 12:9–10).[14] This view answers only a portion of what is meant by rest. While this is one facet of what was meant by God's rest, the author of Hebrews himself argues that while Joshua indeed provided rest, the provision was by no means exhausted and was still available in David's age (4:7–8). "The promise of rest is still available because it was never totally fulfilled. The promise of *rest* in the Old Testament was unfulfilled, but it was not withdrawn; it is available to those who want it now. The entire purpose of this letter to the Hebrews is to get the Jewish believers to enter the fullness of *rest*."[15] An additional point is that the recipients of Hebrews, while presently enjoying their citizenship in the land, had not yet entered into God's rest.

The second view is that of the enjoyment of heaven. The evidence for this interpretation is that Hebrews indicates that enjoyment of rest is still future

(4:1, 11). A piece of additional evidence is the association of the concepts of rest and the experience of heaven as described in Revelation 14:13. While the observation concerning the future aspect of rest that informs this view cannot be disagreed with, this view fails to sufficiently incorporate the specifically Jewish, Old Testament context of the passage.

The third view is that of the enjoyment of a deeper spiritual lifestyle of "faith-rest." The evidence for this position is that God's rest is described in 4:3 as something that we who believe can presently enter into and enjoy through faith (*eiserchometha* is present middle indicative and should be understood as "we are causing ourselves to enter"). Jesus' invitation of participation in His rest may be a parallel idea (Matt. 11:28–30).

The fourth view is that of the enjoyment of the messianic age, for which the text provides several pieces of supporting evidence. First, as with the second, "enjoyment of heaven," view, the idea of a promise that remains certainly indicates the anticipation of future enjoyment (4:1, 11). Second, according to this view, the present middle indicative of *eiserchometha* in 4:3 can be understood as a "futuristic present such as one finds in Matt. 17:11; John 14:3; and 1 Cor. 16:5."[16] Third, while the idea of rest is not limited to enjoyment of the land, neither should it be completely disassociated from it. Fourth, since Psalm 95 is often classified as an "enthronement psalm," one whose subject matter is interpreted as relating to and anticipating the messianic age,[17] it follows that God's rest should be understood in corresponding light. Fifth, there is a strong linkage in Jewish tradition between the messianic kingdom age and the concept of Sabbath celebration (*sabbatismos*, 4:9). A traditional *Shabbat* prayer with a lengthy heritage is, "May the All Merciful let us inherit the day which shall be wholly a Sabbath and rest in the life everlasting."[18] In addition, the early second century's *Epistle of Barnabas* explicitly associates the messianic age with the Sabbath.[19] Indeed, the Old Testament itself associates the messianic age with rest (Ps. 132:12–14; Isa. 11:10; 14:3; 32:18).

A fifth view is presented by Gleason, who synthesizes aspects of several of the previous views.

> The privilege to "enter into My rest" (Ps. 95:11) is best understood as the right to worship before the personal presence of Yahweh (vv. 2, 6), which could be forfeited by hardened, rebellious hearts like those of the Exodus generation (vv. 8–10). This fits the argument of Hebrews 3–4 in which the author encouraged his readers that if they would "hold fast" to their hope (Heb. 3:6) and their assurance (v. 14) in Christ, they could "draw near with confidence to the throne of grace" (i.e., God's resting place) to receive "help" (4:16), "blessing" (6:7), and "reward" (10:35; 11:6).[20]

While several of the above views are commendable, I will now humbly add my voice and issue my own position, which, nonetheless, leans on Gleason's for support. God's rest can be properly understood as the believer's present position of relationship with God and subsequent enjoyment of continual access to His presence and all the associated benefits thereof, such as divine protection, help, blessing, and reward. This rest transcends time, in that it is to be enjoyed and its benefits applied through a limitless procession of "todays," beginning with the seventh day of creation.

In short, there are four temporal aspects to this rest. First, there is the eternal, prototypical facet, which is God's rest following the cessation of His creative labors on the seventh day (4:4, 10). He continues to enjoy this rest, and it serves as the source of the three other available aspects of rest. Second, there is the historical facet, which is the rest associated with Israel's enjoyment of the Land of Promise (3:11, 18–19; also Deut. 3:20; 12:9; 25:19; Josh. 11:23; 21:44; 22:4; 23:1). Third, there is the contemporary facet, which is the present relationship of deep, abiding intimacy and blessing that is available for all believers to enjoy as a lifestyle of faith-rest. Finally, there is the future facet, which is the messianic age when we believers will enjoy the universal reign of the Messiah from the land of Israel.

The author continues his association with his audience, hearkening back to 2:3–4 by referencing his and the community's experience of hearing and responding to the good news that had been preached to them. The actual noun *euaggelion*, which we translate as "gospel," is not employed here, but rather its verb form. Therefore, it may be understood in a technical sense as "gospel," regarding the message enjoyed by the Hebrews recipients, and in the general sense of "good news," regarding the Old Testament message received by the Israelites. That message was the resounding testimony of God, as echoed and reiterated by Moses and the two spies, that He would enable Israel to conquer the land.

It is imperative that God's message of faith take root in His community of faith. When that fails to happen, there is not only an absence of benefit, but in Israel's case, their distrust resulted in a shattering benefit deficit. This marks the first actual occurrence of the word *pistis*, "faith," in the text of Hebrews, although its unseen presence has been felt throughout the previous passage. William Lane defines the use of faith in Hebrews as "confident expectation for the future (cf. 6:12; 10:38–39; 11:1). It is a quality of response that appropriates the divine promise and recognizes the reliability of God."[21]

God's rest is described in 4:3 as something that "we who have believed" (*pisteusantes*, aorist participle, past action with continuing results) can presently enter into and enjoy through faith (*eiserchometha* is present middle indicative and should be understood as "we are causing ourselves to enter"), an audacious confirmation of the present, contemporary aspect of God's rest. It is much less likely that the verb should be understood as a "futuristic present," meant to be understood as future fact.

The author repeats another portion of the quotation from Psalm 95 to demonstrate that God's rest "has primary reference to God's own repose, which precedes and stands outside human history."[22] In 4:4 he immediately links Psalm 95:11 with a quotation of Genesis 2:2, based on the common idea of rest contained in both passages, as well as the common association of these verses in the Shabbat synagogue service.[23] The introduction of the new verse ("He has said somewhere concerning") is again one of a seemingly casual nature, yet the formula has common parallels in Jewish tradition.[24]

Verses 4:5–7 shift back to reiterations of portions of the Psalm 95 quotation interposed with a summary of the author's argument thus far. Hebrews 4:7 contains recognition of the Davidic authorship of the psalm, which, when combined with the previous attribution of the psalm to the Holy Spirit, reveals his understanding of the dual authorship of Scripture. In yet again accentuating the psalm's timelessly contemporary call to respond to God's rest "today," he makes the point that although Scripture testifies that Joshua had provided rest to the generation that came of age in the wilderness (Josh. 21:44; 22:4; 23:1), that did not exhaust the available rest, and there was still some portion available to future generations. In Greek, Joshua and Jesus are both rendered as *Iēsous*, making it easier to see the author's drawing of a parallel between the type and antitype figure of deliverance.

Hebrews 4:9 introduces a new word into the vocabulary of the rest discussion, that of *sabbatismos*, "sabbath celebration." This is the term's only appearance in the New Testament as well as earliest instance in the corpus of our available ancient Greek literature. The fact that the author now chooses a new word, having already repeatedly used the same generic word *katapausis* throughout the section, indicates that it conveyed a nuance necessary to his argument.[25] As previously discussed in the above survey of various interpretive views regarding God's rest, Jewish tradition associates the messianic kingdom age and the concept of Sabbath celebration with examples provided from the Old Testament, the *Epistle of Barnabas*, and the traditional Jewish *siddur* (prayer book). This indicates the future facet of God's rest, and in concert with the archetypical, timeless rest of God (4:4, 10), the historical rest in the land (4:8), and the present available rest (4:3), presents a full-orbed picture of the complexity of the author's concept.

Exhortation to Enter into God's Rest (4:11–13)

The author's practical application links to his immediately previous theological discussion with *oun*, "therefore." Still associating himself with his readers, he urges them to be diligent (*spoudasōmen*, "we might hasten," "we might be zealous or eager") to enter God's rest. The concern is that no one in the recipient community will "fall" through following their ancestors' disobedient example. The term *hupodeigma*, ("example," "model," "pattern") underscores the typological correspondence being drawn between the Exodus generation and the recipient community. The believers are urged to respond to the present, available aspect of God's rest in order to secure their immediate future. It is not that the believers must now either receive God's rest or receive His wrath. It is that through entrance into God's special rest relationship, any propensity to exercise faithlessness through rebellion will be mitigated and prevent receipt of His discipline.

The Word of God is vividly depicted in 4:12–13, portrayed as the sharpest of swords (*tomōteros huper pasan*, "sharper over all"). It is *zaō*, "possessing life" and *energēs*, "operational" (a word from which we derive our word *energy*). Figurative language is used to convey the power of its ability "to pierce, penetrate, and discern even the believer's soul and spirit. While the soul and spirit are two facets of the immaterial part of man, the *joints and marrow* are two facets of the material part of man."[26]

Furthermore, the Word of God "diagnoses the condition of the human heart,"[27] possessing the ability to plumb the depths of the human heart's reflections and intentions and to judge (*kritikos*, the source of our word, "critic"). God's perspective is such that the entirety of creation's population lies vulnerable before Him, naked (*gumnos*, the source of our word for *gym*, and a reminder that Greek athletic events originally played out without clothing) and having their necks stuck out (*trachēlizō*, "to expose the throat," the root source of our anatomical term *trachea*).

Conclusion

In chapters 3 and 4, the author developed the typological connection between the Exodus generation and the recipients of Hebrews through the creative use of Old Testament Scripture, of which Psalm 95:7–11 was primary. This admonition to continued faithfulness was followed by an exhortation for the recipient community to enter into God's rest. The author will now turn his attention to the theological development of Jesus as High Priest.

Study Questions

1. List the connections and points of correspondence between the Exodus generation and the recipients of Hebrews.

2. How was the Exodus generation disciplined for their rebellion? What were the lasting repercussions of this punishment?

3. What evidence is there that the Exodus generation possessed genuine faith? Did they lose their salvation? Why or why not?

4. How would you define "God's rest"?

CHAPTER 6

Superiority of the Messiah to Aaron
Hebrews 4:14–5:10

Preview:

This point in Hebrews marks the beginning of a new major subdivision in the structure of the book that includes the remainder of the first of its two divisions as it extends through 10:18. The author has previously argued the superiority of Jesus in comparison to prior prophetic revelation (1:1–3), angels (1:4–2:18), and Moses (3:1–6). Having thus established the supremacy of Jesus concerning His identity, this section builds on the author's strategy of definitively demonstrating the supremacy of Jesus regarding His priestly ministry in comparison to Aaron and the Levitical priesthood. Although the title "high priest" was previously introduced in 2:17 and reiterated in 3:1, only now, in 4:14–5:10, does the author clarify the intention behind the references.

The Superiority of the Messiah's Position (4:14–16)

The section commences with the author's characteristic connective, *oun*, "therefore," which links the previous exhortation to enter into God's rest (4:11–13) to a more than compelling motivation for doing so. Not deviating from his grammatical choice of a first person plural association with his audience, the author effectively elaborates on Jesus' superior position as the believers' *archeirea megan*, "great high priest." The qualifying adjective *megan* functions just like the idea behind our prefix of "mega," meaning something akin to "intensely awesome and most excellent." What makes this high priest so awesome is our continuous access to him. The word *exchontes* usually is translated as a generic, "since we have." However, its placement as the first word of the sentence along with the participle's present active form indicates a far more emphatic emphasis, such as "we are having" with the sense of a continuous availability.

This Great High Priest has transcended the earth and passed through the heavens and remains there in the presence of God. "Heavens" is plural because the ancient Jewish tradition conceived of heaven as a complex location subdivided into multiple sections. In the first century, it seems that the dominant theology held a tripartite division of the heavens into the atmosphere, outer space, and heaven itself. The Hebrew word for heaven in the Old Testament, *shamayim*, is always plural (Neh. 9:6; 1 Kings 8:27; 2 Chron. 2:6; 6:18; Pss. 33:6; 148:4). Without elaborating, Paul casually refers to three heavens in his letters (2 Cor. 12:2; Eph. 1:10). From a perusal of rabbinic literature, though, it is easy to see that the normatively contentious rabbis could not agree on just how many divisions should be assigned to heaven and experimented with a variety of additional, alternate heavenly divisions, from five to seven to ten in number.

Nonetheless, because the locus of this high priest's ministry is in the very presence of God, He is a far more effective representative agent for his constituency than any earthbound high priest. The recipients are exhorted to cling to their *homologia*, their confession; that is, to hold fast to their prior public expression of commitment and profession of allegiance upon their baptism (see also 3:1; 10:23). The reason for clinging to their prior confession as well as their source of hope is that this High Priest possesses infinite capacity to sympathize with the weaknesses of believers. He understands our weaknesses because He personally experienced the limitations of frail humanity. His ability to identify with believers is grounded in His having been tested (*pepeirasmenon* has an inherent complexity that not only carries the idea of being tempted but of Jesus being placed into the proverbial pressure cooker to see how He holds up, to determine if He could stand the heat).

Jesus' testing, having been tempted in "all things," is qualified with the critical words *xōris hamartias*, "without the result of sin." Lacking an inbred sin nature, Jesus passed the tests without compromising His holiness. The process of Jesus' temptation is often poorly understood. Many are confused as to just how many temptations Jesus was made to experience and equally puzzled as to what variety of temptation He was subjected in order to identify with humanity and sympathize with our weaknesses.[1] Arnold Fruchtenbaum demystifies the issue well:

It does not mean that Jesus suffered every type of temptation men do, and it does not mean that men suffer every type of temptation He did. Other people are not tempted to change stones into bread because Satan will not tempt people to do something they are totally powerless to do. For others that would not be a real temptation, but for Jesus it was a real temptation because He had the power to do just that. On the other hand, Jesus was never tempted to waste His entire day watching soap operas or football on television. The expression tempted *in all points* means "in all areas." 1 John 2:16 states there are three areas of temptation: the lust of the flesh; the lust of the eyes; and the pride of life. Every specific type of temptation will fit into one of these categories.[2]

It is even possible that what the reader is meant to understand by the testing of Jesus referenced in this passage is no more or less than the experiences described in the three Synoptic Gospels concerning the Satanic temptations that Jesus faced immediately prior to the outset of His ministry (Matt. 4:1–11; Mark 1:12, 13; Luke 4:1–13).

Therefore, the author urges the believers to cause themselves to continually draw near (*proserchōmetha*, present middle subjunctive) to the throne of grace, the locus of God's presence, and to do so with an attitude of *parrēsias*, "bold confidence." It is in God's presence that we may, through our High Priest's mercy, obtain an abundant and always sufficient supply of grace to personally appropriate in time of need.

For each believer to possess the ability to approach the "throne of grace" was a radical concept to the Jewish mind of the first century and, indeed, remains revolutionary today. According to the Torah's Levitical stipulations, only one individual, Israel's High Priest, was entitled to approach the physical locus of God's presence, the Holy of Holies in the tabernacle and later the temple. This was an event limited to only one day in the year, Yom Kippur, the Day of Atonement (Lev. 16:1–34). Furthermore, the high priest approached with tremulous awe, not with boldness. Yet through Jesus, the superior High Priest, continual access to the presence of God is universally available to every believer. Hebrews' extensive use of Day of Atonement imagery will be examined in detail in the comments for 9:7.

The Superiority of the Messiah's Priesthood (5:1–10)

The Offices of Priesthood (5:1–4). The new paragraph is linked to the previous declaration of Jesus' high priesthood with the connective *gar*, "for." The author will elaborate on the prerequisites of Levitical high priestly service. The first requirement was that of divine appointment. Every high priest was specially appointed by God as His representative intermediary with Israel. This requirement of divine appointment began with Aaron, Israel's first high priest (Exod. 28:1; Lev. 8:1–2; Num. 3:10).

The high priesthood was intended to be passed down from generation to generation, from the initial high priest, Aaron, through his third son, Eleazar (Num. 3:4), and thereafter to his descendants in direct hereditary succession. It functioned fairly successfully in that fashion until roughly 174 BC, in Israel's Hellenistic era. During this period of Israel's occupation, their Greco-Syrian ruler, Antiochus IV, deposed the high priest Onias III and installed a more amenable replacement of his own choosing. From this point forward, appointment to the high priesthood no longer followed the legitimate hereditary line and became a matter of political circumstance, machination, and maneuver until the abolition of the Levitical system with the temple's destruction in AD 70.

Use of Old Testament Passages in Hebrews 5

Hebrews	Old Testament	Subject
5:3	Lev. 9:7	The Levitical high priest's need for atonement
5:3	Lev. 16:6	The Levitical high priest's need for atonement
5:4	Exod. 28:1	The commissioning of Aaron as high priest
5:5	Ps. 2:7	The sonship of the Messiah
5:6	Ps. 110:4	The Son's Melchizedekian priesthood
5:6	Gen. 14:18–20	Melchizedek
5:9	Isa. 45:17	Eternal salvation
5:10	Ps. 110:4	The Son's Melchizedekian priesthood

The second requirement was a pastoral attitude. Since the Levitical priest had the limitations common to all humanity, he could deal compassionately (*metriopatheio*, to moderate feelings) with those Israelites whose ignorance had caused them to become misguided. The high priest had the responsibility of supervising the offering of both gifts (referencing the burnt grain and peace offerings, Lev. 1–3) and sacrifices for sins (referencing the sin and guilt offerings, Lev. 4–5). Note that the Levitical sacrifices prescribed in the Torah deal only with unintentional sins, not those purposefully intended (Lev. 4:2, 13, 22, 27; 5:17). Sins of defiance were capitally punished (Num. 15:30–31).

As noble as the individual filling the position of Levitical high priest may have been, he was never more than human and was therefore tainted with the imperfection of humanity's common sin nature. Prior to his offering sacrifices on behalf of any other Israelite, he first was required to make sacrifices on his own behalf (Lev. 4:3–12; 9:7). This was particularly evident on the Day of Atonement (Lev. 16:6, 11; see comments on Heb. 9:7).

The Superiority of the Messiah's Qualifications (5:5–10). As the author had previously established the supremacy of Jesus over Moses, he will now proceed with his case and do the same with Moses' brother, Aaron. Jesus' identity as High Priest was not a matter of presumptuously selecting Himself for the position. The Messiah (*christos*, "Christ," "Anointed One") received the high priesthood through the same divine selection as had Aaron. To authenticate and locate this divine call in the record of Scripture, the author now returns to the Psalm 2:7 passage concerning God's Son, a quotation previously included in 1:5 and alluded to in 1:2. Psalm 2:7 is immediately linked together with Psalm 110:4.

In 5:6 he immediately links this verse's topic of God's Son with the topic of the appointment of the eternal priesthood of the order of Melchizedek found in Psalm 110:4. Although he had previously discussed and quoted this psalm's first verse in 1:13, the inclusion of Psalm 110:4 is both new and novel to the argument. By the letter's conclusion, there will be more direct (5:6; 6:20; 7:17, 21) and indirect references to this verse than any other Old Testament passage. Remarkably, no other New Testament book quotes this verse or examines the association between the priesthoods of Jesus and Melchizedek. Melchizedek was the archetypical priest of Genesis 14:18, and he will be employed by the author (Heb. 7:1ff.) as scriptural precedent for the differentiation between the Levitical priesthood and that of Jesus as well as the Levitical priesthood's replacement with that of Jesus.

Focusing on the authenticity of Jesus' human experience during His incarnation "in the days of His flesh," the author illustrates that humanity by underscoring the suffering behind the Messiah's offering of prayers and entreaties as well as their being offered through loud and vocal manifestations of grief. This likely harks back to the extraordinary intensity of Jesus' experience in the Garden of Gethsemane when He sweat blood (Luke 22:44).[3] As a result of the Messiah's reverent awe, His emotional petitions successfully ascended to His Father, the One who ensured that death would hold no dominion over His Son.

The author's declaration of Jesus having learned obedience as a direct result of His suffering (*emathen aph hōn epathen*) is an adaptation of an ancient proverbial saying that appears from time to time in Greek literature[4] and is apparently the first-century equivalent of our popular adage "No pain, no gain." The area of obedience that was learned through His suffering relates to Jesus' death. In Hebrews the verb *paschō*, "to suffer," is only applied in a specialized sense to Jesus' passion. His status as God's Son in no way diminished the need for Jesus to have internalized this lesson through enduring this torment.

The result of Jesus' resolute obedience, however, was the awesome achievement of His perfection (*teleiōtheis*, "having completed a goal," "having accomplished a task"). This is not to say that Jesus was ever in any way or at any time imperfect prior to His passion. To presume any hint of moral malfunction would effectively deny or subvert His divine nature. The level of perfection that He achieved was connected to the complete obedience that characterized His human experience. Paradoxically, the One who shared the very essence of God and was the radiance of His glory (1:3) was to experience through participation in humanity the process of growth—growth that resulted in the balance of perfection between both natures, human and divine.[5]

The achievement of this level of perfection was directly related to His exalted status as the newly installed High Priest of the heavens, commissioned by His Father. As perfect High Priest, Jesus became the source of eternal salvation "to all those who obey Him," i.e., all those who are subject to His authority (*hupakouō*, "to listen to," "to be subject to"). The phrase *sōtērias aiōniou*, "eternal salvation," is exclusively found in only a single Old Testament verse, that of Isaiah 45:17, in a passage that discusses the messianic age. It is impossible to believe that the author of Hebrews anticipated his biblically literate recipients missing the reference.

Clearly, being the fount of eternal salvation was a categorically disparate quality than that which was ever exercised by any member of the Levitical high priesthood. Indeed, Jesus was a high priest in an entirely different class: He was designated by God as a high priest not according to the Aaronic order, but rather according to the order of Melchizedek.

Conclusion

Both the author of Hebrews and of this commentary have more to convey concerning the priest-king Melchizedek, but following the lead of the text of Hebrews, the required follow-up will be delayed until the discussion of Hebrews 7. The next section will serve as a preparatory pause as the author expresses His concern with his recipients' spiritual maturity and their ability to absorb the theological content he intends to convey.

Study Questions

1. What quality or qualities make this Great High Priest so special?

2. Why would this High Priest be particularly effective in His role?

3. How may we understand the testing of Jesus, and what was the result?

4. What are the requirements presented for the office of high priest?

5. What, if anything, is surprising about an admonition for believers to boldly approach the throne of God's grace?

CHAPTER 7

Concerning Spiritual Stagnation
Hebrews 5:11-6:20

Preview:

This section, the third warning passage of Hebrews, examines what has proven to be one of the Bible's most famously troublesome passages to interpret. Here the author warns the recipient community of the danger that could result from their present condition of spiritual stagnation. He first diagnoses their condition of spiritual stagnation. He then provides the community his prescription to correct their malady. This is immediately followed by his pastoral prognosis for recovery from their condition. Notable in this section is the author's distinct alternation between the use of first person community identification and second person distinctiveness. He rotates between speaking in a style that addresses a mutual "us" and one that addresses a very definite "you."

Diagnosis of Stagnation (5:11-14)

The section begins with a continuation of the author's previous line of thought, picking it up with his reference to Melchizedek in the prior verse. The author expresses his desire to communicate a great deal on the topic of Melchizedek to the recipient community using a popular literary idiom (*polus . . . ha logos*, "there is much to say") that draws attention to the importance of the subject to be treated.[1]

However, the author interrupts the progression of his theological argument to express his concern that the subject matter he now wishes to expound on, the Messiah's Melchizedekian priesthood, might prove *dusermēneutos*, "hard to explain" (a word that occurs nowhere else in the New Testament) due to the topic's inherent doctrinal complexity. This challenge is compounded by the recipient community's ability to understand the practical implications of doctrine. They had recently become (*gegonate*, "you have become") what the author describes as *nōthros*, a word that should be translated "lazy," "sluggish" (5:11).

The tone of this section is colored by the author's wielding of a barbed sense of irony in his admonishment. Although the recipients by this time had apparently been believers for no small duration and therefore are sufficiently well educated to be on the teaching end of the spectrum and not the learning end, nonetheless, their recent troubling patterns of behavior and deviation of resolve suggested that it would perhaps be more productive to rehearse a more basic level of doctrine (5:12). This same illustrative contrast between doctrinal "milk" and "meat" is paralleled in Paul's first letter to the Corinthians (1 Cor. 3:2).

That the author really does not truly think his audience immature spiritual infants in need of the repetition of elementary principles of faith is indicated by the fact that, but for brief citations (6:1–2), he completely bypasses those principles and, following this dedicated section of admonishment, immediately returns to expounding on the difficult subject about which he had expressed such effusive concern (7:1–10:18). Furthermore, no one can, without tongue first firmly planted in cheek, characterize the argument of Hebrews thus far as basic material. His point is that the community's spiritual growth had indeed stalled, and while they evidenced some level of regression, it was not terminally advanced. In short, this is a very definite warning for a very real problem, and the author utilizes all his rhetorical skill to persuade his audience toward an appropriate response.

Prescription for Progression (6:1–8)

Having thus diagnosed the community's spiritual malady, the author proceeds to offer a suitable prescription. The first step was not to belabor but rather to build on the doctrinal basics and elementary faith teachings that had already been received, as indicated by 6:1's the *dio*, "therefore," that provides the thrust to launch the argument forward. The community is urged to press on to the goal of spiritual maturity. As Lane underscores, the use of *teleiotēs*, "perfection," "completeness," indicates that immersion in the maturation process itself is not the intended goal; rather, the goal is to arrive at the final result of that process, the completion of divinely orchestrated character transformation.[2]

The author lists six areas of doctrine that he considers to be on an elementary level. First, "repentance from dead works" (*nekrōn ergōn*, a phrase that appears only in Hebrews, also in 9:14), which refers to the Jewish believers having turned from dependence on the Levitical sacrificial system as a means to cover their sin and relate to God. The second area is "faith toward God," which is the result of turning away from dependence on the Levitical system and toward the Messiah. The third area is that of "instruction about baptisms," which refers to a basic understanding and ability to distinguish between water immersion and Spirit baptism.

The fourth area is that of "laying on of hands." The laying on of hands was the ancient Jewish method of commissioning to an office. This ordination procedure, called, in Hebrew, *semikah*, dates back to Moses and Joshua (Num. 27:22–23) and continues today in the ordination of contemporary rabbis.[3] We see this custom exercised in the New Testament for purposes of blessing (Matt. 19:13–15; Mark 10:16; Acts 8:17) and commissioning (Acts 6:6; 1 Tim. 4:14, 5:22; 2 Tim. 1:6). The fifth area of doctrine is "the resurrection of the dead," a teaching firmly rooted in the Old Testament (Isa. 26:19; Dan. 12:2) and fervently believed by the adherents of the Pharisees' populist style of first-century Judaism (Acts 23:8). The sixth and final area of elementary doctrine is "eternal judgment," God's final verdict on humanity (Acts 17:31).

In the original Greek text of Hebrews, the three verses of 6:4–6 actually comprise one remarkably lengthy, run-on sentence. The passage presents a list of four characteristics that were true of the recipient congregation. Each of the four characteristics is modified by 6:4's adverb *hapax*, "once for all" (see also 6:4; 9:7, 26, 27, 28; 10:2; 12:26, 27), meaning that once genuinely possessed, they remain as permanent distinctives.

The first characteristic is that of having been spiritually illuminated (*phō-tizō*, "to give light"). The community's experience of enlightenment is likewise cited in 10:32 and refers to their possession of regenerative faith in the Messiah that has yielded a "once for all" salvation (John 1:9, 12; 8:12; 2 Cor. 4:6; Eph. 5:8; 2 Tim. 1:10; 1 Pet. 2:9).

The second characteristic is that of having "tasted of the heavenly gift." To understand this attribute requires identifying exactly to what "the heavenly gift" refers as well as defining what is meant by having "tasted" it. In context, this gift of heaven must reference salvation. The word *geuomai*, "to taste," provides further confirmation that the community members are genuine believers who enjoy the full experience of salvation's reality.

In an attempt to interpret this warning passage as referencing a group of unbelievers or "partially converted/convicted" believers, some have attempted to argue that the idea of tasting "the heavenly gift" conveys something short of full salvation, that to "taste" does not necessarily entail having "swallowed" and "digested" and perhaps might simply instead indicate a mere nibble of the gospel. The same word was previously used in reference to Jesus' experience of death on our behalf (Heb 2:9). Just as Jesus' experience could in no way be characterized as anything less than full appropriation of death, so too must the community's appropriation of a "once for all" salvation be understood.[4]

This interpretation is further bolstered by the third characteristic, that of the recipient community's having been made "partakers" of the Holy Spirit. The word *metochos*, just as in its previous use in 3:1's, "partakers of a heavenly calling" and 3:14's "partakers of Christ," indicates a full and vital "once for all" participation of the indwelling Holy Spirit with the community.

The fourth characteristic is that the author's audience has tasted the good word of God and the powers of the age to come. The "age to come" refers to the future messianic age. Having just established that what is meant to be conveyed by the idea of tasting is the enjoyment of full experience, we may understand this clause as a declaration that the unforgettable "once for all" experience of those spectacular spiritual manifestations that accompanied the apostolic witness (2:3-4) are merely a down payment, a foretaste, of what will prove normative under the Messiah's rule and reign.

Hebrews 6:6 will add an additional attribute to the author's description of the community. The author chooses a word that uniquely appears only here in the New Testament. The aorist active participle *parapesontas* derives from the verb *parapiptō*, "to fall beside or away." The interpretive dilemma that has proven so challenging over the centuries is to identify with accuracy what transgression the author means to convey through this concept.

First, while some translations append either a temporal "then have" (ASV, NASB, NRSV) or a conditional "if they" to "fall away" (NIV, KJV, NKJV), the actual text provides no such modification, indicating that whatever this sin may refer to, the danger being warned of is not hypothetical in nature but both extreme and actual.

Second, as were the previous four characteristics, this participle is likewise modified by 6:4's *hapax*, "once for all." This means that this sin would be as decisively determinative as was the community's "once for all" experience of salvation. Once this sin is committed, there would be no turning back from its consequences.[5] This is a point of difficulty for those who interpret the "falling away" as an apostasy that results in believer's loss of salvation; if this passage truly teaches that salvation can be forfeited, the "once for all" aspect of it, coupled with 6:6's impossibility of repentance clause, must also teach that salvation, once rejected, is unregainable.

Third, the sin is linked with the previous four characteristics; all five are modified by the same "once for all" concept. This would imply that the community is fully capable of participation in the transgression of "falling away." However, the community had plainly not yet crossed the line of offense. This is indicated in two ways. First, by the author's encouraging great expectations for the community (the "better things" of 6:9) and, second, by the author's uncharacteristic grammatical modification of personal pronouns from the first person "us" and second person "you" to an isolating usage of the third person in 6:4–6.[6]

Assimilation of the above grammatical and contextual evidence, along with the author's previous two warnings of "drifting away" from their trust in Christ (2:1–4) and avoidance of following in the rebellious doubtfulness of their ancestors (3:7–4:13), therefore leads to the conclusion that the falling away being warned of here concerns "the failure to walk by faith;"[7] "a willful 'once for all' . . . refusal to trust God to deliver them from their present troubles" (10:25–34).[8]

An interesting example of the inherent challenge in providing an English translation that conveys both the correct meaning of the language and an accurate representation of authorial emphasis is the fact that most translations do not place the adverb *adunaton*, "impossible," until the second clause of 6:6. In the original text, however, the word actually appears in the emphatic position at the beginning of the sentence initiated in 6:4. What is impossible is the ability to "renew them (those who fall away) again to repentance."

The author is unmistakably stressing that once the sin of falling away has been committed, there can be no turning back from its consequences. Repentance (*metanoia*) means "to change the mind" and, as has previously been established, speaks here not of unbelievers changing their minds about Jesus but of believers' regret for disobedience (as per Paul's usage in 2 Cor. 7:9). Of premium significance is the consideration that an absence of repentance does not equate with an absence of forgiveness. The forgiveness that God extended to Israel at Kadesh Barnea did not result in the recall of His severe discipline.

The "falling away" is an irrevocable and decisive sin that once committed, while it can be forgiven, cannot be undone. God's impending judgment on national Israel's first-century generation for their leaders' rejection of God's messianic provision is as certain as was His judgment on the Exodus generation following their rejection of His provision at Kadesh Barnea. Deviation of the Jewish believers' allegiance from the all-sufficiency of the Messiah to the insufficiency of Judaism's Levitical system would result in their shifting themselves into a category reserved for discipline.

The reason that the discipline for this sin is irrevocable is that the guilty, through their rebellion, thereby crucify to themselves the Son of God and subject Him to public shame. Although commonly translated "re-crucify" or "crucify again," the word *anastaurountas* is used in Greek literature to simply mean "crucify." As Randall C. Gleason cogently explains: "The warning is not against crucifying Christ "again," but rather against reducing Christ's death to the level of a common criminal execution, as the Jewish leaders had originally intended. A public return to the animal sacrifices of the Levitical system would in effect empty Christ's death of any sacrificial redemptive value (cf. Heb. 7:26–27; 10:26)."[9]

To buckle under external community pressure and internal doubt and to fail to stand courageously for the Messiah would cause Jesus an acute loss of face among the general Jewish populace. The believing community's compliance with their persecutors would disgracefully suggest that Christ's sacrificial provision was somehow insufficient and even common, no more effective than any of the thousands of sacrifices offered annually in the temple. This would squarely associate them with the generation already under judgment.

Use of Old Testament Passages in Hebrews 6

Hebrews	Old Testament	Subject
6:8	Gen. 3:17–18	The divine curse of the earth
6:13	Gen. 22:16	The binding of Isaac
6:14	Gen. 22:17	The Abrahamic covenant
6:16	Exod. 22:11	The Mosaic Law concerning oaths
6:18	Num. 23:19	The unchangeable purpose of God
6:18	1 Sam. 15:29	The unchangeable purpose of God
6:19	Lev. 16:2	The high priest's role on the Day of Atonement
6:20	Ps. 110:4	The Son's Melchizedekian priesthood

The author continues his argument in 6:7–8 with a *gar*, "for," that links the previous thought to an explanatory illustration. The illustration is agricultural in nature, contrasting land that yields fruitful results with land that fails to produce anything of profitable consequence. The production of "thorns and thistles" is an allusion to the physical results of humanity's disobedience in the Garden of Eden (Gen. 3:17–18). While productive land receives God's blessing, land deemed worthless (*adokimos*, "unproven," "not standing the test," see 1 Cor. 9:27 and antonym use in 2 Tim. 2:15) is not correspondingly cursed, but rather, "close to being cursed."

This important distinction is often missed or glossed over in the rush to interpret this as an illustration of the final and eternal damnation of an apostate community. While the curse entails fire, it only entails burning off the land's worthless produce and not the destruction of the land itself. This correlates to Moses' warning of covenantal discipline on both the people and land of Israel for future covenantal disobedience (Deut. 29:22–28). It also generates echoes of Paul's description of believers' qualifiedly worthless works being divinely incinerated in the future eschatological judgment (1 Cor. 3:12–15).

In short, the divine discipline of AD 70 is near, at Israel's very door. Unlike the Exodus generation's graciously extended thirty-eight-year disciplinary period of death by natural cause, Israel's imminent period of discipline would be pointedly and violently concentrated.

Prognosis of Salvation (6:9–20)

Nonetheless, the author, now gently addressing them as *agapētoi*, "beloved," expresses his complete confidence of "the better things" concerning the recipient community. The article preceding *kreissona* indicates not just the generic idea of "better things," but the blessing referenced in the previous illustration (6:7). His confidence is based on the prior example of the recipient community's exemplary behavior in bold expression of their faith and loving concern for fellow believers (10:32–34). In fact, they continued to perform the ministry they had performed in God's name, that is, the work and love they had shown fellow believers (*tois hagiois*, "the holy ones").

The author expresses his desire that each member of the community would diligently continue in this fashion in order to appropriate the full wealth of assurance available between now and the inauguration of the messianic age. Conversely, he admonishes the community not to fall prey to a serial progression of the propensity of that which he had previously diagnosed, their spiritual lethargy (5:11). Rather, they are to follow the example of those who inherit "the promises" through an exhibition of the qualities of faithfulness and steadfast patience (6:11–12). The specific promises in question are those that are contained in the Abrahamic covenant. Those who inherit these promises are the patriarchs: Abraham, his son Isaac, and his grandson, Jacob, along with their progeny. Special emphasis is given to the pivotal figure of Abraham in the argument of Hebrews (2:16; 6:13–15; 7:4–5; 11:8–19).

The Abrahamic covenant. Hebrews 6:13 initiates the author's discussion of the patriarchs, specifically Abraham, and the divine covenant the Lord had established with them. The influence of the Abrahamic covenant is woven throughout the tapestry of Scripture, from the twelfth chapter of Genesis through the final chapter of Revelation. It forms the foundational basis for every subsequent covenant in the Bible. This covenant itself is a complex of unconditional divine promises that are stated and reiterated over a period of years, in a series of six recorded encounters between God and Abraham (Gen. 12:1–3; 12:7; 13:14–17; 15:1–21; 17:1–21; 22:15–18). Each successive restatement expanded on and enlarged the promised provisions of the primary, central core of the covenant.

The first passage records God's initial encounter with and commission to Abraham, along with an initial set of promised blessings (Gen. 12:1–3). The narrative records the divine instruction for Abraham to "go forth" to "the land which I will show you." This initial iteration of the covenant contained promises of personal blessing ("I will bless you") in specific relation to numerous offspring ("make you a great nation"), reputation ("make your name great"), and universal influence ("you shall be a blessing" and "in you all the families of the earth shall be blessed"). This universal influence would extend to divine, retributive justice regarding how Abraham (and, by implication, his offspring) was treated by others ("I will bless those who bless you, and the one who curses you I will curse").

The second divine encounter and first expansion of the Abrahamic covenant's promises is revealed in Genesis 12:7. Following Abraham's arrival in the land of Canaan, the Lord promised that Abraham's descendants would inherit the land as a gift ("to your descendants I will give this land"). Abraham later identified this promise as a divine oath, a solemn, unconditional guarantee (Gen. 24:7) that the Lord later intensified through swearing on Himself (Gen. 22:16). This intensification proves of great interest to the author of Hebrews (6:13).

The third divine encounter and second expansion of the Abrahamic covenant's promises is contained in Genesis 13:14–17. The Lord appeared again to Abraham and reconfirmed His intention to give the entirety of the land of Canaan, in every direction, to Abraham and his descendants forever.

The fourth divine encounter and third expansion of the Abrahamic covenant's promises is contained in Genesis 15:1–21. God led Abraham through a solemn covenant ritual, having him place the severed sections of multiple animals in two parallel rows. Normatively, both parties to this type of covenant would walk between the rendered animal pieces, indicating the severe penalty for future infraction. In this unique instance, Abraham was rendered completely passive and unable to move (15:12). God alone bound Himself to the covenant by passing as "a flaming torch" through the animal pieces (15:17), graphically demonstrating the unconditional nature of the covenant.

The fifth divine encounter and fourth expansion of the Abrahamic covenant's promises is contained in Genesis 17:1–21. God added the requirement of circumcision, the physical sign of the covenant, on the eighth day for Abraham and his male descendants (17:10–14). This was to be a vivid reminder, in blood, to every one of Abraham's descendants of God's "everlasting covenant" (17:7). At this time and in conjunction with the reiteration of the promise of innumerable descendants, the Lord changed Abraham's name from Abram ("exalted father") to Abraham ("father of multitudes"). The covenant blessing was expanded to incorporate not just a single nation to issue forth from Abraham, but "nations" as well as kings. Reiterated, as well, was the promise of Abraham's and his descendants' eternal possession of the land (17:1–8). An additional promise was added to the covenant complex, that of a personal relationship with Israel ("I will be their God," 17:8).

The sixth encounter, providing the fifth and climactic expansion of the Abrahamic covenant, is found in Genesis 22:15–18 in conjunction with the famous narrative of Abraham's divinely initiated and subsequently aborted sacrifice of his son, commonly known in Jewish tradition as the *Akedah*, "the binding of Isaac." This event would prove the ultimate test of the faith of Abraham, the "father of multitudes" (22:1–13). The Genesis 22 passage is firmly entrenched in the Jewish imagination and familiar to all. In addition, it is the central and climactic Torah passage in the synagogue liturgy of the Feast of Trumpets, the day celebrated as the anniversary of God's creation and commencement of the new civil calendar year, Rosh Hashanah.

Traditional rabbinic teaching has viewed the willing sacrifice of Abraham, and especially that of Isaac in willingly offering himself, as an act of vicarious atonement throughout the future history of their descendants, the nation of Israel. The righteousness of the patriarchs could be vicariously applied to their descendants in time of spiritual need.[10] The rabbis were not completely off base when they saw a picture of atonement in Isaac. The events of Genesis 22 are a prime example of what Scripture calls "a mere shadow of what is to come" (Col. 2:17). Isaac was a prophetic type, a picture, of the Messiah. Jesus was not only the ultimate Israel, the ultimate David, and the ultimate Moses, but is also the ultimate Isaac. For example, both Isaac and Jesus were the sons of promise. Both men had miraculous births. Both were obedient and willing sons who were prepared and ready to lay down their lives at their Father's behest. Both sons even carried the wood for their own sacrifice.

Indeed, both Isaac and Jesus had Fathers who were prepared to slay them to fulfill a larger purpose. As Abraham was willing to sacrifice His son, so, too,

God was willing to sacrifice His only Son. Yet God did not demand of Abraham what He demanded of himself. The Lord provided a substitute sacrifice for the son of Abraham, a ram caught in the thicket. But there was no alternative sacrifice for the Son of God. Jesus became the Lamb of God, slain for the sin of the world (John 1:29).

Having been thus prepared to obediently sacrifice his only son, the son of promise, Abraham was divinely recognized as the worthy recipient of the covenant promises (Gen. 22:16). Using the most intensive form of divine oath ("by Myself I have sworn"), the Lord restated and ratified four separate components of the covenant. First, hearkening back to the initial promise of Genesis 12:2, the Lord restated His intention of divine blessing. Second, echoing the promises of Genesis 13:16; 15:5; and 17:2–6, God restated His promise of innumerable descendants. Third, summarizing the promises of possession of the land in Genesis 12:7; 13:15; 15:18; 17:8, the Lord promised Abraham's descendants possession of enemy cities. Fourth, hearkening back to the initial set of promises concerning universal influence in Genesis 12:3, the Lord reaffirmed that all nations would be blessed through the seed of Abraham (Gen. 22:15–18).

The Hebrews author's quotation of Genesis highlights the legal intensiveness of God's oath to Abraham. The divine oath made by God and sworn on Himself was the most effective contemporary means to solemnly communicate to Abraham and his progeny the weight behind His resolve concerning the certain eventual fulfillment of these covenant promises (see also Exod. 32:13; Isa. 45:23; Jer. 22:5; 49:13). Having now referenced the divine oath of Genesis 22:16, the author goes on to directly quote Genesis 22:17, the summary verse of God's promises concerning possession of the land, innumerable descendants, and general blessing.

He goes on to contend that Abraham, having patiently waited, finally obtained God's promise. This should be understood as the decades-long development of the Abrahamic covenant from its initial core of promises through the final, climactic procurement of legal confirmation through divine oath. This passage is impregnated with first-century legal terminology. The phrase *eis bebaiosin* (6:16) means "legal confirmation," the word *mesiteuō* (6:17) means "to act as a guarantee," the word *epideiknumi* (6:17) means "to furnish proof," and *ametathetos* (6:18) means "legally non-annullable, completely unchangeable."

The custom of legal oath making, divinely validated in the Mosaic legislation (Exod. 22), was utilized by God to demonstrate His immeasurable level of personal commitment to Israel. Through the two irrevocable, nonannullable facts of divine promise and solemn oath, it is now quite impossible for

God to change His mind (*pseudomai*, "to lie," which is the author's allusion to statements regarding God's unchangeable purpose in both Num. 23:19 and 1 Sam. 15:29). Therefore, those spiritual fugitives (*kataphugontes*, "having fled for refuge") may possess great confidence in taking hold of the object of hope, their salvation, set before them.

This salvation hope is portrayed as "an anchor of the soul." Lane points out that the anchor served as a useful nautical metaphor in the literature of the ancient world.[11] This anchoring hope was firm and secure, stable and unmovable. It is vividly pictured as entering beyond the veil of the tabernacle/temple sanctuary's Holy of Holies (Lev. 16:2, 12, 15) and opening access into the very presence of God Himself (6:19).

As previously discussed, under the Levitical system of the Mosaic covenant, entrance into the Holy of Holies was limited to one day a year, the Day of Atonement, and to one individual, the high priest (see comments at 9:7). Jesus, of course, is the One the author credits with conveyance of our hope through the barrier. He has entered into God's presence as our *prodromos*, "forerunner," a pioneer blazing the trail, encouraging us to follow Him into God's presence as He, our permanent high priest, enables our open access. The section neatly closes with a concluding reference to Jesus' priesthood belonging to the order of Melchizedek, which serves notice that the theological argument, interrupted in 5:10, is about to recommence in the following chapter.

Conclusion

This section of Hebrews not only identified for the community a very problematic area of potential danger facing them, but provided encouragement for the danger's avoidance. Spiritual stagnation and lethargy, both then and today, must be countered with a strong focus on God's solemn promises. A study of God's unconditional covenants with Israel, such as the one regarding the Abrahamic covenant provided in this chapter, can serve to divert our attention from faith's uncertainties and life's steady pressures. Most critically, any successful prognosis for maintaining spiritual health must focus on the all-sufficient provisions of a faithful God.

Study Questions

1. Why does the author pause before advancing his argument concerning Melchizedek and Jesus' high priesthood?

2. What level of instruction is the recipient community ready to receive? Support your answer.

3. In 6:4–6 how does the author describe the recipients of Hebrews?

4. Define what is meant by "falling away."

5. Summarize the promises contained in the Abrahamic covenant, being as specific as possible.

CHAPTER 8

The Priesthood of Melchizedek Hebrews 7:1-28

Preview:

Having successfully discharged the expression of his concern through the contents of the third warning passage, the author of Hebrews now fully concentrates his argument on demonstrating the connection between the respective priesthoods of Jesus and the enigmatic Old Testament figure Melchizedek. On the surface it seems that the author has allotted to Melchizedek, an individual mentioned in only two Old Testament passages (Gen. 14:18–20; Ps. 110:4), and there only briefly, a somewhat disproportionate amount of literary real estate in the text's argument. However, relative to Melchizedek's conceptual importance in relation to the Messiah, the substantial allotment of space seems ideal. Melchizedek is the theological key to understanding the basis of the messianic priesthood's replacement of the inferior Levitical priesthood.

Comparison of Melchizedek and Jesus (7:1–3)

Melchizedek. Melchizedek appears but once in the historical narrative of Hebrew Scripture (Gen. 14:18–20). Abraham, returning home from successful military conquest (Gen. 14:1–17), is met in the Valley of the Kings by the enigmatic figure of Melchizedek. The passage reveals a mere three facts to dispel some measure of mystery.

First, he is identified as being the king of the city of Salem (Heb. "peace"), a city later known as Jerusalem. Melchizedek is a compound Hebrew name meaning "righteous king." This should be understood as a literal name and not some sort of spiritual code name. The second half of the name, *zedek*, "righteous," is shared with another Jebusite king of Jerusalem who appears relatively early in Scripture, Adonizedek, "righteous lord" (Josh. 10:1). It is reasonable to conclude that *zedek* may have been a dynastic name or title. Second, Melchizedek is further identified in the Genesis passage as being a priest of "God Most High" (see Mark 5:7; Acts 7:48; 16:17). As such, Melchizedek pronounced priestly blessing on Abraham. Third, Abraham contributed one-tenth of his military spoils to Melchizedek in recognition of his priesthood.

Melchizedek rates discussion in the first-century works of both Josephus[1] and Philo.[2] It is the traditional rabbinic custom to fill every contextual void left in the text of Scripture with creative embellishment. They constructed their own imaginative solution for reconciling the Melchizedekian and Levitical priesthoods that removes any need for further comparison or theological reflection. According to legend, Melchizedek is a pseudonym for Noah's son Shem, still surprisingly spry all those centuries after the flood.[3] On his encounter with Abraham and pronouncement of blessing over him, Melchizedek reversed the proper order of the recitation of the names of God and Abraham. Abraham corrected Melchizedek, pointing out his breach of priestly protocol. Consequently, God wrested the priesthood from Melchizedek and passed it in perpetuity to Abraham and his descendants.[4] Therefore, according to some rabbis, Psalm 110:4's priesthood of the order of Melchizedek belongs to the peerless Levites! It is unclear just how far back beyond Talmudic times this legend circulated, but it does cause one to raise a suspicious eyebrow of speculation as to whether it is a lame attempt at a response to the argument of Hebrews.

If the legend was contemporary to Hebrews, the author of Hebrews for some reason chooses to ignore it in his treatment. Nonetheless, through the inspiration of the Holy Spirit and the utilization of first-century Jewish interpretive practice, he is able to extract every last juicy drop of theological significance from the Torah's brief description of Abraham and Melchizedek's encounter. He mines the significance of Melchizedek's name, translating it as "king of righteousness," who, ruling Salem, functions as the "king of peace." The typological application to Jesus is obvious. He also capitalizes on the brevity of the Genesis passage and lack of supplied biographical and genealogical detail. In the absence of such specifics, the author argues that Melchizedek should be recognized as a prophetic type of "the Son of God," whose priesthood can therefore be understood as functioning perpetually.

The Melchizedek passage is often thought of as a preincarnate appearance of the Messiah. This idea, although a delightful speculation to preachers in particular, must be laid to rest for several reasons. First, if one can argue that Melchizedek's name is an indication of his messianic identity, then an even stronger case could be made for Joshua 10:1's king, Adonizedek, trumping "king of righteousness" with "lord of righteousness." However, I have never heard that sermon preached; no one thinks of Adonizedek as a preincarnate appearance of Christ.

Second, the text states that Melchizedek is *like* the Son of God, not that he actually *is* the Son of God, describing Melchizedek's similarity to Jesus with the word *aphomoioō*, "to make like," not the words *charaktēr*, "image," or *hupostasis*, "essence" (1:3).

Third, a requirement for priesthood was the possession of humanity (5:1ff.). By definition, at no time prior to His incarnation did Jesus possess the attribute of humanity, thus disqualifying Him from being the one making a brief cameo appearance in Genesis 14:18–20. Furthermore, theophanies, or preincarnate appearances of Christ in the Old Testament, were characteristically brief episodes and not of sufficiently lengthy duration to allow the governing of a city.

Fourth, in Psalm 110:4, the Lord appoints the Messiah as a priest of the order of Melchizedek, thereby distinguishing the two personalities. In short, if Melchizedek had actually been a preincarnate appearance of Jesus, the Lord would have appointed the Messiah as a priest of His own order, an appointment to literal nonsense.

Use of Old Testament Passages in Hebrews 7

Hebrews	Old Testament	Subject
7:1–2	Gen. 14:17–20	Melchizedek and Abraham
7:3	Ps. 110:4	The Melchizedekian priesthood
7:5	Num. 18:21	The Mosaic Law concerning Israel's Levitical tithe
7:14	Gen. 49:10	Prophecy regarding Messiah's descent from Judah
7:14	Isa. 11:1	Prophecy regarding Messiah's descent from Jesse
7:17	Ps. 110:4	The Son's Melchizedekian priesthood
7:21	Ps. 110:4	The Son's Melchizedekian priesthood
7:27	Lev. 9:7; 16:6	The Levitical high priest's need for atonement

Comparison of the Levitical Priesthood and the Priesthood of Melchizedek (7:4–10)

Having rehearsed the historical Melchizedek account and established the man's quality, the author now turns his attention to providing interpretive theological analysis of Genesis 14:18–20 as filtered through the lens of Psalm 110:4. His rhetorical goal is to demonstrate the superiority of the Melchizedekian priesthood over the Levitical. To do so, he must first establish the superiority of Melchizedek to Abraham. He will accomplish this, though, by first underscoring Abraham's inherent greatness. The author directs his recipients to "consider" (the imperative form of *theōreō*, "to observe") Abraham's greatness (*pēlikos*, "how great"). Abraham is "the patriarch," the original and preeminent Hebrew, the father of the nation of Israel and its symbolic embodiment. As great as Abraham may have been, Israel's exalted patriarch nonetheless gave Melchizedek one-tenth of the spoils of his successful military activity (7:4). Furthermore, the spoils that were given were the crème de la crème (*akrothiniōn*, literally, "the top of the heap").

The author now builds his argument through establishing the greatness of the Levitical priests (7:5). His use of present tense in describing the Levitical activities indicates that the temple is still standing at the time of his authorship. According to the Torah, the Levitical system was supported through Israel's tithes. The nation's tithes were given to the Levites for their support, and the Levites, in turn, would present a tithe of those tithes to support the priests (Num. 18:21–28).

In 7:6 the author begins to make his case for the supremacy of the Melchizedekian priesthood. He argues that the Levitical priests receive tithes from their brethren, those with equal status as children of Abraham. However, Melchizedek received his tithe from the great Abraham independent of family or tribal relationship. Furthermore, the Levitical tithe was based on the Torah (*nomos*, "law"), but Melchizedek's tithe was based on *epaggelias*, "the promises," specifically those of the Abrahamic covenant. Throughout the remainder of the text, the author will consistently argue for the dominance of God's unconditional covenants, both the Abrahamic and the new, and their respective promises over the legal system of the Mosaic covenant. Furthermore, as it was an indisputable practice for the greater individual to bless the lesser and not the reverse, Melchizedek's blessing of Abraham demonstrated his preeminence (7:7).

The final point in this section's argument is that the composition of the Levitical priesthood is ever changing, as individual priests die or retire from service at the age of fifty (Num. 8:24–25) and are replaced. Yet Melchizedek, through the absence of biographical data in the Scripture, can be thought of as still living. In short, since the Bible makes no mention of Melchizedek's death, it is acceptable to claim that he is eternal (7:8) for the sake of a very Jewish argument that, while perhaps seeming specious to twenty-first-century readers, would have made perfect sense to Hebrews' first-century recipients. Along the same line of thought and using the same reasoning, the author proposes that in a sense, the father of the Levites, Levi, actually participated in paying the tithe to Melchizedek, as Levi was seminally present in his great-grandfather Abraham's "loins" (*osphus*, "reproductive organ").

Comparison of the Levitical Priesthood and the Priesthood of Jesus (7:11–25)

The Inferiority of the Levitical Priesthood (7:11–19). Having laid the contextual groundwork, the author now launches into the crux of his argument. He conclusively demonstrates the Levitical priesthood's annulment based on the superior merits of the priesthood of Jesus, which serves as its replacement. Filtered through the interpretive lens of Psalm 110:4, Hebrews views the Levitical priesthood as a prophetic type, divinely designed and established for a specific era in history (what some theologians refer to as a dispensation) and to serve a specific, preparatory function. Jesus' priesthood serves as the Levitical priesthood's antitype, fulfilling and replacing the previous system, the typological shadow, with a superior one, the typological substance.

The author literarily brackets his discussion on either end of this section with the use of the two related words *teleiōsis*, "perfection" (7:11), and *eteleiō-sev*, "perfected" (7:19), which are applied relative to the Torah's inherent deficiencies. This bracketing forms an *inclusio* (a clearly demarcated section of text), which is designed to highlight the main point of the argument.

His argument's explosive opening salvo in 7:11 is that *teleiōsis*, "perfection," (or better in the immediate context of its application to believers, "completion," meaning the believer's final arrival at a condition of spiritual maturity, see Use of "Perfect" in Hebrews on p. 247), could never be achieved through means of the Levitical priesthood. Furthermore, he reasons that the entire system of Mosaic legislation is inextricably connected to the priesthood because it finds in the priesthood its very basis of existence ("for on the basis of [preposition *epi*, "upon"] it [*autēs*, personal pronoun related to the previous referent, the Levitical priesthood], the people received the Law"). What this means, practically, is that any conclusions the author will draw concerning the Levitical priesthood will necessarily impact the Mosaic legislation in its totality as well.

God Himself demonstrated the insufficiency of the Levitical priesthood by His announcement in Psalm 110:4 of the installation of a new priest who is identified not with Aaron's order but rather with the order of Melchizedek. It must be kept in mind that this psalm was written by David after the Levitical priesthood had already been functioning for some four centuries. The implications of eventual replacement were unmistakable, even in David's era. If God's true intention was for His chosen people to achieve the spiritual maturity He desired on their behalf through the perpetual continuation of the Levitical priesthood, then there is no explanation, reasonable or otherwise, for the expression of need for a *heteron . . . ierea,* "priest of another, different kind."

This argument is clarified in 7:12, with the author's contention that a change of the priesthood *anagkēs,* ("necessitates") a change of the Torah as well. Of highest significance is that the word translated "change," *metathesis,* conveys not only the generic concept of "a change" or "an alteration," but also of "removal," an example of which is its first-century usage by Philo concerning Genesis 5:24's supernatural transport of Enoch.[5] Replacement of the Levitical priestly system inevitably entailed replacement, even removal, of the entire Torah.

There are some influential voices in the contemporary messianic movement, David H. Stern, author of *The Jewish New Testament Commentary* being one of them, who disagree with this interpretation. Stern writes:

> The context makes it overwhelmingly clear that no change or transformation in *Torah* is envisioned other than in connection with the priesthood and the sacrificial system. The term *"metathesis"* implies retention of the basic structure of *Torah,* with some of its elements rearranged ("transformed"); it does not imply abrogation of either the *Torah* as a whole or of *mitzvot* not connected with the priesthood and the sacrificial system.[6]

Yet what Stern decries is exactly what the passage teaches. The author's use of the particular, loaded word *metathesis,* coupled with the context in which it is employed, makes it difficult to accept that the author intends a mere shuffling of the Torah's deck along with a few selected Levitical edits in order to create a modified, rearranged, abridgment of Torah. Practically speaking, it is a fallacy to suppose that the Torah can be neatly compartmentalized. It was given to Israel as a single legislative unit composed of consistently overlapping ceremonial, civic, and moral legislation. To break one law was to break them all (James 2:10). Indeed, the Torah itself forbids either augmenting or diminishing its contents (Deut. 4:2).

The structure of the Torah's design does not cordon off the legislation pertaining to the priesthood into its own, self-contained Levitical ghetto that lends itself to painless extraction. Rather, the priestly system is inextricably entwined in the very fabric of the Mosaic Law, similar to a metastatic tumor so extensively spread that it cannot be excised without killing the patient. Elimination of the Levitical legislation would be injurious to Torah's construction and would present a system more holey than holy.

Paul explained that the purpose of Torah was to serve as our tutor and diagnostician of our innate condition of sinfulness, educating us of our need and preparing us for the coming of the Messiah (Rom. 3:20; 7:5; Gal. 3:19–4:7). Once Jesus arrived and successfully accomplished His mission, the system previously in place became obsolete (Heb. 8:13).

> Nor was it only the Aaronic priesthood which must be superseded. That priesthood was instituted under the Mosaic law, and was so integral to it that a change in the priesthood carries with it inevitably a change in the law. If the Aaronic priesthood was instituted for a temporary purpose, to be brought to an end when the age of fulfillment dawned, the same must be true of the law under which that priesthood was introduced.[7]

The author builds on his argument, noting the obvious point that Jesus' priesthood is completely independent of the Torah's Levitical legislation and therefore, of the Torah itself. He was demonstrably born of the tribe of Judah (Isa. 11:1; Matt. 1:2–3; 2:6; Luke 3:33; et al.), not Levi. It was illegal for anyone other than a genealogically legitimate Levitical priest to serve at the sanctuary's altar of sacrifice. While, according to Moses, the tribe of Judah was of extreme importance in God's plan and program, the tribe's contribution was not in the area of tabernacle worship. Genesis 49:10 contains a crucial messianic prophecy related to Judah.

Tribe of Judah. On his deathbed, Jacob delivered his final blessing to his twelve sons. His words were fraught with prophetic significance. The patriarch himself emphasized the prophetic content of his remarks by identifying them as revealing what the future held for his family "in the days to come" (Heb., *b'acharit hayyamim,* "the end of days"; Gen. 49:1–2).

It was Jacob's fourth son Judah, the "lion," to whom the mantle of tribal leadership was passed. Judah was recognized as being worthy to receive the privileges of firstborn. In Jacob's prophetic blessings of his twelve sons was the promise that Judah's tribe would rightfully rule (possess the "scepter," the symbol of royalty) over the rest of their brethren until a particular moment in history, expressed with the phrase "the coming of shiloh."

The mysterious term, *shiloh,* can be translated "to whom it belongs,"[8] and has traditionally been understood as a messianic title, a pseudonym for *Messiah.* The first-century Aramaic paraphrases of the Scripture, the Targums, consistently treat this as messianic prophecy. Targum Onkelos reads, "Kings shall not cease from the house of Judah . . . until Messiah come, whose is the kingdom. . . ."[9] The Palestinian Targum likewise reads, "Kings shall not cease from the house of Judah . . . until the time that King Messiah shall come, whose is the kingdom. . . ."[10] In addition, the Midrash,[11] the vast corpus of homiletical commentary, and the Talmud,[12] the oral law, as well as Rashi, the eleventh-century rabbinic "Goliath," all take Shiloh with reference to "King Messiah."[13]

The point is clear by the genealogies recorded in the Gospels, whether through his adopted father (Matt. 1:1–17) or his mother (Luke 3:23–38), that Jesus belongs to the tribe of Judah. Interestingly, if Jesus had not come prior to the destruction of the temple and the accompanying loss of all its stored genealogical records that would occur a mere seventy-five years hence, any claims that he had to tribal descent from Judah would have been hopelessly unverifiable. God's timing was impeccable.

Of special note is the author's reference to Jesus as "our Lord" in 7:14. This is the second of three instances in the Hebrew text where the author explicitly assigns that status to Jesus (also 2:3; 13:20; see Names, Titles, and Descriptions of Jesus in Hebrews on p. 243–245).

As in 7:12 Jesus is again referred to in 7:15 as *hiereus heteros*, "a priest of another, different kind." The Melchizedekian priesthood is completely separate and distinct from the Levitical system. It is a priesthood not based on legislative genealogical requirements, but is based on the power of Jesus' indestructible (*akatalutos*, a word uniquely appearing here in the New Testament) life (7:16). One priesthood is based on Torah (*nomos*), and the other is based on power (*dunamis*).

In 7:17 the author provides another quotation of Psalm 110:4. Only the second half is quoted, emphasizing the eternality of the Melchizedekian priest in contrast to the Levitical priesthood's multiplicity of mere mortals. This quote is the final mention of Melchizedek's name in the text.

Hebrews 7:18 begins with the positively arresting noun *athetēsis*, a legal term that means "annulment," "something set aside," generally used of the annulment of a decree or the cancellation of a debt.[14] The same word is employed by the author in reference to Jesus having removed, set aside, or put away sin through His sacrificial death (9:26). What the author is affirming as having been set aside or annulled is "a former commandment because of its weakness and uselessness."

Just why the author considers the Torah both weak and useless is answered in 7:19's "for the Law made nothing perfect." It was proven ineffective through an almost fifteen-century track record of failure in bringing Israel to a state of spiritual maturity. It was never designed to perfect anything or anyone, but to lead Israel to their Messiah (Gal. 3:24). In contrast, the

Melchizedekian priesthood brings in a better hope, through which believers may draw near to God.

The word translated "bringing in" (*epeisagōgē*) conveys the idea of "bringing in for the purpose of replacement," as found in Josephus, who uses the term in reference to the Persian king Artaxerxes' displacement of his old wife, Vashti, for his new wife, Esther.[15] Artaxerxes did not simply diminish his previous wife's role or alter or abridge her influence in his life. He replaced her with a better model. Just so, the Torah has been annulled, set aside, and replaced by something incomparably superior. We now have a better hope through which we enter God's presence (4:16).

The Superiority of the Priesthood of Jesus (7:20–25). Just as the author created an inclusio through the repeated use of the word *perfect* in the previous section, so, too, he sets the next section apart through the strategic use of the word *horkōmosia*, "oath," in 7:20 and 7:28. The patent superiority of the priesthood of Jesus is demonstrated by its establishment by means of irrevocable divine oath (Ps. 110:4; again quoted in 7:21). The Levitical priesthood was established by means of law, and even the law of God takes second place to the oath of God. According to William Lane, "The divine oath is the impregnable guarantee that excludes all doubt and gives to faith assurance of the promise. The function of the oath is to characterize the promise as final, eternal, and unchangeable."[16]

In 7:22 the author introduces a vitally important theological term to his argument, the word *diathēkē*, "covenant." This term is employed throughout the remainder of Hebrews on a total of seventeen occasions (7:22; 8:6, 8, 9 [2x], 10; 9:4 [2x], 15 [2x], 16, 17, 20; 10:16, 29; 12:24; 13:20), which accounts for almost half of its thirty-seven New Testament appearances. The concept of covenant is inarguably of immense importance in the text of Hebrews.

The contrast the author has been making between the respective Levitical and Melchizedekian priesthoods will now broaden to contrasting the merits of the Mosaic covenant against the new covenant (Jer. 31:31–34). The author will extensively treat the new covenant in the following chapter and for now is content merely to introduce the topic and place it on the conceptual table of Hebrews' discourse, describing it as a *kreittonos diathēkēs*, "a better covenant." This neatly parallels his previous turn of phrase in 7:19, *kreittonos elpidos*, "a better hope," thereby associating the two ideas. Part of the functional weakness of the Mosaic covenant was its lack of a guarantor (*egguos*) to ensure the people's success in following Torah. By contrast, Jesus is the new covenant's guarantee. "The choice of the term, which occurs only here in the NT, is purposeful. In the papyri it can denote a bond, a collateral, or some form of material guarantee that a debt will be paid or a promise fulfilled. But it may also refer to an individual who offers his own life as the guarantor of another person."[17]

In 7:23–24 the author contrasts the continual miasma of impermanence that swirled across the history of Israel's implementation of the Levitical priesthood as high priests either died or were replaced in office. Josephus records that in the fifteen centuries that had ensued from the inauguration of the Levitical priesthood to the destruction of the second temple, Israel was served by eighty-three different high priests.[18] Jesus, however, permanently holds his priesthood because He continues forever. His priesthood is *aparabaton*, "inviolable," "untransferable," and therefore is completely permanent.

In 7:25 the author reaches a logical conclusion based on the previous verses. Jesus is, therefore, "able to save forever." The present tense of *sōzein*, the verb translated "to save," indicates that Jesus' work in salvation goes far beyond that of the single moment in time that the new believer initially received salvation. His salvation power extends throughout each moment of every believer's lifetime, ensuring our salvation for today as well as our eventual arrival into His presence at our final tomorrow (see the section on *Theology of Salvation* in Appendix B: The Theology of Hebrews and New Testament Passages Teaching Assurance of Salvation on p. 54–56).

Those whom Jesus permanently saves are those who "draw near to God through Him." This is a clear reminder that there is no salvation apart from Jesus and there is no relationship with God apart from Him, no matter what our contemporary age of tolerance and ecumenism may claim. Jesus is the sole provision that God has made for humanity's salvation (Acts 4:12).

In addition to Jesus' power to ensure salvation, the author also highlights Jesus' related ministry of high priestly intercession (*entugchanein*, "to appeal," "to petition," "to entreat"). The purpose of His ministry of intercession is to guarantee our salvation and provide the high-priestly mercy and grace promised in 4:14–16.[19] This ministry is part of Isaiah's messianic promise concerning the suffering servant (Isa. 53:12). The gospel of John provides a small sample of what that intercession might sound like (John 17:1–26).

This essential ministry, while active, is not frantic in nature. Jesus' continuous intercession on our behalf does not entail standing, bowing, prostration, waving of arms, or offering of sacrifice. Our perfect High Priest makes intercession for us while seated on a royal throne in immediate proximity to His Father (1:3, 13), who in turn continuously receives the petitions of His Son made on our behalf. David MacLeod's definition is both compact and complete: "Intercession in Hebrews may be defined as the sympathetic appeals and petitions of the ascended, incarnate Son of God to God the Father (on the basis of a finished sacrifice) for the preservation, forgiveness, renovation, and bringing to glory of His people."[20]

The Perfection of the Priesthood of Jesus (7:26–28)

The final three verses of chapter 7 serve to summarize and conclude this segment of the author's argument. Our High Priest, Jesus, is described as being holy, morally innocent, and pure; His qualifications for this singular position are utterly unassailable. His present ministry finds Him separated from sinners by being in the continuous presence of God in the highest of heavens (see the comments on 4:14 for a discussion of plural heavens).

Having made the definitive sacrifice through His offering of Himself, no further sacrifice is necessary. His sacrifice was perfect, complete, sufficient and *ephapax*, "once for all." This is contrasted with the innumerable, never-ending daily stream of sacrifices offered by the high priests of the Levitical system who, through sacrifice, must first cover their own sins prior to offering sacrifice on behalf of the people. On the Day of Atonement, the high priest was specifically commanded to offer sacrifices, first on his own behalf and then on behalf of the nation (Lev. 9:7; 16:6–10, see comments at Heb. 9:7). However, according to Torah, he is to follow the same procedure if he discovers that he is guilty of unintentional sin anytime during the year (Lev. 4:3–12; 6:9–23). According to Josephus, by the first century, the high priests were covering their spiritual bases and offering twice-daily sacrifices (probably a prudent decision, based on Josephus's disclosures).[21]

The section closes with a final "greatest hits," three-pronged comparison. First, God's oath regarding the Melchizedekian priesthood takes precedence over His Torah regarding the Levitical priesthood. Promise trumps Law. Second, while the Torah appoints men to the priesthood, God's oath appoints His Son. Third, while the Torah appoints high priests who are inherently weak through both their mortality and sin nature, Jesus is the perfect high priest. He has victoriously prevailed through thorough testing. He has conquered death after undergoing unimaginable suffering. He is the eternally exalted Son of God whose reign will know no end.

Conclusion

This portion of Hebrews would have served as an immense encouragement to the recipient community. For a group of uncertain Jewish believers plagued by doubt and on the verge of a crisis of faith in God's power to deliver and the Messiah's sufficiency to help in time of need (4:16), this would have served as a much needed corrective. The author of Hebrews capitalized on this opportunity and used it to unveil exceptionally deep theological truths. This is a great example to the twenty-first-century church and a reminder that the solution to a community in faith crisis is not to scale back the teaching of doctrine, which might well be the instinctive response by a worried pastor, but to preach and teach the deeper things concerning our Messiah.

Levitical Priesthood And Jesus' Melchizedekian Priesthood

Levitical	Melchizedekian	Hebrews
Serves as priest only	Serves as Priest and King	1:3, 8; 2:17; 3:1; 4:14–15; 5:5, 9–10; 7:1–2
Ministry is limited to Israel	Ministry is universal in scope	7:1–3
Subordinate to Abraham	Superior to Abraham	7:2, 4–7
Israel tithed to Levi	Levi tithed to Melchizedek	7:9–10
Dependent on Aaronic genealogy	Independent of genealogy	7:3, 6, 11–16
Appointed by Law	Appointed by divine oath	7:28
Requires many appointed men	Requires one appointed Son	4:14; 5:1, 5; 7:23–28
Temporary and limited by mortality	Unlimited by time and duration through immortality	5:6, 9–10; 6:20; 7:3, 8, 15–19, 23–25
Priest needs atonement 7:26–28	Priest is source of atonement	2:9–10, 17; 5:3;
Priest has restricted access to Holy 10:19–22 of Holies	Priest has continual access to the Holy of Holies	9:7, 9–14, 24;
Priest serves in a copy of the divine tabernacle	Priest serves in the divine tabernacle	8:2–5; 9:1–8, 11–12, 24
Priest is chief officiate on the Day of Atonement	Priest is fulfillment of the Day of Atonement	9:7, 11–14
Priest sacrifices animals	Priest sacrifices Himself	2:9–10; 10:4, 10–14

Levitical	Melchizedekian	Hebrews
Priest regularly offers a series of multiple sacrifices	Priest offers one ultimate sacrifice	7:27; 8:3; 9:26; 10:1–4, 10–14
Priest continually standing	Priest now seated	10:11–12
No final remission of sin	Final remission of sin	2:9–10; 5:9–10; 7:27; 9:26; 10:1–4, 10–14, 18
Imperfect salvation results	Perfect salvation results	2:9–10, 17; 7:11–14, 18–19, 28; 10:1–4, 10–14
Provision of external cleansing	Provision of internal cleansing	9:13–14
Priest can never secure salvation	Priest secures eternal salvation	5:9–10; 7:25; 9:12; 10:1–4, 10–14
Appointment dependent on Mosaic Law	Appointment independent of Mosaic Law	5:6, 9–10; 7:1–3, 11–19; 8:4
Inherent deficiency of old legal basis	Inherent perfection of new legal basis	7:11–14, 18–19
Based on a good covenant	Based on a better covenant	7:22
Based on a good hope	Based on a better hope	7:19
One man possessed access to Divine Presence	All believers possess access to Divine Presence	9:7; 10:19–22

Study Questions

1. Do you believe that Melchizedek was a preincarnate appearance of the Messiah? Defend your answer.

2. On what basis and for what reasons was the Torah replaced?

3. Explain how this chapter's contents support the concept of assurance of salvation.

4. Study Comparisons between Levitical and Jesus' Melchizedekian Priesthoods in this chapter. List what you believe to be the five strongest arguments for the superiority of Jesus' priesthood. Explain your reasoning.

CHAPTER 9

Superiority of the New Covenant
Hebrews 8:1–13

Preview:
Following the author of Hebrews' extraordinary tour de force concerning the glorious high priesthood of our Messiah and the encouragement it must have stimulated among his struggling community of readers, he opens this next section with the spectacular literary cheer, "We have such a high priest!" Although chapter 8 contains a mere thirteen verses, each is highly concentrated for maximum theological impact.

The Superior Promises of the New Covenant (8:1–6)

As the eighth chapter commences, the author launches a new expansion of his argument in order to integrate the new covenant with what he had already established regarding Jesus' priesthood. Hebrews 8:1–2 is the letter's central core and provides both a pointed look backward at theological areas already treated as well as a provocative preview of that which still lies ahead. The essential theological point and pinnacle of the argument made thus far has been that "we have such a high priest, who has taken His seat at the right hand of the throne of the Majesty in the heavens, a minister in the sanctuary, and in the true tabernacle, which the Lord pitched, not man." This point will now serve as the foundation to carry his argument forward.

Breaking from the extensively used imagery of Psalm 110:4 and once again employing the imagery of Psalm 110:1, the author reminds the recipient congregation that Jesus is enthroned as High Priest at God's right hand (Heb. 1:3, 13) in the heavens (review comment on 4:14 for a discussion of plural heavens). This description of Jesus being seated finds direct parallel in 12:2, with the only difference between the two verses being 8:1's poetic circumlocution, "throne of the Majesty," in lieu of 12:2's "the throne of God."

Revealingly, Jesus is called a *leitourgos*, "a sacred servant of worship" (from which we derive our word *liturgy*). Of course, this sacred servant could not possibly have served in the existing temple or former tabernacle sanctuaries, which were exclusively reserved for the ministry of the Levitical priesthood. If the Torah's legislation were to be the decisive factor, Jesus would be completely disqualified from service. However, Jesus' high priesthood bypasses Torah, and this priestly scion of the tribe of Judah uniquely performs His sacred duties in the true tabernacle sanctuary located in the heavens, pitched by the Lord and not man.

This far along in the text of Hebrews' argument it is difficult to understand how some in the messianic movement could hold the position that it is unnecessary to think of Jesus' priesthood as having superseded the Levitical one, and that the two priesthoods could perpetually carry on in parallel fashion with Jesus serving in heaven and the Levites serving on earth.[1] This idea flies in the face of everything the author has thus far presented. The sole basis for this view is the Torah's declaration of the perpetuity of the Levitical priesthood (Exod. 29:9; Num. 25:13; et al.). An "everlasting" Levitical priesthood would indeed throw a monkey wrench into the argument for its replacement.

However, Old Testament Hebrew lacks a word that can convey the concept of "eternity" or "everlasting" or "forever" in an absolute sense. The word in question, *olam*, simply means "an indeterminately long duration," as determined by context as when used of the duration of a person's lifetime (Exod. 14:13; 21:6; Lev. 25:46; Deut. 15:17) or that of ten generations (Deut. 23:3). The Mosaic legislation was not designed for eternity, but only for a fifteen-hundred-year preparatory period for Israel prior to the arrival of their Messiah (Gal. 3:19–25). Therefore the Levitical system's abrogation may be argued confidently.

Prior to Israel's construction of the tabernacle, God had supernaturally revealed to Moses on Sinai a visual *tupos*, "an image," "a format," "a pattern," "a model" to illustrate what he was to erect in the wilderness (Exod. 25:40). The wilderness tabernacle, although sanctioned by God for His people's use, was only an imperfect and inferior *hupodeigma* ("example," "model," "replica") and *skia* ("shadow") of the true heavenly tabernacle in which Christ performed His high-priestly ministry. The author of Hebrews develops this thought more fully in the next chapter.

Our Lord's ministry in superior, heavenly surroundings is but one element of His overall superior sacred ministry. His possession of such is the result of His service as mediator (*mesitēs*, "an arbitrator," "a go between") of a better covenant, which has been enacted on better promises.[2] Please do not miss the author's emphatic double usage of "better" (*kreittonos* and *kreittosin*, respectively, see Use of "Better" in Hebrews on p. 39). The better covenant is the new covenant. The covenant to which the new covenant proves superior is the Mosaic. The superior quality of the new covenant is a result of its enactment on superior promises. Jesus' mediation of the new covenant is our guarantee that our salvation remains secure and that our access into God's immediate presence remains assured.

Use of Old Testament Passages in Hebrews 8

Hebrews	Old Testament	Subject
8:1	Ps. 110:1	The divine authority of the Son
8:5	Exod. 25:40	The tabernacle
8:8–12	Jer. 31:31–34	The new covenant

Prophecy of the New Covenant (8:7–12)

This section begins with the author's use of the causal conjunction *gar*, "for," to explain his reasoning in the previous discussion as to the new covenant's superiority. He defends the necessity for the new covenant's establishment by arguing that if the first covenant with Israel, that is, the Mosaic covenant, had been faultless (*amemptos*, "without blame"), there would have been no reason to consider a second covenant. Implicit in God's promise of a new covenant is His recognition of the previous covenant's inadequacy. It is not as if God's plan to establish a new covenant was a midcourse adjustment in His divine master plan for Israel, a celestial "plan B" of sorts. He had always intended to replace the Mosaic covenant with the new covenant. If the nation of Israel's spiritual maturity could be perfected through the Mosaic covenant, another covenant would prove redundant. The new covenant's very existence demonstrates the deficiency and provisional nature of the Mosaic covenant, which could produce neither the justification of humanity nor the internal righteousness that God requires.

It is held by some that to interpret this verse as teaching the innate imperfection of the Mosaic code contradicts Paul's affirmation of the Torah's characteristic holiness, righteousness, and goodness (Rom. 7:12). In a noble attempt to either protect God's character in establishing a flawed covenant or protect the flawed covenant itself, they argue that fault was to be found only in Israel's inadequate ability to keep Torah's requirements and not in the Torah itself.[3] They interpret Hebrews 8:7 in light of the following verse, 8:8, which does indeed underscore Israel's failure. Yet a correct understanding of 8:8 does not provide license to obfuscate the meaning of 8:7. In the first clause of 8:7's conditional ("if . . . then") construction, the adjective *amemptos*, "without blame," modifies *hē prōtē*, "the first." In context "the first" can only refer to the covenant itself and not to its participants, and there is no way to read the clause other than "if the first had been faultless." In short, Hebrews 8:7–8 reveals that there is fault to be found in both covenant and participants.

The New Testament provides a balanced perspective of both the positive and negative qualities of the Torah. Paul's affirmation of its characteristic holiness, righteousness, and goodness (Rom. 7:12) should not be viewed in isolation from his teaching in the very same passage that although the Torah itself per se is good, it nonetheless becomes the base of operations for sin to enslave humanity. It arouses and stimulates our inherent propensity for sin (Rom. 7:5–11). However, just as those who are married are released from their former obligation once widowed, by definition our possession of new life in Christ necessitates our having died to the Torah and been released from its grasp (Rom. 7:1–6).

Furthermore, in conjunction with Paul's identification of himself as a servant of the new covenant, the apostle referred to the Torah as the ministry of condemnation and death engraved in deadly letters on stones (2 Cor. 3:6–11). Indeed, through the Messiah's death, the Torah has been nailed to the cross (Col. 2:14–17). Paul recognized both the need for and the glory of God's new covenant.

The size of the author of Hebrews' massive block quotation of Jeremiah 31:31–34 is without parallel in the New Testament. In the ancient world, the length of scrolls was far from unlimited,[4] and literary "real estate" was always at a premium. The order of the day, particularly regarding the use of supporting quotations from other sources, was efficient brevity (note the limited use of Old Testament quotations in every other New Testament book). Furthermore, such was the first-century Jewish community's level of biblical literacy that the inclusion of a concise phrase or excerpt would suffice to bring to mind the entire Old Testament passage in question. Certainly the inclusion of this quote cannot be explained by audience unfamiliarity with the content of Jeremiah's prophecy. He was not an obscure prophet, and Jeremiah 31:31–34 was not an ambiguous passage. The inclusion of such a generous quotation can only be explained as the author's desire to focus the equivalent of a powerful spotlight on the prophecy, a spotlight so bright that under no circumstances could the passage go unnoticed by the readers.

In introducing his quotation of Jeremiah 31:31–34, the author provides a summary of the immediate context surrounding the prophecy's original announcement some six centuries prior, that of Israel's latest exhibition of disobedience to the Mosaic covenant. Although God had found fault with Israel (for their fault was hard to miss, Israel never having been a paragon of covenantal virtue), nonetheless, he announced His unfailing love and unflagging loyalty to His people. Characteristic of the author of Hebrews, his introduction ignores the human agency of Jeremiah and acknowledges only God's contribution.

The New Covenant. While Jeremiah 31:31–34 is inarguably the central and interpretively determinative oracle of the new covenant, other passages serve to augment the prophecy, including Isaiah 55:3; 61:8; Jeremiah 31:38–40; 32:38–44; 33:7–15; Ezekiel 16:60; 34:24–27; 36:26–38; and 37:26–28. The new covenant's provisions can be examined through synthesis of these collected prophetic passages.

The participating parties to the covenant are God and His chosen people ("the houses of Israel and Judah," Jer. 31:31; Heb. 8:8). God announced to Israel that in the imminent future (that would be six centuries viewed from God's perspective) He would sovereignly effect (*suntelesō*, "to fully accomplish," "to consummate") a new contractual agreement with them. What is meant by "the house of Israel and the house of Judah" is the entirety of the Jewish people, both in Israel and scattered abroad. In no way should this be construed as the church. Although a portion of the church is party to the covenant, that is, the remnant of Israel (Rom. 11:5) of which the Jewish Christian recipients of Hebrews are an example, Gentile believers are not. However, the whole church, Jews and Gentiles alike without distinction, enjoy the covenant's spiritual blessings through means of the Abrahamic covenant as discussed presently.

New Covenant Provisions. The covenant contains eleven provisions, seven of which are touched on in the central Jeremiah 31:31–34 passage and thus repeated in Hebrews 8:8–12, and four of which lay beyond the scope of Hebrews' argument. First, the new covenant is separate and distinct from the inferior Mosaic covenant it was designed to replace (Heb. 8:8–9; Jer. 31:32). The word translated "new" is *kainos*, which conveys the idea of something that is "qualitatively new," "fresh," "unused," "something not previously present," or "a new kind in contrast to an old or obsolete kind." Those who reason that "new" covenant should actually be translated "renewed" covenant, that is, the Mosaic covenant's renewal and not replacement, push beyond the boundaries of the word's usage. While there may be a measure of inherent ambiguity in the original Hebrew word, *chadash*, there is no such flexibility in the Greek. Furthermore, the context rules out the idea of a "renewal." The new covenant is emphatically *ou kata*, "not like," "not according to." In sum, it is discontinuous with the previous covenant made with the Exodus generation (Exod. 24:1–8). The liberating promise of Jeremiah is not that of a "renewed" covenant, but a replaced covenant. Given the choice between a refurbished product and a brand-new one, most people would opt for the new.

The second provision is that this covenant will be characterized by the internalization of God's laws (Heb. 8:10; Jer. 31:33). It is essential to note a key point bearing on translation and interpretation. The standard Masoretic Hebrew text of Jeremiah's prophecy records that God will write on Israel's hearts His Law (singular form), which is often taken to mean God's "Torah." However, we do not find in the corresponding section of the Septuagint's second-century BC Greek translation of Jeremiah a parallel reading of *nomos*, "law" (singular form), but instead, *nomous*, "laws" (plural form).

While this discrepancy cannot be cleverly resolved, it can be explained by one of two possibilities. The first option is that the Jewish translators of the Septuagint intentionally translated Jer. 31:33 with a plural *nomous* to remove the possibility of misunderstanding it in reference to the Torah, intending that it instead be understood as a nonspecific set of God's laws that may or may not overlap with those of the Mosaic legislation. We find an example of this kind of usage in Genesis 26:5, in reference to Abraham's obedience to God's (obviously pre–Mosaic covenant) laws.

The second possibility is that the discrepancy resulted from the translators of the Septuagint working from a divergent text. The second-century BC Septuagint's version of Jeremiah is quite divergent from our tenth-century AD Masoretic Hebrew version in both length and arrangement. A textual variant as minor as a contrary singular/plural noun is relatively small potatoes compared to other issues. However, considering that the Spirit-inspired text of Hebrews quotes at no small length from the Septuagint version of Jeremiah, it seems reasonable to conclude that the plural *nomous* is no accident of translation, but rather the accurately safeguarded and transmitted Word of God.

Further confirmation that a nonspecific set of God's laws and not Torah is intended comes from Hebrews itself. In the Greek text, when an author or translator wants the readers to understand that the Torah, in a technical sense, is meant, the singular form of *nomos* is employed. This is particularly true of both the book of Hebrews and the Septuagint's translation of Jeremiah. In 8:10 the author of Hebrews transferred this quotation verbatim, including the plural *nomous*. Yet, with the exception of this quotation and its repetition in

10:16, the author of Hebrews always (twelve times out of twelve) uses the singular form of *nomos* when he means "the Torah" (7:5, 11, 12, 16, 19, 28; 8:4, 9:19, 22; 10:1, 8, 28).

Moreover, few of our author's Septuagint quotations survived the transfer into his epistle grammatically intact; he habitually adjusts and nudges the quotation's grammar, even substituting or adding a word to rhetorically strengthen his argument. Whether he does so purposefully or because he is quoting from memory is impossible to determine. Nonetheless, it seems clear that if the author had meant to convey through this quotation that God would put the Torah itself, either the unrevised or revised edition, into our hearts, he would have clarified the grammar as he so often does throughout the text of the letter and has done elsewhere in this very quotation of Jeremiah 31:31–34.[5] It is, therefore, altogether reasonable to conclude that the author, writing under the inspiration of the Holy Spirit, intended that "laws" be understood nonspecifically, as in the case of Abraham's obedience (Gen. 26:5). Indeed, God did not invent the concept of law at Sinai.

The third provision of the new covenant is the promise of spiritual regeneration (Heb. 8:11–12; Jer. 31:33–34; Ezek. 36:25–27). From the greatest citizen to the least, intimate knowledge of the Lord will abound. The need to consult legal experts and teachers concerning God's moral requirements will vanish, replaced by the personal, internal awareness of that which God requires and desires as written by Him on our hearts and minds. Ezekiel reveals that God will exchange our hard hearts of stone for those of flesh.

The fourth provision is that the Holy Spirit will indwell all participants (Heb. 8:10; Jer. 31:33; Ezek. 36:26–27). According to Ezekiel, God will place His Spirit in us. It is through the means of the Holy Spirit that hearts and minds will be filled with the knowledge of the Lord.

The new covenant's fifth provision is the promise of Israel's sins being forgiven (Heb. 8:12; Jer. 31:34; 33:8). God promises the compassionate extension of His mercy concerning His people's sins and iniquities.

The sixth provision is that the new covenant's blessings extend to every participating Jewish person (Heb. 8:11; Jer. 31:34). Although the blessings of the new covenant extend to Gentile followers of the Messiah, the covenant was specifically made between God and Israel and therefore has particular significance and application to Jewish believers such as the recipient community of Hebrews. Even so, it is critical to bear in mind that these new covenant blessings do not extend universally to every Jew simply by virtue of them being Jewish. These blessings are restricted to that portion of Israel who choose to participate, that is, the believing remnant of Israel. In their passion to extend love and blessing to the Jewish people, some Christians neglect to share the gospel with them. We must all be ever mindful that there is only one available means to experience the provisions of the new covenant, that is, faith in Jesus as the Messiah.

The seventh provision is that the Old Testament's promise of ideal covenantal relationship ("I will be their God and they shall be My people") will be fully realized (Heb. 8:10; Exod. 6:7; Lev. 26:12; Jer. 31:33; 32:38; Ezek. 37:27). This loving relationship between God and His people will be characterized by intimate access and covenant fidelity.

The final four provisions of the new covenant do not derive from Jeremiah 31:31–34 but from other prophetic passages beyond the scope of Hebrews and mostly relate to the future messianic kingdom. They will be briefly listed as follows. The eighth provision is that Jerusalem will be gloriously rebuilt and Israel made prosperous and secure in their land (Jer. 31:38–40; 32:41–44; 33:7–13; Ezek. 34:25–27; 36:33–38). The ninth provision is that the covenant is both everlasting and irrevocable (Isa. 55:3; 61:8; Jer. 32:40; Ezek. 16:60). The tenth provision is that the covenant promises that the messianic King will one day rule over Israel and the whole earth (Jer. 33:14–15; Ezek 34:24–25). The new covenant's eleventh and final provision is the covenant promise that God will dwell again in His sanctuary in the midst of Israel (Ezek. 37:26–28).

The New Covenant between God and Israel

Passages	Provisions
Jer. 31:32	The new covenant is separate and distinct from the Mosaic covenant, which it was designed to replace
Jer. 31:33	God's new laws will be internalized.
Jer. 31:33–34; Ezek. 36:25–27	There is a promise of Israel's spiritual regeneration.
Jer. 31:33; Ezek. 36:26–27	The Holy Spirit will indwell all.
Jer. 31:34; 33:8	There is a promise of Israel's sins being forgiven.
Jer. 31:34	The covenant blessings extend to every participating Jew.
Jer. 31:33; 32:38; Ezek. 37:28	The ideal covenantal relationship will be fully realized.
Jer. 31:38–40; 32:41–44; 33:7–13; Ezek. 34:25–27; 36:33–38	Jerusalem will be gloriously rebuilt and Israel will be prosperous and secure in their land

Passages	Provisions
Isa. 55:3; 61:8; Jer. 32:40; Ezek. 16:60	Everlasting and irrevocable
Jer. 33:14–15; Ezek 34:24–25	The messianic King will rule over Israel and the whole earth
Ezek. 37:26–28	God will dwell in His sanctuary in the midst of Israel

Passages	Importance
Gen 12:1–3, 7; 13:14–17; 15:1–21; 17:1–21; 22:16–18; Eph. 2:11–16; 3:5–6	These references amplify and explain how both Jews and Gentiles participate in the application of the Abrahamic covenant's blessing component

Passages	NT Confirmation
Matt. 26:28; Mark 14:24; Luke 22:20; 1 Cor. 11:25; Heb. 10:29; 13:20	Jesus' shed blood is the means of ratifying the new covenant.
Rom 11:26–27	The new covenant is the guarantee of Israel's salvation.
2 Cor. 3:6–7; Heb. 8:6–13	There is need for the new covenant and the new law.
Heb. 7:22; 8:6; 9:15; 12:24	Jesus is the guarantee and mediator of the superior covenant.
Heb. 10:16–18	There is forgiveness through the new covenant.

New Covenant Significance. The foundation of the new covenant is found in the components of land, seed, relationship, and especially blessing contained in God's covenant with Abraham. The significance of the new covenant is that it provides both amplification and explanation as to how both Jews and Gentiles participate in the application of the Abrahamic covenant's blessing component (Gen. 12:1–3, 7; 13:14–17; 15:1–21; 17:1–21; 22:16–18; Eph. 2:11–16; 3:5–6).

While the new covenant abrogated the Mosaic covenant the moment it was inaugurated by means of Jesus' death, it had no similar effect on any of God's other covenants. If anything, rather than annulling the Abrahamic covenant, the new covenant upheld and more firmly established God's foundational covenant with Abraham. Every promise God had made to Abraham and later affirmed with Isaac and again with Jacob still securely held. After all, these covenant promises were conditioned on God's own solemn oath (Heb, 6:16–17; 7:20–21, 28). As the Abrahamic covenant had preceded the giving of Torah by over four centuries, the Torah's practical obsolescence as a way of life with the coming of the new covenant did nothing to invalidate God's promises to the Jewish nation through His covenant with Abraham.

New Covenant Confirmation. The new covenant is confirmed in the New Testament through five means. First, Jesus' shed blood on the cross is the means of new covenant inauguration and ratification (Heb. 10:29; 13:20; Matt. 26:28; Mark 14:24; Luke 22:20; 1 Cor. 11:25). During His Last Supper, which was a Passover seder, Jesus identified the traditional third cup, the "cup of redemption," as symbolizing the new covenant in His own blood, which was poured out on behalf of many for the forgiveness of their sins.

Second, as has been previously discussed, the New Testament affirms the need for a new covenant and a new set of laws (Heb. 8:6–13; 2 Cor. 3:6–7). Third, as has also been touched on, Jesus is the guarantee and mediator of the superior covenant (Heb. 7:22; 8:6; 9:15; 12:24). Fourth, God's forgiveness is only available through the means of the new covenant (Heb. 10:16–18). This area will be commented on shortly, in context. Finally, the new covenant is the guarantee of Israel's salvation at the conclusion of the time of Jacob's trouble and inauguration of the messianic age (Rom. 11:26–27).

The Obsolescence of the Old Covenant (8:13)

The author wraps up his discussion of the new covenant with a final, conclusive thought. The moment God announced the coming establishment of a "new" covenant, He was simultaneously broadcasting that the covenant made at Sinai was *palaioō*, "obsolete," "antiquated," "useless through being worn out." The Mosaic covenant had automatically become the *old* covenant. Paul likewise employs the phrase "old covenant" (2 Cor. 3:14). Universally, in any field, area of life, body of personnel, or collection of equipment, once the announcement has been made that "the new" is on its way, it is obvious to all that "the old" now possesses only temporary status. At the arrival of "the new," "the old" must necessarily give way.

The verb *palaioō* is employed twice in this verse, first conjugated as a perfect active indicative, "He has made old," and again as a present passive participle, "being made old," both forms leading to the inevitable conclusion that God Himself was the responsible agent of the Mosaic covenant's obsolescence. In short, God exercised His divine prerogative to pull the plug on His own covenant, but only after having established its superior replacement.

It is important to recognize that if time were the fundamental issue, and if what God meant to imply was that the Mosaic covenant was only "old in point of lapsed time," then His word choice would have been *archaios*, from which we derive the English *archaic*, as previously discussed in commenting on Hebrews 1:11. That is a perfectly appropriate word to distinguish between that which is older or younger, as in "I still drive our old car, but my wife gets to drive the new model."

From the moment Jeremiah proclaimed, "Behold, days are coming," every Israelite should have anticipated that the Mosaic covenant's days were numbered. It became antiquated in Jeremiah's day, and it was "ready to disappear" when Hebrews was written almost two millennia ago. The Mosaic covenant has been in a state of abrogation for five centuries longer than it was in a state of activation.

Conclusion

No matter the contextual or grammatical evidence, many believers, particularly in the messianic community, hold fast tenaciously to their misunderstanding that the new covenant inscribes onto our inner being a copy of the "the one and only Torah,"[6] albeit an abridged version that excludes the priestly legislation and that is interpreted through our Jesus-centric perspective. This position views the Torah as eternal in an absolute sense and rejects that God would ever contemplate a replacement.

To hold a conflicting position means opening oneself up to accusations of malevolent, even "invidious,"[7] motivations or, in the case of a messianic believer, disloyalty to one's Jewish heritage for abandoning Torah, as if adherence to the Torah was ever the premium hallmark of Jewish identity. According to Stephen's presentation in Acts, Jewish identity might more accurately be indicated not through adherence to Torah but by rebellion against God (Acts 7:51–53). That is precisely the reason that the Mosaic legislation, as a package, was found by God to be deficient and in need of replacement with the superior new covenant. In reality, for Jewish believers in Jesus, it is their participation in this better covenant along with that of the Abrahamic covenant that defines genuine Jewish identity according to the New Testament (Rom. 9:6–8).

Indeed, the idea of the Torah's replacement reverberates throughout the ancient rabbinic texts. There has always been a stream in Jewish tradition that anticipated the Torah's replacement with the coming of the Messiah. One rabbi taught that God would seat the Messiah not on a throne at God's right hand, as per Hebrews (1:3, 13), but in a heavenly Yeshiva where his students would call him, "the Lord." He is quoted, "and the Messiah will sit in the

Yeshiva, and all those who walk on earth will come and sit before him to hear a new Torah and new commandments."[8] Another rabbi imagined that on the Messiah's arrival, he would "gather the exiles of Israel and give them thirty new commandments."[9]

Other rabbis speculated that "only the totality of all the letters contained in the Torah has been fixed for all eternity, and that the same complement of hundreds of thousands of letters can be and will be rearranged into different words expressing different instructions. This is what will happen in the Messianic days."[10]

In contrast, the renowned thirteenth-century rabbi Maimonides attempted to put the breaks on Jewish speculation (as well as respond to the evangelistic efforts of Hebrews-reading Christians) through the ninth of his famous *Thirteen Principles of Faith*, "I believe with a complete faith that this Torah will not be exchanged and there will be no other Torah from the creator."[11]

Ultimately, the conclusive issue is not about whether being under the new covenant means that particular sections of Mosaic legislation are to be abridged, excised, or revised. That discussion is aimed squarely at the trees and not the forest. The point of Hebrews 8 does not involve specific areas of Mosaic legislation or even the Torah itself. The issue is not one of law but of the covenant from which they are derived. Hebrews 8 argues that the whole Mosaic covenant, as an entire contractual, constitutional system of relationship between God and His people, has been replaced. While there may be some areas of overlap between old and new constitutional systems, only one contract is capable of yielding dividends.

It is difficult to comprehend why some believers, Jewish and Gentile alike, who so obviously love the Messiah and recognize their participation in the new covenant, continue to cling to the Mosaic covenant. To propose that continued participation in following any portion of the Torah's legislative system is mandatory, obligatory, or otherwise compulsory for believers is a tacit offense to the sufficiency of our High Priest's ministry and His new covenant provisions as outlined in the text of Hebrews.

Jesus' priesthood was not designed to be inserted into the Mosaic covenant's preexisting mold; it broke the mold. The Mosaic covenant is not modular in construction. Believers cannot swap out one priesthood for another, like upgrading the components of an obsolete computer. The new covenant is not an upgrade but a comprehensive replacement. The reason that new wine cannot be poured into old wineskins is that the old wineskins are compositionally inadequate for the task.

What, then, is the role of the Mosaic legislation in the life of a new covenant believer who, through the death of the Messiah, has himself been released from all obligation to Torah (Rom. 7:1–6)? Shall he slice out the contributions of Moses from His copy of Scripture? May it never be! Rather, Paul's words should be decisively instructive regarding practical, daily application of Scripture (including Moses) to our lives: "All Scripture is inspired by God and profitable for teaching, for reproof, for correction, for training in righteousness; that the man of God may be adequate, equipped for every good work" (2 Tim. 3:16–17).

The Torah, along with the entirety of the Old Testament, can and should play a central role in all new covenant believers' spiritual lives. We possess the liberty to obey any of Torah's precepts that do not patently contradict New Testament instruction (Col. 2:14–17). However, while we are free to venerate the instructions of Torah as God's Word, it is the New Testament that God has provided to be our spiritual lodestone as we, the bondservants of Messiah (Rom. 6:16–22), now submit ourselves to His law (1 Cor. 9:21; Gal. 6:2).

Study Questions

1. Is there any significance to the length of Hebrews' quotation of Jeremiah 31:31–34?

2. Who are the parties to the new covenant? To what extent can the church participate, and to what extent may they do so?

3. Explain whether this covenant should be thought of as "new" or "renewed."

4. Of the eleven provisions of the new covenant, which are most significant? List the top four and defend your choices.

5. What is the relationship between the Abrahamic, Mosaic, and new covenants?

6. Describe the present status of the Mosaic covenant.

CHAPTER 10

Superiority of the Messiah's Priestly Service
Hebrews 9:1-10

Preview:
This next section is demarcated with another inclusio, setting this unit apart through his use of the phrases dikaiomata latreias, "regulations for worship" (9:1) and dikaiomata sarkos, "regulations for the body" (9:10). In this unit, both the wilderness tabernacle and the requirements of its priestly ministry are discussed, although neither at length. A detailed treatment of Israel's worship practices as instituted by Moses would not serve to advance his argument; therefore he swiftly transitions to the point he wishes to accentuate, which is the superiority of the Messiah's priestly service. The author shows little concern to bring contemporary temple service into his treatment, opting instead to focus on Israel's divinely disclosed "template" for worship, the tabernacle. He capitalizes and builds on his previously introduced line of reasoning regarding God's supernatural revelation to Moses of a tabernacle replica prior to construction (Exod. 25:40) and the typological connections he had drawn between Levitical worship and Christ's priesthood (8:2-5). This section is the latest entry in the writer's expanding collection of contrasts between elements of the respective old and new covenants.

Components of the Levitical Sanctuary (9:1-5)

The author begins with a straightforward introduction to the subject at hand, which is the worship regulations set forth under the Mosaic covenant. These, of course, were centered on the tabernacle, here referred to as "the earthly sanctuary," a pointed contrast to 8:2's sanctuary, "which the Lord pitched, not man."

139

Use of Old Testament Passages in Hebrews 9

Hebrews	Old Testament	Subject
9:2	Exod. 25:23–26:30	The tabernacle and its components
9:3	Lev. 16:3	The Holy of Holies
9:4	Exod. 16:33	The jar of manna
9:4	Exod. 30:1–6	The altar of incense
9:4	Num. 17:8–10	The rod of Aaron
9:4	Deut. 10:3–5	The two stone tablets
9:4–5	Exod. 25:10–22	The ark of the covenant
9:6	Num. 18:2–6	The service of the Levitical priesthood
9:7	Lev. 16:2	The High Priest's role on the Day of Atonement
9:10	Lev. 11:2	The Mosaic Law concerning food
9:10	Lev. 11:25	The Mosaic Law concerning uncleanness
9:10	Lev. 15:18	The Mosaic Law concerning uncleanness
9:10	Num. 19:13	The Mosaic Law concerning uncleanness
9:13	Lev. 16:6–7	The Day of Atonement
9:13	Num. 19:9	The ashes of the red heifer
9:19–20	Exod. 24:3–8	The ratification of the Mosaic covenant
9:21	Lev. 8:15	The consecration of the Levitical priesthood
9:22	Lev. 17:11	The necessity of blood for atonement
9:28	Isa. 53:12	Isaiah's suffering servant

The Tabernacle. The tabernacle was the central location of Israel's worship, a sanctuary in which God's Shekinah glory could take up permanent residence among the nation. As the writer had previously highlighted, the tabernacle was designed as a representation of the true tabernacle in heaven as divinely revealed to Moses (Heb. 8:5; Exod. 25:40). It was here that the Israelites would gather for worship, generation after generation, for over four centuries, until it was replaced by the temple.

There are five names given to the tabernacle in Scripture, each name reflecting a specific purpose or function. It is referred to as "the tabernacle" (Exod. 25:9), which underscores its main purpose as the place where God dwells among His people; "the sanctuary" (Exod. 25:8), which accentuates its holy character; "the tent" (Exod. 26:36), which accentuates its temporary character; "the tent of meeting" (Exod. 27:21), which emphasizes its function; along with "the tabernacle of the testimony" (Exod. 38:21) and "the tent of the testimony" (Num. 9:15), which both serve to highlight its housing of the ark of the covenant, which contained the two tablets of the Law.

Including the spacious, surrounding outer courtyard, the tabernacle's total dimensions were 150 feet long on the southern and northern perimeters by 75 feet wide on the western and eastern perimeters. The total enclosed area of the rectangular tabernacle complex was roughly 11,250 square feet. The Egyptians used similarly designed portable structures in this period for both sacred and secular use, and their royal tents were likewise subdivided into two rooms, with the outer chamber twice the length of the inner.

The structure of the tabernacle was that of a reinforced, flat-roofed, rectangular tent with dimensions forty-five feet in length by fifteen feet in width by fifteen feet in height. Always oriented facing eastward, the structure was divided into two sections, the larger called *Hagia*, the "Holy Place," and the second, smaller subdivision *Hagia Hagion*, the "Holy of Holies." The Holy Place was the tabernacle's initial room and served as the locus of service for the priests' daily sanctuary ministry. Behind the Holy Place was the second subdivision, the Holy of Holies, entered only by the high priest on the Day of Atonement. This inner sanctum was cube-shaped, measuring fifteen feet on each side and (as with the entire structure) fifteen feet in height.

These subdivisions were separated by a veil constructed of linen interwoven with cloth that was vibrantly dyed in blue, purple, and scarlet and decorated with embroidered, artistic renderings of cherubim. It was hung from gold-covered hooks on gold-covered acacia wood posts set in silver sockets (Exod. 26:31–35). Hebrews calls this the "second veil," in contrast to the veil at the entrance that separated the inner courtyard from the sanctuary (9:3).

The author provides his readers with a survey of the tabernacle furniture, beginning with two of the three pieces in the Holy Place.

Menorah. This was the seven-branched candlestick (Heb., *menorah*), referred to here as *luchnia*, "the lampstand." It was constructed from one massive, solid piece of pure gold. Estimates of its weight range from approximately 75 to 125 pounds.[1] It was positioned in the Holy Place's south side opposite the table of showbread and diagonally across from the table of incense.

The ornate components of the menorah were patterned after the almond tree, the first of the Promised Land's trees to blossom in spring. On either side of the main shaft were six branches, together making seven branches. At the top of each of the seven ornate branches was a little pinch-ended bowl that held olive oil and a wick. The purpose of the menorah was to provide a perpetual light source in the windowless tabernacle (Exod. 25:31–40).

The menorah was never to be completely extinguished and was, therefore, tended morning and evening by the priests (Lev. 24:3–4). Its undying flame symbolized the presence of God among His people. Twice a day, evening and morning, the priests were to clean the menorah's seven lamps, trimming the wicks and replenishing the olive oil (Exod. 27:20–21).

Table of Showbread. This table, constructed of acacia wood and overlaid with gold, was designed to hold the twelve loaves of "show bread," or "bread of the presence," which were twelve loaves of unleavened bread arranged in two rows on perpetual display before the Lord. These loaves were eventually eaten by the ministering priests who replaced the bread weekly on the Sabbath (Lev. 24:5–9). The table's dimensions were three feet long by eighteen inches wide by two feet three inches high.[2] An ornamental edging of gold ran around the four-footed table, and attached to the table's corners were four gold-covered rings, into which two gold-covered acacia wood poles would be inserted on either side to transport it (Exod. 25:23–30). It was positioned in the Holy Place's north side opposite the menorah and diagonally across from the table of incense.

Altar of Incense. Although the author transitions in 9:3 to the Holy of Holies, the altar of incense was actually in the Holy Place, directly in front of the veil leading to the inner sanctum of the Holy of Holies. Nonetheless, it functionally related to the ministry in the interior room, and that is likely what the author has in mind here. Incense was burned on it every morning and evening in conjunction with the maintenance of the menorah. Each year on the Day of Atonement, the high priest was to apply the blood of the sin offering on the horns of the table (Lev. 16:18–19). The altar was made of gold-covered acacia wood. The top was eighteen inches square, and it was three feet tall. It had horns and an ornamental edging of gold. Attached to the table's corners were four gold-covered rings, into which two gold-covered acacia wood poles would be inserted on either side to transport it (Exod. 30:1–10), just as with the table of showbread.

Ark of the Covenant. This was the sole furnishing in the Holy of Holies and was the most important of the tabernacle elements because it served as God's throne (1 Sam 4:4; 2 Sam. 6:2). The ark was an open-topped chest constructed of acacia wood and overlaid inside and out with gold. It was rectangular, with dimensions of three feet nine inches in length and two feet three inches in both width and height.[3] An ornamental molding of gold ran along the top of the chest. Attached to the chest's corners were four gold-covered rings, into which two gold-covered acacia wood poles would be left inserted on either side in order to transport it without actually having to make physical contact with the chest itself (Exod. 25:10–18; 26:33).

The chest contained the two stone tablets of the Ten Commandments (Exod. 25:16–21; 40:20). The ark also contained a golden jar of manna (Exod. 16:33; Heb. 9:4–5) and Aaron's rod (Num. 17:10). It was common practice in the ancient world to house important documents, such as covenants, law codes, treaties, and the like in specially constructed containers. A chest of similar dimensions, on which the same sort of carrying rings were attached, was one of the treasures discovered in the tomb of Tutankhamen.

The ark had a lid fashioned of solid gold. This was the mercy seat, the atonement cover, the throne of God's grace (Heb 4:16), the place over which the Shekinah glory would dwell and meet with the high priest once a year on the Day of Atonement as he sprinkled blood on the lid for Israel's propitiation (Lev. 16:14). On either end of the lid, either attached or constructed as one solid piece with the golden cover, were two cherubim of gold. These celestial beings faced each other with their wings spread toward one another and overshadowing the lid (Exod. 25:18–22). God would thereafter be poetically pictured as the One enthroned between the cherubim (1 Sam. 4:4; Ps. 80:1–3).

The ark of the covenant went missing after the destruction of the temple in 586 BC. When the temple was rebuilt, the Holy of Holies remained empty. The absence of the ark, of course, has spawned immeasurable speculation, several dozen books, and a smashingly terrific film. Often going unnoticed amid all the imaginative theorizing and intrepid investigating is Jeremiah 3:16, which states, "It shall be in those days when you are multiplied and increased in the land . . . they shall no more say, 'The ark of the covenant of the LORD.' And it shall not come to mind, nor shall they remember it, nor shall they miss it, nor shall it be made again."

Having simply itemized the tabernacle furniture, the author neglects to fill in any details, much less draw out elaborate typological significance between the Messiah and every Christological detail of the tabernacle's elements, both small and great. He was not writing his version of *Christ in the Tabernacle*, but rather was providing a "big picture" overview of how the tabernacle was designed and how it functioned in order to arrive at his point, the superiority of the Messiah's priestly ministry over the Levitical.

Components of Levitical Service (9:6–7)

Having surveyed the components of the Levitical sanctuary, the author proceeds to summarize the components of Levitical service. Prior to penetrating beyond the veil and into the activities in the inner sanctum, he first focuses on the activities of the outer room. In 9:6 he stresses the daily grind of the never-ending, continual activity required of the priests to properly maintain the sanctuary. The menorah's perpetual flame needed tending, and incense needed to be offered twice daily, each morning and evening. In addition, the showbread required replacement every week. The faces of the individual priests would change with each cycle of service, but the requirements of the priesthood were monotonously incessant.

Day of Atonement. Day of Atonement imagery flows freely through Hebrews, both prior to this point in the text and afterward. For the sake of fostering better appreciation of this topic's importance, comprehensive treatment will be provided here in one, uninterrupted segment. This is the most sacred day on Israel's liturgical calendar. Its purpose was to make atonement for the holy sanctuary, the tabernacle, the congregation, the altar, the priests, and the people of Israel. It was to be a time for a national confession for sins not confessed and forgiven throughout the year, a reminder that the normal, everyday sacrifices were insufficient to atone for sin (Lev. 16:29–34).

The Day of Atonement (Heb., *Yom Kippurim*), commonly called Yom Kippur, is more accurately rendered "The Day of Coverings." The term *kippurim* conveys a slightly different nuance than what is normally understood as the meaning of the theological term *atonement*. *Kippurim* does not denote the removal of sins as much as the covering over of them. As the author of Hebrews so keenly stresses in 9:9–10, the cleansing provided through the Levitical system was exclusively external. Yom Kippurim refers to the great "holy carpet" under which God swept Israel's sins during His annual fall cleaning.

The covering for the sin of God's people was blood, the symbol of life, for "it is the blood . . . that makes atonement" (Lev. 17:11; Heb. 9:22). A basic yet vital concept of Scripture is that without blood there can be no atonement. The shedding of blood is the only means of covering or atonement the Bible recognizes. The word *blood* (*haima*) appears for the first time in Hebrews 9:7. Throughout the remainder of Hebrews from this point forward, the need for blood as the means of approach to God is underscored time and again (9:12, 13, 14, 18, 20, 21, 22; 10:4, 19, 29; 11:28; 12:24; 13:11, 12, 20).

Israel's propensity toward sin created estrangement between them and the Lord. God, in His grace, gave Israel the sacrificial system in order to restore their relationship, to cover over their sin on an annual basis. Each year the

Israelites got a clean slate, a fresh start before God, a literal recovery. Of course, Israel's annual atonement lasted only as long as individuals remained free from committing sinful acts. Following all the Day of Atonement's elaborate and meticulous rituals, the daily and weekly Levitical sacrifices immediately recommenced on the following morning.

As to congregational responsibilities (Lev. 23:26–32), on this day absolutely no labor of any kind is to be performed. In fact, the performance of any work is an infraction of capital consequence. This day is to function like a sabbath of sabbaths (Heb., *shabbat shabbaton*), a super-Sabbath. The Israelites were to "afflict" their "souls," traditionally understood as indicating the practice of self-denial, primarily reflected in a fast, a complete avoidance of food and water for a twenty-five-hour period (an additional hour is added to the day at the front end, as per Lev. 23:32).

Leviticus 16, the central chapter of not only Leviticus but the very center point of Torah, is devoted to enumerating the high priest's rituals and practices for the day. The chapter commences with the clear affirmation that only one man could approach God, Israel's high priest, who served as the central figure on that day's stage. Furthermore, while the high priest was the only individual authorized to approach the divine presence, he was not free to do so anytime or in any way he desired. He could only enter God's presence on the day and in the manner that God had approved. Any deviation would mean certain death (16:1–2). This is a solemn reminder to our contemporary society, which is continually bombarded with the popular myth that there are many ways to God and that individuals are free to choose their own paths. The Day of Atonement reminds us that God alone determines the means of our access to Him.

The high priest acted as the representative of the people of Israel. This portentous responsibility of a nation's atonement before their God rested squarely on His priestly shoulders. Israel's most sacred figure was to enter into the nation's most sacred place to perform its most sacred rituals on its most sacred day.

During the New Testament era, the high priests played more of a political role than a religious one. Therefore, the high priest would be sequestered in the temple courts a full week prior to the big day in order to study and rehearse. The Sanhedrin and the priests trained and drilled him incessantly throughout the week on the minutia of the Atonement rituals. One wrong move would be disastrous for an entire nation! The high priest was forced to stay awake all through the night before the Holy Day, reading and discussing Scripture with his assistants. If they noticed him nodding off, the assistants snapped their fingers and made him stand up on the cold stone floor with his bare feet to rouse him. An understudy priest was also appointed at this time to wait in the wings in case of emergency.[4]

After performing the standard morning sacrifice in the beautiful, golden robes of the high priest, he laid them aside and, after the first of what will be several ritual washings throughout the day, exchanged them for a simple white linen garment similar to that of an ordinary priest.

The high priest would sacrifice a male bull for himself, his family, and his fellow priests. Prior to making atonement for the people, he first had to take care of his own sin. Placing two hands on the bull's head, he made confession for himself and his family (Lev. 16:3–6). Following the bull's sacrifice, the blood would be collected in a bowl and carried by an assistant priest into the sanctuary, being stirred all the while so that it did not coagulate. Concurrently, the high priest would carry into the sanctuary an incense censer filled with burning coals from the altar of sacrifice and solemnly approach the veil separating the Holy Place from the Holy of Holies. Behind the thick veil separating the Holy Place from the interior of the Holy of Holies, the small, windowless room was pitch black, illuminated only by the glow of the still-burning coals held in the priest's fire pan.

Laying the fire pan on the floor, the high priest would place a measure of incense on the hot coals, immediately creating a vast amount of fragrant smoke that filled the room. Exiting the Holy of Holies, he would emerge from behind the veil to take the bowl of blood that his assistant had been stirring. Reentering the Holy of Holies, the high priest sprinkled blood on the mercy seat (or, during Second Temple days, where the mercy seat had once been) as well as on the ground in front of the ark of the covenant (Lev. 16:11–14).

A special lottery was created involving two identical goats brought before the high priest. The priest would put his hands into a box where there were two lots, small tablets on which were written the Hebrew words *l'YHWH* ("to the Lord"), and *l'azazel* ("to *azazel*," or "removal"). The high priest would pull the lots out and determine the fate of the goats. The lot on the right was assigned to the goat on the right, the one on the left to the goat on the left. The one designated as to the Lord was destined for sacrifice. The one designated to *azazel*, commonly referred to as the "scapegoat," would be driven out into the wilderness (Lev. 16:7–10).

The high priest would sacrifice the male goat on behalf of the nation. Reentering the Holy of Holies a third time, he would sprinkle the blood of the goat in the Holy of Holies. This was followed by retaking the bowl containing the bull's blood and sprinkling the veil outside the Holy of Holies. He would then purify the altar of sacrifice by mixing together the blood of the sacrificed bull and goat. These rituals served to "reboot" the altar, the tabernacle or temple, and the congregation of Israel for a fresh year (Lev. 16:15–19).

The high priest would then turn his attention to the second goat. By placing his two hands on the head of the goat and making public confession on behalf of all Israel, the high priest transferred the sins, transgressions, and iniquities of the nation onto the scapegoat. The goat now served as a substitute for the Jewish people. The scapegoat was escorted by another priest outside of the camp and far into the wilderness, where it was to be set free (Lev. 16:20–22). In the New Testament era, however, the scapegoat was escorted outside of Jerusalem and into the Judean desert. An innovation had been added to assuage the nation's nagging fear that the scapegoat, having had Israel's sins transferred on it, might, like a stray dog finding its way back home again, somehow find his way back into the midst of Israel. The goat was led to a high cliff top and was given a healthy, two-handed shove off the edge to remove all doubt of his possible return.

Hebrews portrays Jesus as the fulfillment of the Day of Atonement throughout its argument. In chapters 2, 7, 9, and 10, two facets of this connection are explored. The initial fulfillment of the Day of Atonement is through Jesus serving as God's perfect High Priest (Heb. 2:17). In Israel's history, high priests came and went as they died or were replaced. As a resurrected High Priest, Jesus will minister permanently. There is not one moment of any day when Christ is not serving as High Priest. Therefore our salvation is secured eternally (Heb. 7:23).

There was no need for Jesus to first make a sacrifice for Himself before He could minister on our behalf, because He Himself was the perfect, sinless sacrifice. Furthermore, unlike the priestly sacrifice of animals, His sacrifice did not need to be continually offered on a daily, weekly, or annual basis, but was a perfect offering for the total and complete eradication of sin, sacrificed once for all (Heb. 7:26; 9:25–26).

In addition, Jesus does not serve as High Priest in "a holy place made with hands, a mere copy of the true one." Jesus' high priesthood functions in the Holy Place in heaven itself. The Holy of Holies in which he enters is the heavenly presence of God. The atoning blood that this high priest bears is not the inferior blood of animals but His own blood, the blood of the Messiah (Heb. 9:11, 24).

Just as the high priest exchanged his normative, glorious garments for humble robes, so, too, did Jesus exchange His glory for humble human flesh (Phil. 2:5–8). Furthermore, no weeklong, all-night study sessions were necessary for this High Priest, nor was an understudy waiting in the wings. He had no need to memorize the Word of God. He is the incarnate Word of God.

The second facet of Jesus' typological fulfillment of the Day of Atonement is as God's perfect sacrifice. Not only was Jesus the perfect High Priest, but He offered up blood superior to that possessed by "bulls and goats." Animal blood could only cover up sin but never completely remove it. The Messiah's sacrifice, by contrast, thoroughly sanctifies us in the sight of God. This perfect sacrifice, indeed makes us holy. No one could possibly pretend that his sins were definitively dealt with on the Day of Atonement. The Levitical high priest only cleansed the external, the flesh. The fact that the Day of Atonement sacrifices were annually repeatable proved that they were insufficient. If they had truly cleansed sin, they would not need repetition. The rituals contained a very abbreviated expiration date. However, Jesus, offering this perfect sacrifice, cleansed the heart as well (Heb. 10:1–10).

Finally, the author of Hebrews also sees a typological connection between Jesus and the scapegoat. Just as it was necessary for the scapegoat, bearing the sin of the nation, to be executed outside of the camp, so, too, Jesus, bearing Israel's (and the world's) sin, was executed outside the walls of Jerusalem (Heb. 13:10–16). In a stunning foreshadowing of the circumstances surrounding Jesus' sacrifice, the Mishnah records the Jewish population's abusive hitting and plucking out of the scapegoat's hair as the doomed animal departed the city.[5]

The Inferiority of Levitical Worship (9:8–10)

Quite interestingly, in 9:8 the author explains to his readers his awareness that his insight into the typological relationship between Jesus and the Levitical worship was not of himself but was through the inspiration of the Holy Spirit. He had not drawn these connections on his own; God Himself had revealed the truths he now shared. The substance of this supernatural insight was that as long as the Levitical system of worship remained in place, the high priest was the only person who would ever enjoy access into the personal presence of God. The common people could only get as close as the courtyard. The priests could only get as close as the veil. Access was restricted to all but one man for the duration of but one day each year. Open access to God's presence for all people could only be achieved by the abolition of the Levitical system of worship.

Calling the tabernacle a *parabole*, an "illustration" or "symbol" (a term from whence we derive both our word *parable* and the mathematical concept) for our present age, he reasons that offerings made through the Levitical system could never make the worshiper perfect (*teleioō*, "to complete," see Use of "Perfect" in Hebrews on p. 247) in conscience (9:9). The Levitical system's many rituals only cleansed the external component of humans from sin's defilement. It possessed no power to affect their internal nature.

He argues that God never intended for the system to be in place permanently. The inferior Levitical system was only to be imposed until what the author calls "a time of reformation." The word translated "reformation" is the noun *diorthōsis*, "to correct," "to make right." It is the latest example of our author's 154 vocabulary words that appear only once in the New Testament. Once this new age of "making things right" between God and His people arrived, the Levitical system of worship became superfluous.

Conclusion

According to Hebrews, the death, resurrection, and exaltation of Jesus caused a new and superior covenant to be inaugurated. With that new covenant, a superior priesthood was established and a superior High Priest installed. Yet, as the author put quill to scroll some two thousand years ago, the Levitical system was still fully functional. The glorious temple in Jerusalem was a marvel of the ancient world. The Levitical system of worship must have exerted an extremely powerful political, social, and emotional pull on the readers to reaffirm their trust in the sacrificial system. They needed the author's reminder that while to humans eyes the Mosaic system, as exercised in the Second Temple, appeared to be at the pinnacle of its grandeur, in God's eyes it was already superfluous, obsolete, and ineffective.

Study Questions

1. Describe the basic structure of the tabernacle.
2. List and describe the tabernacle furniture.
3. Describe the activities of the high priest on the Day of Atonement.
4. What was the purpose and function of the Day of Atonement? What was it designed to accomplish?
5. What evidence has Hebrews presented to indicate that Jesus is the fulfillment of the Day of Atonement?

CHAPTER 11

Superiority of the Messiah's Sacrifice
Hebrews 9:11–9:28

Preview:

The author now builds on his previous establishment of the superiority of the Messiah's high priesthood over that of the Levitical as regards sanctuary, service, and worship (9:1–10). Having thus far accentuated Christ's high priestly intercessory ministry (2:18; 4:15–16; 7:25; 8:1–2), he now focuses on the unique sacrifice that enabled Jesus' successful intercession. The author had previously laid the seeds for this discussion (5:1; 7:27; 8:3), and now he takes up the topic of messianic sacrifice in earnest. Foundational to the discussion and assumed by the author is his readers' familiarity with basic Levitical ritual and in particular the high priest's activity on the Day of Atonement (see comment on 9:6–7) as well as the Levitical system's fundamental reliance on the necessity of animal blood (9:12, 13, 14, 18, 19, 20, 21, 22, 25) in atonement's provision. He argues that the Melchizedekian priesthood of Jesus retains that fundamental reliance on blood; however, the required blood is now that of Jesus Himself and not that of animals.

Superior Elements of the Messiah's Sacrifice (9:11–12)

The section continues the author's prior reflection that the Levitical priesthood had possessed a definite shelf life, divinely designed to function until the arrival of "the time of reformation" (9:10). However, now that Christ has appeared as the High Priest "of the good things which have come," the transition between the two systems has been accomplished. The author's articulation of these two distinct stages in history, separated through a major activity of God, serves as an outstanding example of what many call "dispensations." Other biblical examples of such clearly marked transitions between historic ages that are set apart from one another through groundbreaking, divine action would be the respective pre– and post–Garden of Eden eras, the respective eras pre- and post-Flood, and the present church age versus the future messianic kingdom.

The "good things which have come" are the three superior elements of Christ's sacrifice enumerated against a backdrop of the Day of Atonement. First, the heavenly tabernacle into which Jesus entered was superior to the earthly tabernacle "made with hands" into which the Levitical high priest entered annually.

Second, the associated sacrificial blood of Jesus (His own) was superior to the blood borne by the Levitical high priest, that of goats sacrificed on behalf of the nation (Lev. 16:15) and calves sacrificed on behalf of the priests (Lev. 16:11). The Levitical high priest never dared to gain entry beyond the veil and into the Holy of Holies without blood. Yet as Fruchtenbaum notes, while the Levitical high priest entered into the earthly tabernacle *with* blood, Jesus entered the heavenly tabernacle *through* blood. "The priest had to come carrying blood for his own sins, and the blood he carried was not his own. Jesus had no sins, and therefore He went *through blood*, and this blood was His own."[1] Hebrew 9:12's instrumental preposition *dia* should be understood as indicating that Jesus entered by means of, or by virtue of, His own blood, not "along with" His own blood. We are not to gruesomely suggest that Jesus' blood was somehow collected as it dripped down the cross for His later presentation and offering to His Father.[2] No, Jesus entered God's presence empty-handed, but those empty hands were nail-scarred.

Third, while the Levitical high priests were required to repeatedly appear before the Lord's presence in the Holy of Holies every year, Jesus entered into God's presence *ephapax*, "once for all," the same word the author previously used in reference to Jesus' sacrifice (7:27). Jesus' superior sacrificial work, once accomplished, was never to be repeated. Since the redemption He obtained was eternal, He permanently broke the ineffective annual Levitical cycle.

Superior Results of the Messiah's Sacrifice (9:13–28)

In comparison to the Levitical sacrifices, the Messiah's sacrifice produced a superior ability to sanctify (9:13–14) and the ratification of a superior covenant (9:15–22) through ministry in a superior location (9:23–28).

Superior Sanctification (9:13–14). Under the Levitical system, ceremonial defilement prohibited ceremonial participation. No one, therefore, could worship God unless ceremonially clean (Num 19:13, 20). The author cites the goat and bull sacrifices of the Day of Atonement ceremony (Lev. 16:6–7) along with sprinkled red heifer ashes (Num. 19:9) to summarize that the Levitical process of ceremonial cleansing was effective only regarding the external component of humans ("the flesh") and had no effect on their inner being ("the conscience").

Red Heifer. Like the search for the ark of the covenant, the quest to locate a perfect red heifer has captured the imagination of a large segment of the contemporary church.[3] These raiders of the lost ashes also ponder the whereabouts of the ancient vessel containing the ashes of a red heifer used in temple times.

According to the Torah (Num. 19:1–22), God commanded Israel to sacrifice outside the camp a perfect, never yoked, red heifer (a young cow that has never given birth). After sprinkling its blood seven times toward the tabernacle/temple, the carcass was incinerated. As it burned, cedar wood and hyssop bound with scarlet wool were added to the fire. When the fire had gone out, the remaining heap of carcass and wood was to be pulverized and sifted until only ashes remained.[4] These ashes were to be collected in a vessel, and one portion at a time, as needed, was to be mixed in water to create the "water of sanctification" (Num. 19:9; Heb. 9:13). Anyone rendered ceremonially unclean through contact with a corpse or in some other manner, could be cleansed by being sprinkled by the priest with this ashy liquid.

As outlined in Numbers 19, the procedure was a rather straightforward affair. However, as with most of the Mosaic legislation in the accumulated centuries beyond the days of the tabernacle, the rabbinic tendency was to complicate the uncomplicated, to create Gordian knots where once there were only simple slipknots. By the time of the New Testament, this procedure could be considered the poster child for rabbinic legislative excess.

The Mishnah devotes an entire tractate, *Parah*, to the procedure, recording that in the Second Temple era the red heifer was sacrificed on the Mount of Olives, which was east of the temple, across the Kidron Valley.[5] The ashes were collected into three containers, one for present use, one for safekeeping, and one for the use of future generations. The supply of each heifer's ashes was carefully apportioned out and lasted for generations. In the fifteen centuries from Moses to the destruction of the temple in AD 70, only nine red heifers were sacrificed. The final sacrifice was performed just prior to the composition of Hebrews by the high priest who served from AD 59–61, Ishmael ben Phiabi.[6]

Years earlier, in preparation for the ceremony, special housing was constructed in Jerusalem on isolated, elevated courtyards that made no contact with the bedrock beneath. This was in order for pregnant women to bear and raise their children without the risk of any child's possible defilement through contact with an unmarked grave. Once they were eight years old, these youngsters, without ever making contact with the ground, sat on boards mounted across oxen and rode to the pool of Siloam. There they collected the required amount of water in stone vessels and rode up to the Temple Mount.[7] They dismounted, entered the temple, and poured the water into a trough. One of the children took the ashes of the red heifer and mixed them in with the water, creating the "water of sanctification." David Stern points out a connection between the water of sanctification and the Day of Atonement that may explain its mention in 9:13 alongside bull and goat sacrifice. He notes that according to the renowned thirteenth-century rabbi Maimonides, the high priest was sprinkled with this water to assure purity before his entrance into the Holy of Holies.[8] It was Maimonides' opinion that the ceremony of immolating the red heifer and recreating the water of purification would resume at the coming of the Messiah.[9]

In 9:14 the author employs the rabbinic rhetorical technique of *qal vachomer*, "light and heavy"; the application of truth about that with lesser significance to that with greater significance, which is usually recognizable by the telltale "How much more so?" comparisons (2:1–4; 10:28–29; 12:25). He reasons that if animal blood and ashes (the lesser) can have a physical cleansing effect, then the cleansing effect of the Messiah's blood (the greater) would be exponentially superior, extending beyond the flesh to the conscience.

The issue has less to do with the physical composition of the blood itself than the means by which it was shed. One can be reasonably assured that, given a choice, the assortment of bulls and goats targeted for sacrifice would not have volunteered for the assignment. Yet Jesus willingly offered Himself, a perfect sacrifice without spot or blemish (1 Pet. 1:19). No one constrained or forced Him into this action; He willingly chose His destiny. He offered Himself "through the eternal spirit," an expression occurring nowhere else in the New Testament, and which most likely should be understood as the Holy Spirit,[10] making 9:14 an example of a New Testament verse that includes all three members of the Trinity.

Ratification of a Superior Covenant (9:15–22). With 9:15's connective *kai dia touto*, "and for this reason," the argument now progresses to the superior covenant ratified through the Messiah's sacrifice. Building on the foundation previously laid in 8:6–13's discussion of the new covenant, the author reiterates his previous identification (8:6) of Jesus as the covenant mediator (*mesitēs*, "an arbitrator," "a go between"). His death was compulsory to the ratification of the new covenant, as it both qualified and enabled Him to hold this office.

The Mosaic covenant, called here "the first covenant," was not designed to provide *apolutrōsin*, "redemption," as was the new covenant. Whereas the new covenant's *raison d'être* was the definitive removal of sin (Jer. 31:34, Heb. 8:12), the Mosaic covenant's limitations only allowed for the covering of sin. Now, however, through His death, the promise of an eternal inheritance, salvation (1:14), may be realized for all those who have been divinely designated (*keklēmenoi*, perfect passive participle, "having been designated, called, summoned"). This is the same word previously used of believers' "heavenly calling" (3:1) and anticipates imminent discussion of Abraham's call (11:8).

In 9:16–17 the author's mention of inheritance plays off the dual aspect of the meaning of the Greek word *diathēkē*, which possesses both the ideas of "covenant" and of "testament," a legal will. This clever rhetorical nuance is literally lost in translation. His point is that the stipulations of the new covenant, like that of a will, provide for the heirs' inheritance. No matter how extensive the promises of inheritance may be, as expressed in the will, nothing is actually inherited until the death of the testator. The covenant/testament remains invalid (*mēpote ischuei*, "no force") until that moment. Ergo, for believers to receive the distribution of their eternal inheritance, that is, their salvation, they must first receive the redemption that only became available to them through the Messiah's sacrifice. As F. F. Bruce notes, Jesus was "testator and executor in one, surety and mediator alike."[11]

Covenant affirmation and ratification through means of blood is the theme of 9:18–22. The author summarizes the events surrounding the inauguration of the Mosaic covenant, recorded in Exodus 24:1–8. Having recorded God's commands in a scroll, Moses had an altar built at the foot of Sinai alongside twelve pillars erected to represent the twelve tribes of Israel. As the Levitical priesthood had not yet been initiated, selected young men, likely comprised of firstborn sons (Exod. 13:1–2), offered several sacrifices. For this unique occasion, Moses himself assumed the duties of a high priest, sprinkling half of the collected blood from the sacrifices on the altar.

After Moses read the book of the covenant to the people, the congregation of Israel unanimously responded as they had willingly done the preceding day, declaring that they would be obedient to all that the Lord had said. With the nation having officially consented to the covenant, Moses took the remainder of the blood and sprinkled it toward the people. Hebrews 9:19 adds that the scroll of the covenant was also included in the sprinkling and that the sprinkled blood was mixed with water, scarlet wool, and hyssop, two details not included in the Exodus account. He also sprinkled the tabernacle and all the vessels of the ministry (Lev. 8:10–15).

This act of sprinkling symbolically bound the nation to the stipulations of the covenant, as it was now the most solemn of covenants, a covenant ratified by blood. The author paraphrases Moses' statement of covenant ratification in 9:20, massaging the quotation a bit for it to clearly prefigure Jesus' announcement of new covenant inauguration at His Last Supper (Matt. 26:28; Mark 14:24; Luke 22:20). The discussion of blood is brought to a climax with the declaration in 9:22 that there can be no forgiveness (*aphesis*, "dismissal," "release," "pardon from or cancellation of debt") absent the shedding of blood, a citation of Leviticus 17:11, which is the key verse in the book of Leviticus as well as the central concept of the entire Levitical system of worship. Interestingly, the word translated "shedding of blood" is *haimatekchusia* and appears here for the first time in the known corpus of ancient Greek literature.[12]

In sum, the author has argued for the centrality of blood as the means of divine access (9:7), the basis of ratification for both old covenant (9:18) and new (9:14), and the exclusive means of divine forgiveness (9:22).

Superior Location (9:23–28). The ratification of a better covenant provides the ability for the Messiah to exercise His ministry in a better location. The worship environment of the first covenant was the central sanctuary, first the tabernacle and later the temple. A concept inherent in the Levitical system of worship is that the sanctuary and every implement related to the function of sanctuary worship would become corrupted over time through the sin of individual worshipers (Lev. 16:16; 20:3; 21:23; Num. 19:20). Once a year it was necessary for the sanctuary to be ceremonially cleansed (*katharizesthai*, "to be purged"). The means of cleansing, as the author has so well established by this point in his argument, was the sacrificial blood of animals. The day on which this cleansing was performed was, of course, the Day of Atonement.

While the blood of sacrificial animals was adequate to cleanse "the copies of the things in the heavens" (9:23), the requirements for cleansing the heavenly reality behind the copies were understandably more stringent, requiring Christ's blood. The need for the heavenly sanctuary's purification may quite understandably raise many an eyebrow. Some, perhaps uncomfortable with viewing the author's image of the heavenly sanctuary in material terms, instead see the sanctuary as spiritual in essence and define it as God's dwelling place in the midst of His people. Their position seeks to explain the author's statement regarding the cleansing of the heavenly sanctuary as simply indicating the cleansing of the "defiled conscience of men and women."[13]

However, the author gives no indication that he intends for his readers to interpret his matter of fact, unambiguous statement in a spiritual sense. Hebrews presents the church as "God's household" (3:6), not His tabernacle.[14] After all, this is not the first time the author has written of the heavenly sanctuary in which Jesus ministers as High Priest in the presence of God. If the heavenly reality behind the earthly tabernacle is devoid of material essence, then the divine revelation to Moses of a pattern/model/blueprints fails to make sense (Exod. 25:40; Heb. 8:5). Furthermore, the explicit teaching of the New Testament is that since the resurrection, Jesus has been in possession of a glorified physical body. That physical body is seated on a real throne at God's right hand (Heb. 1:3, 13; 8:1; 10:12–13; Ps. 110:1). This requires the heavenly sanctuary to be, in some fashion far beyond mortal comprehension, material in nature.

The difficulty with this position, however, is that it raises the very pointed question as to just how the heavenly sanctuary, wherein dwells the presence of God, came to need cleansing. Arnold Fruchtenbaum sets forth two provocative possibilities to ponder:

> First, when Satan rebelled against God, he did so while he was still in Heaven, and, thus, Satan's rebellion brought sin into Heaven itself (Isa. 14:12–14; Ezek. 28:11–19). The Ezekiel passage states that he defiled the Sanctuary in Heaven. For this reason, the heavens were not clean (Job 4:18; 15:15; 25:5). Second, man is united with creation. When man sinned, his sin reached even unto Heaven. That is why Colossians 1:20 teaches that when Jesus died He reconciled things in Heaven as well as on earth. For these reasons, the Heavenly Tabernacle needed the cleansing of better blood.[15]

The typological connection with the earthly tabernacle necessitates the material nature of the heavenly sanctuary, and it is that material nature that is stressed in 9:24. When the Messiah appeared in the presence of God on our behalf, it was not into the temple's Holy of Holies that He entered. He was no Levitical high priest tremulously piercing the darkness beyond the veil in observance of the rituals of the Day of Atonement. He Himself was the Atonement. The inferior copy was bypassed in favor of the superior original, as Jesus entered heaven itself. For the first and only time in the text, the author substitutes a singular reference to heaven instead of his customary plural "heavens" (1:10; 4:14; 7:26; 8:1; 9:23; et al.). The author had already made the point that Jesus had passed through the heavens (see comments on 4:14 for a discussion of multiple heavens). However many "heavens" there may be, the author's use here emphasizes Jesus triumphal entrance into the *highest* heaven, the final level, the top floor, the last stop.

The author's use of comparison with the Day of Atonement continues with his assertion that, unlike the Levitical high priests who must repeatedly, once each year, enter the Holy of Holies, Jesus' entrance into heaven was a "once in an eternity," unrepeatable event. Hebrews 9:25–26 contains the unequivocal declaration *oud' hina pollakis prospherē heauton*, that Jesus would not offer Himself repeatedly. One of the central aspects underscored here that makes His sacrifice superior is that He appeared *hapax*, "once," at the climax of history to cancel the force of sin through his sacrifice.[16] The very fact that that it was necessary to annually observe the Day of Atonement exposes the inherent insufficiency of every Levitical offering ever presented over the prior fifteen-century period. Furthermore, no animal's blood would ever prove adequate to do more than cover sin. Indeed, no high priest's blood would have proven sufficient. Only Jesus' sacrifice proved a satisfactory offering in the presence of God.

This passage precludes any concept of the Messiah, in any fashion, now repeatedly offering Himself as a sacrifice in heaven or, alternatively, reenacting His sacrifice, in any fashion, here on earth. The author affirms that if sacrificial repetition were a required element in the process, Jesus "would have needed to suffer often since the foundation of the world" (9:26). The clarity and lack of ambiguity in which the finality, unrepeatability, and nonreproducable nature of Jesus' definitive accomplishment on the cross is expressed precludes the notion of an eternal sacrifice, a perpetual sacrifice, or even a single representation of that sacrifice before the throne of God. The author has vehemently argued that the intrinsic inadequacy of the Day of Atonement lay not only in the inferiority of the blood that was offered but also in the ritual's need for annual repetition. The text, therefore, precludes as inferior any conception of Christ's sacrifice requiring moment by moment, hourly, daily, or weekly repetition. Furthermore, neither the earthly nor the heavenly Holy of Holies contains an altar on which to offer sacrifice.[17]

The declaration of 9:26 provides a summary of this segment. In one historic moment, "the consummation of the ages," Jesus appeared before the Father *hapax*, "once for all time," for the accomplishment of one purpose, "to put away sin," by one means, "the sacrifice of Himself." "The consummation of the ages" harks back to the announcement of "these last days" in 1:2, that Jewish idiom for the messianic age, the time for the fulfillment of God's yet unfulfilled promises. The sharp division between dispensations (BC and AD, if you will) has been drawn by the Messiah and His supreme accomplishment. The phrase translated "to put away sin" (*eis athetēsin tēs hamartias*) contains a word used nowhere else in the New Testament but Hebrews, *athetēsin*, which was previously employed by the author in 7:18 with reference to the annulment of the Torah. It is a legal term that means "annulment," "something set aside," generally used of the annulment of a decree or the cancellation of a debt. Through His bloody, sacrificial death, Jesus has removed sin, set it aside, forever annulled its power, and sent it a notice of cancellation.

In case his readers failed to either understand or appreciate the one-time nature of Jesus' sacrifice, in 9:27–28 the writer employs the term *hapax*, "once," an additional two times in reference to the finality of Jesus' sacrifice. People frequently cite 9:27's statement concerning men being appointed to die once with judgment to follow as support against nonbiblical teachings like reincarnation and the possibility of postmortem second opportunities for salvation. While that usage is indeed good, in the actual context of Hebrews, the statement is a declaration confirming that Jesus would never be resacrificed. Jesus, being a man who had already tasted death (2:9), would never again repeat the experience.

Christ was "offered once to bear the sins of many" (9:28). This is the language of the prophet Isaiah writing of God's suffering servant who took upon Himself the guilt of Israel and vicariously bore their iniquity (Isa. 53:12). Jesus accomplished His messianic mission with one noble, sacrificial act. Therefore, the days of His suffering are over, never to return, as they have been replaced by the unending age of His exaltation (5:8–10).

In addition to the use of 9:27 with regard to the refutation of false doctrine, some have instead used the verse to innovate new doctrine. Fruchtenbaum notes that the statement that "it is appointed for men to die once" has been taken to an extreme in certain quarters without regard to the two categories of exceptions provided in Scripture.[18] First, unlike James Bond, who "only lives twice," any ordinary person miraculously resurrected during his lifetime, such as Lazarus or poor, sleepy Eutychus, experienced death twice. Second, neither Enoch nor Elijah died, but were taken by the Lord. Yet, since it is appointed for men to die once," embedded in some people's understanding of the book of Revelation is the necessity of these fellows to return as the two martyred witnesses (Rev. 11) in order to get what's coming to them! It is hard to imagine how that interpretation squares with the multitudes of believers who never die because they experience the rapture (1 Cor. 15:51).

The author completes this section with an encouraging reminder that the Messiah is indeed planning to return. When He does so, it will not be to provide an additional act of sacrifice. His return engagement will have no reference to solving the problem of sin. That problem has already been solved, and that aspect of His ministry is definitively behind Him. He is coming for "to those who eagerly await Him" to bring salvation from this age and the inauguration of the next as He establishes His rule and reign over His kingdom.

Conclusion

Jesus' second coming will serve as the final typological fulfillment of the Day of Atonement. The tribulation, "the time of Jacob's trouble," when the nation of Israel will experience an unprecedented affliction of both body and soul, will powerfully conclude with Israel's repentance and salvation as they recognize their ultimate King and High Priest and receive His atonement (Zech. 12:1–13:1) at the dawn of the messianic age.

Study Questions

1. List the three superior elements of the Messiah's sacrifice.

2. Describe the Levitical ritual of the red heifer.

3. What is the role of blood to the Mosaic and new covenants?

4. Explain the typological connection between the earthly and heavenly tabernacles.

CHAPTER 12

Sufficiency of the Messiah's Sacrifice
Hebrews 10:1-18

Preview:
The writer proves himself a skillful first-century rhetorician through his habitual use of repetition, restatement, and summary. In this section, continuing through 10:18, he approaches the same ideas he has previously established from an objective perspective and this time emphasizes the subjective perspective of his readers. In effect, he answers any anticipated concern from his readers as to just what Jesus' high priesthood means to their community.

The Insufficiency of Levitical Sacrifice (10:1-4)

He begins by connecting (*gar*, "for") what he is about to articulate about the insufficiency of the Levitical sacrifice with what he has just previously communicated concerning the "once for all" nature of Jesus' sacrifice in 9:11–28. Once again, he pounds the drum of typological correspondence between the elements of old and new covenants and old and new priesthoods. He does this by using two contrasting designations, the word *skia*, "shadow," and *eikōn*, "image," or "substantive reality." Just as he had previously used *skia* in reference to the tabernacle (8:5), he now applies the term to the Torah. The Mosaic Law was a foreshadowing of "the good things to come," that is, the substantive image.

Eikōn is employed by Paul in reference to Christ's being the image of God (2 Cor. 4:4; Col. 1:15) and to the conforming of believers into Christ's image

(Rom. 8:29; 2 Cor. 3:18). *Skia* is also employed by Paul in reference to practical Jewish observances, such as festivals, Sabbaths, and food laws (Col. 2:16–17). These he calls *skia tōn mellontōn,* "a shadow of things to come," a remarkably similar phrasing to that of Hebrews 10:1. Both "what is to come" in Colossians 2:17 and "the good things to come" of 10:1 refer to the completed work of the Messiah.

Use of Old Testament Passages in Hebrews 10

Hebrews	Old Testament	Subject
10:4	Lev. 16:6–7	The Day of Atonement
10:5–9	Ps. 40:6–8	The Levitical sacrificial system
10:11	Exod. 29:38	The Levitical priestly service
10:12	Isa. 53:10–12	Isaiah's suffering servant
10:12–13	Ps. 110:1	The divine authority of the Son
10:16–17	Jer. 31:33–34	The new covenant
10:22	Ezek. 36:25	The new covenant
10:25	Lev. 23:27; 25:9	The Day of Atonement
10:26	Num. 15:30–31	The sin of defiance
10:27	Isa. 26:11	Divine judgment against God's enemies
10:28	Deut. 17:6; 19:15	The Mosaic Law concerning testimony
10:29	Exod. 24:8	The ratification of the Mosaic covenant
10:30	Deut. 32:35–36	Divine judgment against God's enemies
10:30	Ps. 135:14	Divine justice for God's people
10:37	Isa. 26:20–21	Divine judgment against God's enemies
10:37–38	Hab. 2:3–4	Admonition to faithfulness

Please note that the English translations sometimes add words that do not directly correspond to the original Greek text for the sake of explication and reader clarity. Such is the case with the NASB translation of Colossians 2:17 (in which the word "mere" modifies "shadow") and similarly with Hebrews 10:1 (in which "a shadow" is modified by "only"). On the one hand, I appreciate the translators' attempt to help the reader absorb the nuance of the contextual arguments in these respective passages, which are both centered on comparisons, through adding words like "mere" and "only." Yet, on the other hand, the addition of these "helping" words ends up making the verse say more than it should. Specifically, in 10:1 the Torah, as "only" a shadow, can now be seen only as deficient because of the word addition. While it is true that the Torah as shadow is deficient when compared against the substance of Messiah's ministry, the shadow of Torah should not always be viewed pejoratively.

An example is when my son's attempt to sneak up on me is foiled because I notice his approaching shadow. The casting of his shadow should be considered a good thing and not disparaged simply because it is not my son's actual substance. His shadow prepares me for "things to come" (in this case, the ambush of old Dad), and therefore I am quite pleased that the shadow arrived prior to the substance. Likewise, we must be careful to appreciate the shadowy nature of the Torah in 10:1. While it could never bring anyone to a state of spiritual maturity, that was as much a divinely included feature as it was a defect. The Law was God's gift, not His mistake, and was given to prepare us for the good things to come (Gal. 3:19–25).

Nonetheless, the annual repetition of the Day of Atonement sacrifices demonstrated their insufficiency by their very recurrence. In short, if the Day of Atonement had truly been adequate for the cleansing of sin, the ritual would have been performed only once. The first ceremony would have been the last ceremony. The very fact that the daily Levitical system cranked right back up again the following morning, leading one year later to another Day of Atonement, indicated that nothing had spiritually changed from the previous year. The fact that the worshipers came away on the Day of Atonement with a retained consciousness of their sins proves that they had not experienced a *hapax*, "once for all," final cleansing.

The Day of Atonement's bulls and goats, sacrificed for the priesthood and people, respectively (Lev. 16:3, 6–7, 11, 14–16, 18–19), could never take away sins. Rather, these sacrifices and the physical, ceremonial cleansing wrought by their blood served as an annual reminder of their inefficiency in dealing with the congregation of Israel's most pressing problem, their sin. As F. F. Bruce points out, the insufficiency of animal blood in decisively dealing with sin was not an exclusively messianic insight. This is seen in the relative ease with which the rabbis, following the temple's destruction, were able to reinvent a synagogue-centered Judaism that was completely devoid of blood sacrifice.[1]

The entire Yom Kippur ritual, from its initiation to its completion, was designed to focus on each Israelite's consciousness of sin. The twenty-five-hour period of fasting (Lev. 23:26–32), the repeated confession of sins (Lev.

16:20–22), and the marked exclusivity of the high priest's entrance into the Holy of Holies all served to remind each participant, including the high priest himself, that his guilt still remained and was only covered over. This stands in stark contrast to the ministry of our Great High Priest who, as mediator, testator, executor, and guarantor of the new covenant, has ensured our forgiveness and God's permanent removal of our sins from the divine record. We have received pardon; our consciences are clean. In the words of the Horatio Spafford's hymn "It Is Well with My Soul,"

> My sin—O, the bliss of this glorious thought,
> My sin—not in part but the whole,
> Is nailed to the cross and I bear it no more,
> Praise the Lord, praise the Lord, O my soul!

Worthy of special attention is the author's consistent use of the present tense throughout this section's discussion of Levitical practice, indicating that temple worship was still functional at the time of composition. Pointing out the reduction of Israel's incomparable temple to inglorious ruin and rubble would have been the crowning illustration for this master of rhetorical persuasion's argument. Of all possible moments to cite the temple's destruction in the letter's argument, placement in 10:1–4 would have possessed the most rhetorical force. The question he asks in 10:2, concerning whether the Day of Atonement sacrifices would not have ceased to be offered, provided a veritable superhighway-wide opening for him to answer a resounding, "As indeed the sacrifices have ceased to be offered since Rome destroyed the Levitical sanctuary!" His failure to mention or allude to anything of the kind makes a post–AD 70 publication of Hebrews quite inconceivable.

The Replacement of the Levitical with Messiah's Perfect Sacrifice (10:5–10)

The argument is seasoned at this point with a quotation from Psalm 40:6–8, on which the author then comments. The context of Psalm 40 contains David's self-disclosure of sacrificial devotion to the ways of the Lord and to following His Torah. However, much of the psalm extends beyond any probable personal experience of David and into the prophetic realm of the future Messiah to come. Indeed, the author of Hebrews places the words of David typologically into the mouth of his descendant at His incarnation, applying them to the Messiah's perfect obedience to the Torah as well as His definitive sacrificial devotion to the Lord through His death (Heb. 10:5–7).

The author has inserted a quotation from this particular psalm to serve his rhetorical purpose, which was to demonstrate the superiority of the Messiah's sacrifice based on its voluntary nature and His willful participation.[2] The prerequisite to the Atonement, by design, was the Incarnation, to accomplish the specific purpose of God that otherwise never could have been achieved through the sacrifices of dumb animals. The ultimate form of sacrifice would necessarily take the form of the Son of God becoming man and intentionally obediently giving Himself over to death at His Father's behest.

This particular quotation is notoriously challenging as it diverges in phrasing and word choice from both the text of the original Hebrew and the Septuagint. Various suggestions have been proposed to explain the variations, such as the author's use of a different manuscript or the resulting imprecision of quoting from memory. An alternative, highly compelling proposal is the author's use of "phonetic manipulation . . . rhetorical techniques of rhythmic arrangement and ornamentation of style . . . to attract the ear of the audience and thereby to draw their attention to that element of the argument."[3]

In 10:9b the author adds an explanatory comment that usually receives an undemanding milquetoast translation, such as, "He takes away the first in order to establish the second." This is not the first instance, after all, of the author affirming the replacement of the old covenant with the new (8:7-13). However, the reader must appreciate that this explosive comment represents the author's launch of a theological grenade. The Greek word behind the phrase translated "He takes away" is the present active indicative form of *anaireō*, which means "to destroy," "to kill," "to slay," "to put to death," "to do away with." This word is used only this once in Hebrews and is the equivalent of the author's having "gone nuclear." In the words of Paul Ellingworth, it is "the strongest negative statement the author has made or will make about the Old Testament cultus."[4] By means of the Messiah's sacrifice, He has destroyed the Mosaic covenant; He has killed the Torah's legislation. According to 10:7, the Messiah has thus achieved "the will of God."

Although this is the word's sole use in Hebrews, *anaireō* appears elsewhere throughout the New Testament, employed mostly by Luke. As demonstrated through its usage, *anaireō* is a word that drips blood. Proceed through the following list and appreciate its usage in context. It is used of the plot to kill Jesus (Luke 22:2), the multiple plots to kill Paul (Acts 9:23–24, 29; 23:15, 21; 23:27; 25:3), the Sanhedrin's intent to kill the apostles (Acts 5:33), Jesus' execution (Luke 23:32; Acts 2:23; 10:39; 13:28), James's execution (Acts 12:2), Stephen's execution (Acts 22:20), Herod's slaughter of the children (Matt. 2:16), Moses' killing of the Egyptian (Acts 7:28), and the Lord's slaying of the Antichrist (2 Thess. 2:8).

In 10:10 the author shifts to first person plural ("we") from the previous section's use of third person, indicating the augmentation of the theological with the applicational. In this short verse, he affirms four points. First, believers have been sanctified (*hēgiasmenoi*, "having been made holy, consecrated," perfect passive participle, which indicates past action with continuing result). Second, we enjoy our consecration through (*dia*, "by means of") the offering of the physical body of Jesus the Messiah. Third, both believers' sanctification and Christ's sacrifice are qualified by the word *ephapax*, "once for all." His voluntary offering of Himself on the cross has permanently sanctified us in the sight of God. "It is a sanctification which has taken place once for all; in this sense it is as unrepeatable as the sacrifice which effects it."[5] Fourth, both His once for all sacrifice and believers' once for all consecration were accomplished *en hō thelēmati*, "by the will of God."

The Finality of the Messiah's Sacrifice (10:11–14)

As the writer begins climactically drawing his themes together toward a conclusion, he summarizes a select range of dissimilarities that exist between the Levitical priesthood and that of Jesus (see Comparisons between Levitical and Jesus' Melchizedekian Priesthoods). The first set of distinctions concerns posture and activity. According to Levitical practice and the stipulations of Torah (Deut. 18:5), Levitical priests are required to continuously stand in their ministry as, each day and in the same way, the exact same sacrifices are repeatedly offered in an unremitting, continuous cycle (Exod. 29:38). By way of contrast, Jesus has offered (*prosenegkas*, aorist tense, indicating previous completed action) a single, sufficient sacrifice. Having managed, therefore, through this one act of sacrifice to realize thoroughly the goal and purpose of His ministry and with no further offerings to perform, Jesus sat down at the right hand of God (Heb. 1:3, 13; 8:1). In again taking up the imagery of Psalm 110:1, the readers are reminded of the enthroned priest concept of 8:1–2's major purpose statement.

The second set of distinctions concerns quantity and sufficiency. The Levitical system required the activity of innumerable priests offering multiple sacrifices over an unremitting period of time. In contrast, one single Priest, Jesus, offered one single sacrifice one single time. Moreover, it was necessary for Levitical sacrifices to be offered in a continuous loop because of their innate insufficiency to atone for sins. Animal blood served to cover sin temporarily but was powerless to remove it permanently. It would be like getting a giant ink stain from a leaky pen on the front pocket of your favorite white shirt. Good luck getting out that unsightly blue blotch in the laundry cycle! Since it is your favorite shirt, you cannot bring yourself to part with it, so you decide to place a clean white sticker over the stain and hope no one notices. Although this tactic may possibly fool some of your friends and fellow employees, you remain acutely sensitive to the fact that you continue to walk around the workplace carrying a temporarily covered big blue stain of imperfection over your heart, removal of which would stymie even the finest of infomercial cleansing products.

In contrast to the inadequacy of the Levitical system, the stain of our sin has been effectively and permanently removed through the voluntary sacrifice of God's Son. By this one offering, Jesus has perfected (*teteleiōken*, perfect tense, indicating past action with continuing result) for all time those who are sanctified. The expression *eis to diēnekes*, "for all time," "in perpetuity," is the equivalent of Buzz Lightyear's slogan "To infinity and beyond!" It is so essential to the author's point that after having employed the temporal phrase in 10:12, he repeats it two verses later in 10:14 to unambiguously accentuate the permanent quality and effect of the perfection of those consecrated through His sacrifice. His achievement was foretold by the prophet Isaiah, who revealed that God's suffering servant's death as a sacrificial guilt offering would result in the justification of sinners (Isa. 53:10–12).

Since His exaltation and entrance into heaven as High Priest, Jesus sits enthroned at His Father's right hand, "waiting from that time onward" until His enemies are subjugated (Heb. 10:13; Ps. 110:1). This is the usual New Testament description of the posture of the exalted Jesus (Rom. 8:34; Eph. 1:20; Col. 3:1; Heb. 1:3; 13; 8:1; 10:12; 12:2; 1 Pet. 3:22). Only one time in the New Testament is Jesus portrayed in any other posture, and that is when He rises from His throne at God's right hand to receive the spirit of Stephen, the first believer martyred for His name (Acts 7:56). Sometime in the future, Jesus will again rise to His feet when He descends from heaven as the awe-inspiring Judge of the earth.

The Superiority of the New Covenant (10:15–18)

The extensive discussion that the author first began in 7:1 is now brought to a conclusion with a repetition of Jeremiah's prophecy of the new covenant (Jer. 31:31–34). Unlike the original quotation in 8:7–12, when the central prophecy was quoted in full, this time Jeremiah 31:31–32 is economically omitted. The focus is not on the establishment of a new covenant but rather on two of its specific provisions, that of the internalization of God's laws and God's compassionate extension of forgiveness and mercy concerning His people's sins and iniquities. The quotation's introductory formula is phrased so that attribution is given to the Holy Spirit as both the original witness of this proclamation and as its current witness. The author's use of a present active indicative form of the verb *martureō*, "to testify," "to bear witness," indicates that this is not simply the Holy Spirit's historical testimony from Jeremiah's day but His current testimony to first-century believers. The new covenant is now operational, and its provisions, especially that of forgiveness, accessible.

The writer's final summation is that where there is divine forgiveness (*aphesis*, "dismissal," "release," "pardon from or cancellation of debt") of "these things," that is, our sins, then logically there is no longer any need for the Mosaic covenant's Levitical legislation. When God's comprehensive internal cleansing is available through the Messiah, no one would settle for the ceremonial external cleansing of Moses.

Conclusion

The letter of Hebrews has scrutinized the priesthood of Melchizedek (7:1–28) and demonstrated its superiority over the priesthood of Aaron in both the realm of priestly service (9:1–10) and the sufficiency of sacrifice (9:11–10:18). In addition, it has established the new covenant's superiority over that of the Mosaic covenant (8:1–13), which has been slain by the Messiah's death (10:9).

This leaves, however, the very pragmatic question of how the stipulations, customs, and traditions of the Mosaic covenant may be practiced by those who care to do so. In a passage that has previously been cited (Col. 2:16–17), Paul explained in his letter to the Colossians that no one was to judge anyone else in his or her personal preferences regarding observance of Jewish customs and practices. The examples he provides of celebration of annual festivals, monthly new moons, weekly Sabbaths, and even the laws of *kashrut*, food laws, were all acceptable, even profitable activities in which the Christian believer might engage. These, he wrote, are "shadows of things to come," prophetic pictures or typological images whose underlying substance is none other than Jesus Himself.

It is telling that the maintenance of Jewish custom and tradition as described in Acts is not qualified as something negative, ill advised, or unenlightened. Rather, Luke describes such practices as normative in the early decades of the church. The only aspects of the church's Jewish culture that later required adaptation were those that interfered with the incorporation of Gentiles into the church and their acceptance as equals, such as inflexible adherence to kosher food regulations.

It must be remembered that in first-century Israel, Judaism was not only a religious system but also a national way of life, the ancient law of the land. It would have been exceedingly difficult to extricate religious responsibilities from national duties or even from simple cultural expression.[6] Indeed, there is no evidence in the New Testament of any kind of "legalism police squad" insisting that the Jewish believers give up temple worship or sabbath observance, or eat a sandwich of ham on rye. Indeed, quite the opposite is in view.

For example, Peter and John are recorded in the account as customarily attending the temple prayer service (Acts 3:1). Paul, the apostle of liberty himself, the Hebrew of Hebrews (Phil. 3:5) and Pharisee of Pharisees (Acts 23:6), clearly continued the practice of Jewish customs, even exercising a vow of dedication (Acts 18:18). The most casual perusal of Acts reveals how Paul lived as a Jew when among Jews (1 Cor. 9:20). Paul's life simply does not read as that of an apostate Jew. Paul affirmed that he was innocent of offense against Torah or temple (Acts 25:8) or the Jewish nation or their customs (Acts 28:17). When he was falsely accused of teaching the diaspora Jews to abandon (*apostasia*, "to apostatize from") the Law of Moses, he publicly complied with Jewish customs of observance.

James called the Jewish Christians gathered in Jerusalem to celebrate Pentecost "zealous for the Law" (Acts 21:20), underscoring their passionate commitment to continued observance of the Torah. That these first-century Jewish believers still conformed to the precepts of Torah even though no longer under obligation to do so (Rom. 10:4; 2 Cor. 3:6–11; Gal. 3:10–25; Heb. 8:1–13) demonstrates the strong connection between Torah, the nation of Israel, and Jewish identity. To Jewish residents of Israel, Torah observance was not just a theological commitment but also a national and cultural one. To abandon the Torah not only would have been disloyal and unpatriotic, but it was viewed as tantamount to the discarding of Jewish identity.

Freedom from the Law must entail the freedom either to keep the Law or not; otherwise it is not true freedom. The testimony of the New Testament is that under most circumstances, the early Jewish Christians chose to exercise their freedom in Christ by practicing either Torah-observant or semi-Torah-observant lifestyles. At a minimum, Paul's words should be decisively instructive regarding practical, daily application of both Testaments to our lives. "All Scripture is inspired by God and profitable for teaching, for reproof, for correction, for training in righteousness; that the man of God may be adequate, equipped for every good work" (2 Tim. 3:16–17).

Where, then, does this leave the observance of Hebrews' recipient community of Jewish Christians and the concerns of its author? Was he not advocating a complete abandonment of all Jewish customs and a complete separation from Jewish observance? May it never be! The letter of Hebrews is less concerned with what is practiced by the community than who is trusted (or distrusted) by them. It is one thing to enjoy the observance of Jewish customs and incorporate them into the faith lifestyle of a confident and identifiable believer in the Messiah; it is quite another to abandon open messianic commitment by slinking back into Judaism as a system of faith. That level of disobedience represents an altogether different paradigm than what we see exemplified through Peter, James, and Paul. It is a failure of faith in Christ, a collapse of messianic trust, and is rightly considered by God to be rebellion.

Study Questions

1. Explain what is meant in Hebrews by image and substance. How do these concepts apply to the author's argument?

2. What indication does the text provide that the Levitical system is still functioning at the time of Hebrews' composition?

3. What makes Jesus' sacrifice superior?

4. What prompted this commentary to describe the author of Hebrews as having "gone nuclear" in his argument?

5. What is the evidence that Jesus' sacrifice has finality?

6. What is the role of Torah, if any, in the lifestyle of believers in Jesus?

Section II

Practical Application
Of the Supremacy
Of the Messiah

Hebrews 10:19–13:25

CHAPTER 13

Exhortation to a Lifestyle of Faith
Hebrews 10:19–39

Preview:

Hebrews 10:19 marks a new concentration and approach in the letter. While the previous division was primarily theological in nature with occasional patches of application, the final division is the opposite. Now the focus is on the application and integration of the letter's abundance of theological truths concerning the Messiah's supremacy into the community's lifestyle and outlook. This section is loosely structured as an inclusio framed by the repetition of the noun parresian, "boldness," "freedom of access," in 10:19 and 10:35. Hebrews 10:19–39 argues that the theology laid forth in 7:1–10:18 must find practical expression in the recipient community. Specifically, the writer contends that the superior access to God that believers now possess through Jesus should result in a superior lifestyle of faith (10:19–25); he warns of the danger inherent in living an inferior lifestyle of faithlessness (10:26–31); and finally, he encourages his readers to persevere in their still characteristically faithful lifestyle (10:32–39).

Superior Access to God Must Yield a Superior Lifestyle of Faith (10:19–25)

Hebrews 10:19 heralds the commencement of a new section with a sprightly "therefore" (an inferential *ouv*) that takes the entirety of 7:1–10:18's argument and thrusts it forward toward the writer's fresh discussion of practical application. The section is neatly structured around three exhortations (10:22–24) that are connected to the three great Christian virtues, faith (10:22), hope (10:23), and love (10:24).

173

As he has done previously (3:1, 12), the author articulates his emotional connection to his readers as fellow believers by appealing to them as brothers prior to making his case as well as by using the first person plural ("we"). In preparation for his issuing forth of three exhortations, he first supplies the motivational source underlying the exhortations.

The believers are now in possession (*echontes*, "since we have") of two magnificent certainties. First, we have a "great priest" (*hierea megan*, a thematic echo of 4:14's *archierea megan*, "great high priest") supervising "the house of God" (3:1–6). Jesus is firmly managing the affairs of His people.

The second magnificent certainty possessed by believers is the "confidence to enter the holy place by the blood of Jesus." The word *parrēsian*, usually straightforwardly translated "confidence" or "boldness," actually conveys the more robust idea of "freedom of access" and "openness." The reason we can possess a bold or confident attitude is that we possess superior access to God's throne of grace (4:16). We need not be as the Levitical high priests, annually approaching the Holy of Holies in a spirit of tentative timidity. Rather, our approach should be characterized by temerity as we daily enter into the very presence of God. This special access is something of which Israel's high priests could only have dreamed, that of unlimited daily, intimate, ever available authorization to enjoy a personal audience with the Most High. This superior access, of course, has only been made possible *en tō haimati Iesou*, "by means of Jesus' blood."

This access is by a new (*prosphaton*, "fresh," a word that appears only here in the New Testament) and living pathway (*hodos*, "road") that the Messiah has inaugurated (*enekainisen*, a word that appears in the New Testament only here and in 9:18) on our behalf. Jesus Himself tutored his disciples in this concept, teaching that He exclusively is "the way, and the truth, and the life" (John 14:6).

This pathway runs directly through the heavenly sanctuary's veil (9:3), which is identified here as His flesh. Typological or metaphorical language is employed to make the point that just as a thick curtain restrained free access into God's presence in the earthly tabernacle, so, too, in His incarnation, Jesus' human body served as a barrier to God's presence. At Jesus' death, the veil in the temple was torn and access into the Holy of Holies was opened, temporarily (Matt. 27:51; Mark 15:38; Luke 23:45). The breaking of Jesus' body, like the tearing of the veil, opened the way into God's presence, permanently.[1] Jesus has unveiled God for us.[2]

The first of three exhortations is with respect to faith (10:22), calling believers to continually draw near (*proserchōmetha*, present middle subjunctive) to God. This is the exact same word and tense as used in 4:16's earlier, parallel invitation to draw near to the throne of grace. God's presence may be entered with a sincere heart and in full assurance of faith. The phrase "having our hearts sprinkled from an evil conscience" is the author's use of ritualistic, priestly language to indicate the justification and positional sanctification that believers possess through the metaphorical application of Christ's blood. "Having been sprinkled," reflects the perfect passive form of *rhantizō*, "to sprinkle." This signifies that our salvation occurred at a previous moment in time yet has continuing effect, as well as that that this cleansing process was something that was done to us by another party and that we ourselves played no role in making it happen.

The phrase "our bodies washed with pure water" has engendered a variety of interpretations, with some seeing it metaphorically related to Levitical ritual and most others taking it as a reference to baptism. As with the related parallel phrase, "having been sprinkled," the word translated "washed," *louō*, is likewise in the perfect passive form. This signifies, first, that the washing occurred at a previous moment in time yet possesses continuing effect, and second, as with the parallel phrase concerning sprinkling, this cleansing process was something that was done to us by another party and we ourselves played no role in making it happen. Most likely it is an allusion to one of Ezekiel's prophetic contributions to the provisions of the new covenant, specifically that of spiritual regeneration. God promised through the prophet that He would "sprinkle clean water on you, and you will be clean; I will cleanse you from all your filthiness" (Ezek. 36:25).

The second of the three exhortations is with respect to hope (10:23), calling believers to "hold fast the confession of our hope without wavering" (3:6, 14; 4:14). The content of our hope is, of course, our Great High Priest Jesus who, through cleansing us, has enabled our access to God. The adjective *aklinē*, "without wavering," "steady," is used nowhere else in the New Testament, appearing here to remind us to remain steadfast in our faith. When trouble presents itself and faith begins to swerve, steering into the spiritual skid requires the retention of our focus on Jesus, for "he who promised is faithful." We can hold fast to our hope because the object of our hope, Jesus, will never let us go.

The third of the three exhortations is with respect to love (10:24). The author calls his readers to carefully consider (*katanoeō*, "to ponder," "to study," a word used in 3:1) how to stimulate one another to love and good deeds. This admonition precludes the sort of casual "hail fellow, well met" attitude one experiences so frequently in the twenty-first-century church. So many of us consider the weekend a certified success by simply dragging our bodies (and those of our kids) into the church sanctuary, smiling pleasantly (if plastically) at our neighbors, and enduring the ensuing service. If while we are sitting there we carefully consider or ponder anything, it is what we intend to eat for lunch, and if we were to study anything, it might be the clock.

The sort of mutual encouragement and stimulation spoken of in Hebrews is miles away from the congregational experience of many believers. The word translated "stimulate" is *paroxusmos*, from which we get our word *paroxysm*. The English word means "to convulse" as well as "a sudden violent emotion or action." Unfortunately, many of us can probably agree that this definition is more congruent with a typical church experience than the stimulation of anyone to love and good deeds. The definition of *paroxusmos* as "stimulation" conveys both a positive and negative connotation. It is used only one other time in the New Testament, and that is of the "sharp disagreement" between Paul and Barnabas (Acts 15:39). May this exhortation in Hebrews energetically be taken to heart in churches and serve as a much needed corrective to any deficiencies in our congregational fellowship.

Requisite to the development of any manner of deep, mutual, and encouraging fellowship among believers is their regularly coming together in assembly. Hebrew 10:24's exhortation with respect to love would be stillborn if all believers followed the "habit of some" in "forsaking" their "assembling together" (10:25). What might provoke a contingent of believers to abandon regular communion with their fellow house church members is not revealed here and may only be surmised based on the forthcoming information in this passage concerning persecution and hardship (10:32–36). In an echo of 3:13's parallel exhortation, the believers are called to battle doubt, indifference, and apathy with mutual encouragement (*parakaleō*, a meaning-rich word that, along with encouragement, also encompasses the idea of exhortation, correction, help, and counsel) of community members toward one another.

The reference in 10:25 to "the day" has been understood in various ways. There are only three other such absolute references in the New Testament where the phrase "the day" stands alone without modification (Rom. 13:12; 1 Cor. 3:13; 1 Thess. 5:4), and in each of these uses the meaning is clear in context.[3] Hebrews' citation of "the day" is unique in that it appears in the text apparently independent of context, at least upon first glance.

The phrase is usually understood as Jesus' second coming, a shortened form of the well-used formula "the Day of the Lord." However, since the immediate context of Hebrews 10 has not been particularly eschatological, this identification should be seen as a reasonable, but inconclusive, choice.

Alternatively, in the specific context of the warning passages, "the day" may refer to the impending judgment on the Jewish nation resulting from its leaders' imprudent actions in falsely attributing the power of Jesus to Satan.

This gathering political storm was certainly foreseeable ("as you see the day drawing near") by Judean and Jerusalem residents as the seeds of the Roman revolt began to be sown. This identification is another reasonable choice.

A final possibility is that what the original readers were meant to understand by "the day" is how the term is used in Jewish tradition, as shorthand for the Day of Atonement. Rabbinic literature often refers to this holiday as simply *ha Yom*, "the Day," the ultimate, definitive day. The name the Mishnah gives to its tractate entirely devoted to the Day of Atonement is *Yoma*, "Day." Certainly, Day of Atonement ritual and concern have been interwoven throughout the immediate context and that which precedes it. This identification seems the most reasonable and combines thematic elements of the previous two interpretations. The return of Jesus at the dawn of the messianic age to both judge the world and rescue His people Israel, along with the nation's repentance and salvation, will be the ultimate fulfillment of the Day of Atonement.

Fourth Resultant Warning of Danger: Concerning the Inferior Lifestyle of Faithlessness (10:26–31)

The argument now arrives at its fourth warning, which arises from the immediately previous discussion of the lifestyle of faith. The possible failure of the community to exhibit a faithful lifestyle, to allow themselves to buckle under and give in to external pressure and internal doubt, fear, indifference, or apathy would prove a most hazardous course. In short, the product of an inferior lifestyle would be an abbreviated life. This warning should be considered a parallel, complementary treatment of that previously issued in 6:4–6. The more impassioned, sophisticated restatement of concern of 10:26–31 reflects the theological foundation the author has laid since the prior warning in the intervening text of the argument (7:1–10:18).

This fourth warning may be correctly assessed through synthesizing its content with that of the three warnings issued thus far and interpreting that content in the contextual framework of the author's argument. His expressed concern has centered on the danger of his readers "drifting away" from their trust in Christ (2:1–4), their following in the rebellious doubtfulness of their ancestors (3:7–4:13), and their stubborn refusal to trust God's power to deliver (6:4–6).

It has already been established that the danger to the community lay not in the presence of isolated instances of doubt, apathy, fear, and so on, nor even in these trends beginning to form a problematic, habitual pattern. The true danger rested in the accelerated coalescing of these trends and patterns into the spiritual equivalent of "the perfect storm," one single irrevocable and decisive sin, that of "falling away" (6:6). Once committed, while it can be forgiven, it will nonetheless unleash a devastating consequence that cannot be undone. Deviation of allegiance from the all-sufficiency of the Messiah to the insufficiency of Judaism's Levitical system would result in their shifting themselves into a category reserved for discipline. God held that specific generation of national Israel responsible for their leadership's rejection of His messianic provision, and they would be severely judged for their sin. The gravity of this fourth warning and its tension is heightened through the author's repetition of the adjective *phoberos*, "terrifying," in 10:27 and 10:31.

The section begins in 10:26 with *gar*, "for," connecting the forthcoming warning of danger with the author's previously expressed concern regarding the failure of community members to assemble for messianic worship (10:25). The author begins with a conditional ("if") statement, using the first person plural and including himself with his readers ("if we"). The expressed condition is the community's continuance in sin (*hamartanonton*, present active participle meaning "to go on sinning").

This is no ordinary sin, however. The sin is modified by the adverb *hekousios*, "willfully," "deliberately," "intentionally," a word that appears in the New Testament only here and in 1 Peter 5:2. In the Greek text, *hekousios*, "willfully," is actually the first, and therefore most emphatic, word in the sentence and expresses a conscious, intentional attitude "that displays contempt for God."[4] The word suggests the idea of deliberation. That the author of Hebrews framed the initial concern as conditional indicates that thus far no member of the community had yet committed this sin. However, it was under consideration.

Under their present circumstances, a calculated return to Levitical Judaism possessed an undeniable appeal—the same powerful appeal to doubt and fear that seduced the Exodus generation into turning back from the Land of Promise (Num. 14:1–35). The Exodus generation's decision to yield to their fear instead of to their God proved ruinous to the nation. An entire generation had not only deprived themselves of the enjoyment of God's blessing but had grievously incurred his wrath. The Jewish Christian addressees of Hebrews were likewise flirting with disaster. To abandon the Christian community was no mere social decision; it was first a theological denunciation of their Christian confession; second, a declaration that they had found the Messiah's ability to save somehow deficient; and third, an endorsement of their preference for the Mosaic over the new covenant.

At the climax of Hebrews' theological argument (10:18), the author's final summation was that since Christ provides a level of divine forgiveness, of comprehensive internal cleansing, that was unavailable through the Levitical priesthood, no one in his or her right mind would settle for the inferior external cleansing of the Mosaic covenant. Yet settling is just what this sin entails, and not without grave consequences. In this instance, those who choose to live by the Law will die by it as well.

The Torah's legislation made no provision for those guilty of willful, deliberate sin, that sin defiantly committed with a rebellious, high-handed attitude (Num. 15:29–31), such as idolatry, murder, adultery, or blasphemy. There was no available Levitical sacrifice for covenant infidelity of such magnitude that it warranted capital punishment. This "temporal discipline"[5] for covenant infidelity entailed the termination of the offender's physical life, not his or her eternal rejection by God.

For Jewish believers of this generation who deliberately choose this defective path of defection after having received full knowledge of the saving truth of the Messiah, "there no longer remains sacrifice for sins." Note that although many translations modify "sacrifice" by adding the indefinite article "a," it is absent in the original Greek text.[6] Instead of being a helpful addition to make clearer the meaning, it has instead confused some into thinking this verse teaches that Christ's sacrifice is somehow rescinded through commitment of this willful sin. This is nonsense and a view based not on the text but on a translation. What this does mean, however, is that none of the Mosaic legislation's 613 commandments, stipulations, and statutes had the power to address the rebels' situation and cover this specific sin. They would trade the all-sufficient for the insufficient, and exchange a potentate for the impotent.

Those believers guilty of this sin should not expect absolution but rather "a certain terrifying expectation of judgment." In 10:27 the author includes a quotation from Isaiah 26:11 concerning the outpouring of fiery judgment on God's adversaries. Fire, or the promise of fire, as the divine means of physical judgment is found often in the Old Testament, especially in the Torah (Lev. 10:1–2; Num. 11:1–2; 16:35; Deut. 32:21–22). By committing this sin, the Jewish believers have placed themselves in an adversarial position toward God; this is not a healthy choice, all things considered.

According to a quoted combination of Deuteronomy 13:8 and either 17:6 or 19:15 (the latter two verses containing parallel content), anyone who has set aside (*athetasas*, "to have violated") the Law of Moses as established by the testimony of two or three witnesses would die without mercy (10:28). The author employs the rabbinic rhetorical technique of *qal vachomer*, "light and heavy," the application of truth about that with lesser significance to that with greater significance, which is usually recognizable by the telltale "How much more so?" comparisons (2:1–4; 10:28–29; 12:25). He reasons that if Jesus is superior to Moses and the new covenant superior to the Mosaic, then it stands to reason that the punishment for violation of the superior would be much severer than for that which is inferior.

The problem for interpreters of these warning passages has always been this: When execution is the comparative starting point, how much qualitative room is left for an escalation in severity? A greater sin necessarily requires a greater punishment. Yet the punishment for violation of the Torah is death. What is the nature of the punishment that fits this particular crime spoken of in Hebrews? This interpretive challenge, plus the reference to fiery judgment in 10:27, is why so many see in this passage eternal damnation.[7]

> However, it is better, both in light of the content of the previous three warning passages and contextually, to reject the notion that a "severer punishment" necessarily entails damnation and that fiery judgment necessitates hellfire. As previously discussed in the comments on 2:1–4, to see spiritual death here as opposed to physical death overvalues the *qal vachomer* ("lesser and greater") contrast, imagining that since the punishment for disobedience to the lesser covenant resulted in physical death that disobedience to the far greater covenant would logically result in that which transcends the physical realm, eternal damnation. The text in no way warrants this level of escalation. Randall Gleason reasons: "Rather than greater in 'kind' (i.e., spiritual death rather than physical death), the severity could refer to a physical punishment greater in degree or force than that previously experienced by the Old Testament examples."[8]

The nation of Israel and the residents of Jerusalem in particular would face an unprecedented outpouring of wrath sometime within the next decade. How soon that would be depends on the proximity of Hebrews' composition to AD 70 (see *Date of Composition* in Background of Hebrews). The unpardonable sin of Jewish national rejection of Jesus and the consequent forthcoming judgment (Matt. 23:35–36; Luke 11:50–51: Acts 2:40) would result in the devastation of the entire region of Judea. Jerusalem, the city that kills her prophets (Matt. 23:37), was destined to be ravaged with fire and left desolate; its vaunted temple would be destroyed (Matt 24:2). The severity of this concentrated outpouring of God's wrath is incontestable. With an estimated first-century Jewish world population of some eight million of whom three million lived in Israel, almost one million Jews were killed in the war against Rome and another ninety-seven thousand led away as slaves.[9] It was, as Josephus recorded, the most catastrophic war that had been waged to date in recorded history.[10]

Note that the rebellious sin of the Jewish believers would cause the forfeit of their lives, not of their salvation. Salvation, once divinely granted, is never ours to forfeit. As those who had once trusted in the Messiah, they enjoyed irrevocable spiritual benefits and therefore would never be deprived of God's eternal salvation.

In 10:29 the author explains the far-reaching extent of this sin. It demands nothing less than the rejection of the ministry of the entire Trinity, reflecting on the ministry of all three members of the Godhead. First, it affects the Father in that His Son's ministry is treated with contempt. Those who dishonor the Son dishonor the Father as well (John 5:23). The sinner is one who "has trampled under foot" (*katapateo*, "to tread upon," "to treat with disdain") the very Son of God, an example of the epitome of flagrant spiritual chutzpah. The word *katapateo* is used only here and twice each by Matthew and Luke in reference to treating something of great value as if it were contemptibly powerless, like trampling insipid salt (Matt. 5:13), or worthless, like throwing pearls before pigs (Matt. 7:6) or trampling casually disseminated seed (Luke 8:5).

Second, it affects the Son in that not only has He been "trampled under foot," but also His blood has been regarded as unclean. Christ's blood is called "the blood of the covenant," which is an allusion to the Exodus 24:8 quotation the author previously cited in 9:20. At His Last Supper, Jesus Himself identified the third cup of Passover wine as symbolizing "the new covenant in His blood" and thereby announced the covenant's inauguration (Matt. 26:28; Mark 14:24; Luke 22:20).

The adjective translated "unclean" is *koinos*, "common," which is used in the New Testament to indicate that which is ceremonially impure, unholy, or common, such as unwashed hands (Mark 7:2, 5), nonkosher food (Acts 10:14), or unsaved Gentiles (Acts 10:28). To regard the Messiah's blood as being *koinos* is to regard it as ordinary, no better or superior than any other sacrificial blood, which is completely contrary to what the author of Hebrews has been arguing throughout his letter (9:7, 12–14, 18, 20–22; 10:4, 19, 29; 11:28; 12:24; 13:11, 12, 20).

For known believers to imagine either that the Messiah's sacrifice was no better than the Levitical sacrifices or to question its unique sufficiency to provide a definitive purification for sins and then to openly reassociate with the Levitical system of worship would be a humiliating affront to the Son of God, one that would require punishment. This action would unambiguously associate them with the generation already under judgment. The word translated "punishment," *timorias*, appears nowhere else in the New Testament. In other ancient Greek literature, it conveys a sense of vindictiveness or retribution, "a punishment meant to satisfy a sense of outraged justice, the defense of one's honor or that of a violated law."[11]

The idea of regarding the Messiah's blood as common is parallel to 6:6's warning against reducing Christ's death to the level of a common criminal execution. A public return to the animal sacrifices of the Levitical system would, in effect, empty Christ's death of any sacrificial, redemptive value (cf. Heb. 7:26–27; 10:26). The extraordinary irony is that this is the very blood by which these same believers have received their positional sanctification and retain their eternal salvation ("by which he was sanctified").

Third, it affects the Holy Spirit, called here "the Spirit of grace," in that the sinner has insulted Him (*enubrizo*, "to insult," "to abuse," "to treat with reproach," a word that appears only here in the New Testament). This is a direct reference to the unpardonable sin, the sin for which that generation of Israel was under judgment (Matt. 3:7; 12:22–45; 23:35–36; Luke 11:50–51; Acts 2:40). The Jewish leadership had dismissed Jesus' messianic identity and, consequently, the messianic kingdom, through their ruinous accusation that His miracles were demonically empowered. Jesus identified their rejection as blasphemy against the Holy Spirit. This was considered Israel's formal, national rejection of their Messiah, and Jesus consequently pronounced irrevocable divine judgment on the entire generation (Matt. 12:22–45).

Divine discipline is required for a believer who is guilty of this sin and of the accompanying theological implications enumerated above concerning offense to the ministry of the Trinity. This sin reidentifies the rebellious Jewish Christian with the faithless nation. The author, to ensure that his readers do not miss the substance of this warning (as if he had been at all obscure at any point in the argument), links together two consecutive Old Testament quotes dealing with God's vengeance (Deut. 32:25) and judgment (Deut. 32:36 or perhaps the parallel text of Ps. 135:14), once again underscoring the adversarial position toward God into which they were placing themselves.

He closes this fourth warning with another use of the adjective *phoberos*, "terrifying," declaring that it is "a terrifying thing to fall into the hands of the living God" (10:31). This is an evocative echo of David's words in 2 Samuel 24:14 when, after sinning by commissioning a national census, he was forced to chose between three forms of judgment. He reasoned that the best choice was to "fall into the hand of the LORD for His mercies are great." Consequently, seventy thousand Israelites died by pestilence within the three allotted days of wrath. The lesson from that passage is that even though God's mercies are great, tens of thousands of Israelites still suffered death for a sin that their king had committed. A nation is always held responsible for the actions of its leaders. God's justice was satisfied by seventy thousand deaths; His mercy was exercised by the fact that the rest of the nation survived, including David and His family. The judgment encroaching on Israel in the first century would likewise reveal that even when He shows mercy, it is nonetheless terrifying to fall into the hands of the living God.

Encouragement to Persevere in a Faithful Lifestyle (10:32–39)

This section provides a fleeting insight into the possible motivation for the sort of failure the community is warned against in 10:25–31. The author begins 10:32 with *de*, "but," in order to contrast the nightmarish scenario he has just described with his confidence in the community based on his personal knowledge of them and their history. He urges them to remember (*anamimnēskesthe*, a mouthful in any language, meaning, "to remind," "to recall") their early days as believers, the period subsequent to their "being enlightened" (*photizō*, the same word used to describe their having come to faith in 6:4). As an aid to this "walk down memory lane," the author leaves no possibility that they will fail to grasp his point and spells out for them the specific areas of recollection he has in mind.

He turns to the language of sports metaphor to describe their experience, reminding them that they had endured (*hupomenō*, "to endure") a period of persecution ("sufferings"), likening it to having successfully competed in a grueling wrestling match (*athlēsis*, a word that appears only here in the New Testament, meaning "athletic contest," "fight"). Their persecution was characterized in three ways.

First, they had been made a public spectacle (*theatrizō*, "to hold up to derision," "to bring up on stage to be stared at," a word that appears only here in the New Testament and from which we derive the word "theater"). The community, as the talk of the town, had been publicly mocked and ridiculed through verbal insults (*oneidismois*, "revilings," "reproaches") and through abusive acts of violence and confiscation of property (*thlipsesin*, "afflictions," "tribulation").

Second, the community had expressed passionate solidarity (*koinōnos*, "partners") with other believers who had likewise experienced persecution. Here is another indication that this particular church was part of a much larger network of house churches in the immediate surrounding community of Jerusalem or nearby Judea (see Recipients in the introduction). To those who had been imprisoned for their faith, the community had exhibited sympathy (*sumpatheō*, "to suffer alongside," "to show compassion," a word used in the New Testament only here and in 4:15 of Jesus' quality as High Priest).

Third, upon having their possessions either looted by the neighborhood or seized by the authorities (*harpagēn*, "plunder"), they nonetheless retained an attitude of joy properly aligned with their messianic perspective. In the midst of callous persecution, they remembered that no matter what temporary possessions had been lost to them, they had the divine promise of superior (*kreittōn*, "better," see Use of "Better" in Hebrews on p. 39), permanent (*menō*, "to remain") property (*huparxis*, "goods," "wealth," "possessions") that could never be stolen.

This permanent property or possession has been understood in two ways. The first view is that the "community property" is eternal salvation. However, in 10:35–36, this same property is again referenced along with the disclosure that its receipt is conditioned on obedience. Eternal salvation, which is never conditioned on performance (Eph. 2:8–9; Titus 3:5–7), cannot be in view.[12] The alternative, preferable view is that of eschatological reward. This view sees the property as an echo both of Jesus' appeal to store up treasures in heaven (Matt. 6.20) as well as the crowns awarded to faithful believers at the judgment seat of Christ (2 Cor. 5:10). The readers' previous experience of persecution can be connected to incidents described in Acts (8:1; 12:1ff.; 22:19; 26:11), each of which included the requisite elements of public slander, abuse, imprisonment, and confiscation of personal property.

Based on his readers' commendable track record of faithfulness under pressing circumstances (*ouv*, "therefore"), the author encourages his readers to "stay in the game" and avoid losing heart. Just as their previous behavior in crisis proved exemplary, so, too, they must not discard (*apoballō*, "to throw off") their attitude of *parrēsian*, "bold confidence" (that quality to which they were urged to hold fast [3:6] and with which they were to draw near to God's throne [4:16], as well as the word recently used [10:19] to convey their "access" to that throne).

Their exercise of this confidence is characterized as inherently possessing *megalēn misthapodosian*, "a great reward." This should be understood as synonymous with the "better possession" of the previous verse. The qualifying adjective, *megas*, functions just like the idea behind our prefix of "mega," meaning something akin to "intensely awesome and most excellent." The word translated "reward" appears only in Hebrews 2:2; 10:35; and 11:26 and nowhere else in the New Testament, the Septuagint, the Apocrypha, or any known Greek literature prior to the first century.[13]

This whole chapter, thus far, has been characterized by the author's dazzling use of language.[14] The reason for his fast and furious, concentrated burst of ten-shekel vocabulary words was not to show off his education; that was evident from the initial lines of the epistle. The use of rare vocabulary words was a rhetorical technique designed to captivate an audience. It would have been especially effective in an orally delivered letter like Hebrews. This is in contrast with prevailing twenty-first-century communication theory, which directs communicators to speak on an eighth-grade level and, at all cost, avoid the use of highfalutin' language for fear of coming off as pretentious or being misunderstood.

In 10:36 the author returned to the previous matter of endurance (10:32). The community would need this quality to accomplish God's will, which is to exercise the sustained obedience He desires for them. Through obedient endurance, they will receive "what was promised."

The author bolsters his encouragement through the use of two Old Testament quotations linked together in 10:37-38 for rhetorical effect. The first quote is a brief snippet of Isaiah 26:20, which highlights the imminence of the Messiah's return, "in a little while." This is immediately followed by a modified citation (again, to enhance the author's rhetorical effectiveness) of Habakkuk 2:3-4. The original prophecy of Israel patiently waiting for God's deliverance has been massaged to instead reference God's deliverer, "He who is coming." Until the Messiah's return, not only is the community directed to live by faith, but also the Messiah Himself ("My righteous One") is so described. His faithfulness will not diminish or "shrink back," providing for the believers an example of perfect messianic faith for them to emulate.

This example will strengthen the readers' resolve not to fall away (6:6) through the commission of the defiant sin of rebellion (10:26). It will hearten them on to their eventual receipt of a great and permanent reward (10:34-36). The exercise of their faith will keep them from aligning themselves with the nation under judgment and will therefore preserve their lives (*psuchē*, a word with a complex meaning that ranges from the material, "lives," to the immaterial, "souls," and every nuance in between; the context and theology of Hebrews necessitates the physical aspect). Alternatively, as they already had been warned four times, a failure of faith and a triumph of fear would lead to their "destruction"[15] (10:39) in the impending outpouring of divine wrath against the Jewish generation who had rejected His Son.

This section concludes with the author's confident, even boisterous, assertion (*hēmeis de,* "but we," in the emphatic position at the top of the sentence) that neither he nor his readers are of a temperament to withdraw (*hupostolēs,* "to shrink back," a word that appears nowhere else in the New Testament, the Septuagint, the Apocrypha, or any known Greek literature prior to the first century) from their Christian commitment. Both writer and readers would persevere in a faithful lifestyle.

Conclusion

In 10:38-39's references to the faith of both Christ and of the readers, the author has subtly introduced the main theme of his subsequent chapter—

faith. There his readers will be reminded of their ancestor's lifestyles of faith to encourage them toward perseverance.

Study Questions

1. What two certainties are believers in possession of in 10:19–21?

2. What are the advantages of assembling together with other believers? The disadvantages of not assembling? Defend your answers.

3. What is the willful sin, and how does it reflect on the members of the Trinity?

4. What does this chapter reveal about the history of the community?

5. What incentives, positive or negative, has the author provided to persevere in a lifestyle of faithfulness?

CHAPTER 14

Evidence of the Lifestyle of Faith
Hebrews 11:1–40

Preview:

In the previous section, the author encouraged his readers to patiently endure their present circumstances in light of their receipt of future promises. He now provides a cornucopia of biblical examples of men and women whose faithful lifestyles evidenced this pattern of patience. This whole section can be considered a follow-up to and a development of his previous reference to "those who through faith and patience inherit the promises" (6:12). What follows is a brisk saunter through select Old Testament personalities from Genesis through Joshua followed by a swift canter through the remaining books as praiseworthy witness after witness is presented in chronological sequence for the readers' consideration. Each witness shares the common trait of possessing an enduring faith that powerfully sustains his (or her) confident hope that God's promises will find eventual fulfillment.

This chapter contains a textbook example of rhetorical anaphora, the concentrated repetition of a key word at the beginning of a sentence or clause for heightened effect, in this case, pistis, "faith," which is employed twenty-three times. The distinctive style of this division of Hebrews sets it apart from the rest of the letter. While it is a necessary development of the letter's argument between chapters 10 and 12, respectively, it nonetheless could stand alone as a literary unit quite nicely. It neatly takes its place in that culture's common literary subgenre of cataloging noteworthy personages for motivational purposes.[1] Antiquity provides two excellent Hellenistic Jewish examples from that era. First is the second-century BC's apocryphal Sirach, whose catalog commences with the quotation borrowed by James Agee, "Let us now praise famous men and our fathers that begat us."[2] Second is the intertestamental book of 1 Maccabees, which recounts the events surrounding the origins of the holiday Hanukkah and contains a catalog of biblical personalities, articulated by dying patriarch Mattathias, which appears cut from the same literary template as that of Hebrews 11.[3]

187

The Outcome of Faith (11:1–3)

Hebrews 11:1 is perhaps the most familiar verse in the entirety of Hebrews, and with good reason. The statement succinctly and timelessly synthesizes the author's heartfelt admonition to the recipient community of readers and, by extension, every subsequent reader as well. The understanding of five key words in this verse and the next, as well, is critical to correctly grasping the point of the writer.

The first word is *pistis*, translated "faith," or "faithfulness." This is confident belief directed toward the Lord, specifically a trust or reliance on His ability to fulfill His promise(s). The faith exercised in these examples is not completely blind faith in the absence of tangible evidence. Faith is not the optimistic fruit of imagination; it is the reasonable extrapolation of existing evidence into a realistic hope. In short, it is the belief that since God has done *this* in the past, we may possess confidence that He will also do *that* in the future.

Use of Old Testament Passages in Hebrews 11

Hebrews	Old Testament	Subject
11:3	Ps. 33:6–9	Divine creation
11:4	Gen. 4:3–10	Cain and Abel
11:5	Gen. 5:24	Enoch
11:7	Gen. 6:13–7:1	Noah
11:8	Gen. 12:1–5	Abraham
11:9	Gen. 23:4; 26:3; 35:12–27	The patriarchs
11:11	Gen. 18:11–14	Sarah
11:12	Gen. 22:17	The Abrahamic covenant
11:13	Gen. 23:4	The patriarchs
11:17	Gen. 22:1–10	The binding of Isaac
11:18	Gen. 21:12	The Abrahamic covenant
11:20	Gen. 27:27–29, 39–40	Isaac's blessing of Jacob and Esau
11:21	Gen. 47:31; 48:15–16	Jacob's blessing of Joseph's sons
11:22	Gen. 50:24–25	The death of Joseph

Hebrews	Old Testament	Subject
11:23	Exod. 1:22–2:2	The birth of Moses
11:24	Exod. 2:10–15	The maturity of Moses
11:28	Exod. 12:21–30	The Passover
11:29	Exod. 14:21–31	The Exodus
11:30	Josh. 6:12–21	The conquest of Jericho
11:31	Josh. 2:11–12; 6:21–25	Rahab
11:32	Judg. 6–8	Gideon
11:32	Judg. 4–5	Barak
11:32	Judg. 13–16	Samson
11:32	Judg. 11–12	Jephthah
11:32	1–2 Samuel; 1 Chronicles	David
11:32	1 Sam. 1–16	Samuel
11:33	Dan. 6:1–27	Daniel
11:34	Dan. 3:23–25	Shadrach, Meshach, and Abed-nego
11:35	2 Kings 4:32–37	Elisha and the Shunammite's son
11:36	Jer. 20:2; 37:15	Jeremiah
11:37	2 Chron. 24:21	Zechariah the son of Jehoiada

The second word is *hupostasis*, a word that was previously discussed in the comments relating to 1:3 and 3:14. While it is often translated in a subjective sense as "confidence or "assurance," it is best in Hebrews to consistently focus on its more objective sense of "substance," "essence," or "nature." Of the five appearances of the word in the New Testament, three of those occasions fall within the pages of Hebrews, so interpretive caution must be exercised. While in the case of 3:14 and 11:1 it may be understood to vaguely convey either confidence or assurance, it is, nonetheless, best to carefully translate the term consistently with its previous usage at the top of the book, that is, as a foundational basis or grounding substance from which our assurance may amply flow.

The third word is *elpizō*, "to hope." This is the expectation of desire. The objects of hope in Hebrews are the fulfillment of God's promises. The fourth word is *elegchos*, properly translated "conviction" or "proof." The fifth word, found in 11:2, is *martureō*, "to testify," "to witness," which was previously employed in reference to the Holy Spirit's testimony of the new covenant (10:15). This word is often translated in 11:2 as "commended," "received commendation," or "gained approval." However, since there is no compelling reason to assign the word anything other than its primary definition of "witness," nor any compelling reason to deviate from the author's usage in the immediately preceding context, it is best to understand this aorist passive verb as "received a testimony." Chapter 11 is, after all, a testimonial to those whose lives operated by means of faith.

With this understanding of these five key words, Hebrews 11:1–2 should be understood to read, "Now faith (the confident belief in God's ability to carry out His expressed purpose) is the substance (the foundational basis or essence underlying any attitude of assurance) of that which is hoped for (our certain expectation that God will make good His promises), the personal conviction that what is at present not yet personally seen, enjoyed, or grasped will, nonetheless, become objectively realized in the future. This is the testimony of our predecessors in faith." For the readers, this meant that life in the present could and should be lived in the confident light of the glorious future God had planned for them. God's promises are not theoretical, but certain; it is this guarantee that can fuel the engine of a faithful lifestyle dedicated to patient endurance.

Hebrews 11:3 initiates the unit's pattern of beginning a series of sentences with the emphatic placement of the dative noun *pistei*, "by faith," at the head of a series of sentences. He begins his ode to the outcome of faith with the preliminary premise that faith commences in each life with the initial recognition that God is the creator of the time-space continuum. The term *aiōnas*, generally translated "universe" or "worlds," finds its primary meaning in the concept of "ages" (see comments on 1:2). This is, of course, a "shout out" to the Genesis 1:1–2:1 account as well as a patent allusion to the poetic description of creation in Psalm 33:6–9. The recognition of divine handiwork echoes Paul's observation in Romans (Rom. 1:20).

Paragons of Faith (11:4–40)

Paragons of Faith: Prior to the Patriarchs (11:4–7). Having established the necessary introduction to the outcome of the faith lifestyle, the author begins his series of testimonials to those Old Testament figures, "paragons of faith," who exemplified this model. This list illustrates what the author had in mind when he mentioned the men of old who received a testimony (11:2). He underscores these testimonials with the thematic affirmation that it is impossible to please God in the absence of faith. Two elements of faith are categorically absolute, in that not only must one believe in the existence of God, but that for those who seek Him, He is "a rewarder" (*misthapodotēs*, "wage payer," which appears only here in the New Testament)—that is, one who is characteristically and reliably in the business of keeping His promises.

The excursion through the Old Testament begins with the faith of Abel in contrast to that of his brother Cain (Gen. 4:3–10). While both brothers offered sacrifices to God, Abel's was considered by God to be "a better sacrifice." Over the millennia, countless efforts have been expended in the attempt to demonstrate what made Abel's sacrifice superior to that of Cain. As the Hebrew text provides no explanation for the discrimination, speculation has extended from content of the sacrifices (livestock versus agriculture) to execution of proper sacrificial ritual. The answer lies in this very text. Abel's sacrifice was considered acceptable because it was offered by means of faith; it was his faith that enabled him to receive a "testimony" (*martureō*, aorist passive form just as in 11:2) "that he was righteous." This correlates with the Lord's statement to Cain, encouraging him to do what was right and be accepted (Gen. 4:7). The author encourages his readers by affirming that Abel's faith timelessly continues to testify to all subsequent faithful generations.

The second paragon of prepatriarchal faith is Enoch. Although this mysterious figure is mentioned only briefly in the Old Testament as one who "walked with God" (Gen. 5:24), Enoch has nonetheless played a disproportionately hefty role in Jewish thought, with good reason. The author of Hebrews' point is that Enoch is the epitome of the faith lifestyle under discussion. According to Genesis, so great was his righteousness that Enoch completely bypassed death through being taken or translated (*metatithēmi*, "to transfer," "to translate," "to change") by God into His presence. This action of divine translation, along with the case of Elijah and the chariots of fire (2 Kings 2:11), provides substantive Old Testament precedent for the New Testament expectation of a future Christian rapture (1 Cor 15:51–52; 1 Thess. 4:16–17), which would have been a significant hope for the readers of Hebrews.

Enoch plays a large role in the writing of the intertestamental period, particularly in the apocryphal book bearing his name, 1 Enoch, in which he evolves into the superhuman figure Metatron, the chief of angels, and is later seemingly identified as the Messiah (1 Enoch 71:14–17).[4] Enoch rates specific mention in additional apocryphal works, such as Jubilees (4:17; 10:17) and especially Sirach (44:16; 49:14), which speaks of Enoch's unique example of repentance. Most notable is the New Testament's quotation of 1 Enoch 1:9 in the book of Jude.

The third paragon of faith is Noah, the exemplar of those who exhibit the personal conviction that what is at present not yet personally seen will, nonetheless, become objectively realized in the future (1:11). Through faith, Noah saw the future as present certainty. Having received divine warning of future disaster, Noah reverently snapped into action, preparing "an ark for the salvation of his household." If construction had been delayed until after the initial raindrops had splashed the ground, Noah's family would have been lost. This extraordinary, unprecedented venture surely invited community ridicule, but scorn never trumps faith; rather, faith condemns the faithless.

Paragons of Faith: The Patriarchs (11:8–22). The next paragons of faith are the patriarchs, of whom, of course, Abraham, the "the believer" (Gal. 3:9), or man of faith, takes pride of place. Of all the testimonials to faith provided in this chapter, Abraham receives the most extensive treatment. The origin of the Abrahamic covenant is highlighted, along with Abraham's eager willingness to be a charter participant in God's enduring plan. God's promises to Abraham required of the patriarch the possession of a long-term perspective, for in the short-term, that of the life spans of Abraham and his immediate descendants, nothing tangible was realized except their own obedience.

Having received the Lord's call and completely lacking acquaintance with his final destination, Abraham abandoned his home country for a new home-land, one that was promised by God Himself. For this patriarch of patriarchs, God's promise of a future inheritance was sufficient cause to take the initial steps of the journey and each subsequent step thereafter (Gen. 12:1–5). Abraham's faith was "a response of trust to the God who had promised."[5] Explains F. F. Bruce, "Even when he received the promise of the inheritance, it was the promise that he received, not the visible possession of the land; but to Abraham the promise of God was as substantial as its realization."[6]

Throughout his lifetime, Abraham lived in his own land (*gēn tēs epaggelias,* "the land of promise"; the only time this familiar phrase actually appears in either Old or New Testaments) as a tent-dwelling transient (*paroikeō,* "to dwell alongside, to reside as a foreigner"). Although the Abrahamic covenant granted ownership of the land by divine decree to the patriarch and his son Isaac (Gen. 23:4; 26:3) and grandson Jacob (35:12–27), they only formally owned one diminutive portion, the cave of Machpelah (Gen. 23:17).

The author explains that Abraham's perspective was based on expectations that far exceeded that of a receipt of a national homeland in which to pitch his extended family's tents. Abraham's faith involved a forward-looking perspective that realized the "certainty of future hope."[7] The Promised Land was just an appetizer. For Abraham the main course was the heavenly Jerusalem, the transcendent city of cities, the apex of architectural contemplation, whose *technitēs*, "designer," and *dēmiourgos*, "builder" (a word used only here in the New Testament), is God Himself. The heavenly Jerusalem, the crowning climax of God's provision, is no innovation by the writer of Hebrews retroactively foisted upon the hopes of the patriarchal heroes. Rather, this very natural Jewish expectation is briefly described in John's Revelation (3:12; 21:1–22:5), and the author cites, without explanation, clarification, or qualification, his own expectation of this city (Heb. 12:28; 13:14).

In 11:11 the writer transitions from the Abrahamic covenant's Land of Promise to that of promised son. Based on the English translation, it is relatively easy to misread this verse as concentrating more on the faith of Sarah than on that of Abraham. Nonetheless, the focus remains on Abraham's faith. His wife, who was undoubtedly dubious about the enterprise of a first-time pregnancy at her advanced age (Gen. 18:11–14), merits mention in association with Abraham. Based on the Genesis account, it appears that by this stage in their marriage, certain activities had ceased. However, since it takes two to tango, the sufficient faith of both partners in once again donning their dancing shoes and reacquainting themselves with the dance warrants mention.

In the Greek text, it is clear that Abraham was the one who, by faith, *dunamin eis katabolēn spermatos elaben*, "received power to produce sperm," a graphic detail often smoothed over in translations designed for public pulpit consumption. That Abraham's potency is in view is confirmed by the following verse's characterization of Abraham as one who was "as good as dead." The author cites Genesis 22:17 to make the point that Abraham and Sarah's faithful participation in extraordinary circumstances would be the instrumental means through which God would fulfill the Abrahamic covenant's promise of innumerable descendants.

In 11:13, the writer argues that Abraham and his family died without experiencing the fulfillment of any covenant promises, whether of land, nation, or universal blessing (Gen. 12:1–3, 7; 13:14–17; 15:1–21; 17:1–21; 22:15–18; see comments on Heb. 6:13ff.). Rather, this delay of covenant realization did not shake their faith, for they recognized their current status as *zenoi kai parepidēmoi*, "strangers and sojourners," on the *gēs*, "land" (not earth, as in some translations, since the context is the land promises of the Abrahamic covenant [Gen. 23:4]). Their faith was of a quality that assumed their *patris*, "homeland," would be theirs to enjoy in a future age of resurrection. Never looking backwards to their ancestral Haran or Ur, the patriarchs looked forward to their receipt of the Promised Land and beyond that to their aspiration (*oregō*, "to strive after") of citizenship in the heavenly city of Jerusalem.

The testing of Abraham through the attempted offering of his son Isaac (Gen. 22:1–10) provides the climactic illustration of faith by which to conclude the author's discussion of Abraham. As discussed earlier in the detailed comments on 6:13ff. regarding the Abrahamic covenant, the "binding of Isaac," traditional Jewish thought and liturgy have seen the patriarchs' righteous acts of faith as a means of atonement that could be vicariously applied throughout the future history of their descendants, the entire nation of Israel, in time of spiritual need. This view developed through early rabbinic teaching that Abraham actually went through with the sacrifice of his son, shedding Isaac's blood and then immolating him. Michael Brown comments:

> This same thought is also carried over in a prayer still included in the additional service for the Jewish New Year (Rosh Hashanah), which culminates with the words, "Remember today the Binding of Isaac with mercy to his descendants." We are forgiven through the merit of the sacrifice of Isaac! The rabbis even taught that the final resurrection of the dead would take place "through the merits of Isaac, who offered himself upon the altar" (Pesiqta deRav Kahana, 32).[8]

According to *Encyclopedia Judaica*, medieval rabbi Ibn Ezra "quotes an opinion that Abraham actually did kill Isaac . . . and he was later resurrected from the dead. Ibn Ezra rejects this as completely contrary to the biblical text. . . . Such views enjoyed a wide circulation and occasionally found expression in medieval writings."[9]

The traditional Jewish connection of the Genesis story to the concept of bodily resurrection neatly aligns with the understanding of the writer of Hebrews. The author firmly asserts that as Abraham and son set forth upon their portentous journey, the patriarch's expectation of the eventual outcome was nothing less than that of a divine undoing of Abraham's sacrificial act. As the Lord had affirmed earlier to Abraham, it would only be through Isaac that the chosen nation of covenantal promise would be called (Gen. 21:12). Therefore, in order for the program to proceed as divinely pledged, any harm that was to come upon Isaac, the son of promise, even to the extreme extent of loss of life, would necessitate the Lord's intervention. Indeed, the author points to the account of "the binding of Isaac" as a prophetic type (*en parabolē*, "in a foreshadowing").

In 11:20 the author logically propels his argument forward by transitioning from the faith of Abraham to that of his son. Isaac is the next paragon of faith in this chapter. While a continued focus on the "binding," this time from the son's perspective, certainly would have been satisfactory to illustrate the point, the author instead shifts the focus of Isaac's faith chronologically forward to his covenantally charged blessing of his own son of promise, Jacob

(Gen. 27:27–29), and the prophetically charged blessing of his firstborn, Esau (Gen. 27:39–40), regarding things to come.

The reversal of the normal genealogical order of priority in Isaac's first blessing the younger son (albeit unintentionally) is again exhibited, this time with acute intention, in Jacob's blessing of his grandsons through Joseph (Gen. 48:15–16). Ephraim is purposely given preferential position by his grandfather over Ephraim's older brother, Manasseh, through the location of Jacob's hands during the blessing. Although Joseph, prior to the blessing, attempted to correct his father through repositioning Jacob's right hand from atop the younger grandson's head to that of the elder, Jacob persisted in his intention to testify to God's unambiguous preference for Ephraim. The author's reference in 11:21 to Genesis 47:31's reference to "Jacob leaning on his staff" reflects the inherent ambiguity of the original unpointed, vowel-less Hebrew text. While the Septuagint's Greek translation reads "staff," the same word is alternatively understood by the Masoretic Hebrew text as "bed."

Having transitioned from Abraham to both son and grandson of Abraham, the patriarch's great-grandson Joseph is the next example of the author's enumerated paragons of faith. Genesis 50:24–25 reveals that while on his deathbed, Joseph's faith was penetratingly manifested. Aware of the divine promises made to his family through the Abrahamic covenant, Joseph reminded his children of the future certainty of their eventual exodus from Egypt, instructing them to return his body to their homeland for burial in the Land of Promise.

Paragons of Faith: The Exodus Generation (11:23–31). The next section concerns that giant in Jewish life, thought, and imagination, Moses, as well as those in both his immediate and extended sphere of influence. Moses was literally birthed and nurtured in an atmosphere of acute faith. He came into the world at a critical turning point in the Israelites' history, in the year 1526 BC. Paralyzing fear and devastating loss swept through Egypt's Jewish slave community as they were compelled to comply with Pharaoh's decree that all male Jewish babies be destroyed. However, Moses' parents, Amram and Jochebed, realized that their son was a unique and special child of destiny (*asteios*, "externally elegant," "possessing nobility of form," a word used elsewhere only once in the New Testament, also of Moses [Acts 7:20]). Their perception enabled faith to surmount fear (a spiritual lesson of no small importance to the recipients of the epistle of Hebrews). After keeping the baby hidden for three months, it became clear that his family could no longer protect him. Jochebed preserved her son's life by placing him in a basket and floating him down the Nile to the royal house of Pharaoh (Exod. 1:22–2:3).

From the faith of Moses' parents, the author transitions to that of Moses himself. Having been raised for four decades in the royal court and possessing the elevated legal designation as "the son of Pharaoh's daughter," Moses nonetheless renounced his royal position and accompanying power by choosing to associate instead with the Hebrew slaves (Exod. 2:10–15). Continued maintenance of his Egyptian privileges would have constituted his participation in "the passing pleasures of sin" (11:25). As did his parents before him, Moses possessed a future perspective (*apeblepen . . . eis*, "continually looking forward to") that enabled him to withstand Egypt's temporary abuse and mistreatment of a slave in order to receive God's permanent reward. The treasures of Egypt paled in comparison to the bounteous provision of the Lord. The author refers to Moses' suffering as *ton oneidismon tou christou*, "the reproach of the anointed one." Although some translations read *christos* here as "Christ," that is, Jesus, it is better to understand this as referring to Moses himself, God's chosen vessel to both liberate and lead His people. In successfully delivering Israel from Egyptian bondage, even after enduring great suffering, Moses serves as a type of Christ, who delivered the church from the bondage of sin.

Having slain an Egyptian and been rejected by the Hebrews (Exod. 2:13–15), Moses exercised his faith by fleeing Egypt and entering into exile in the unfamiliar wilderness of Midian. Once again the author explicitly underscores the principle of faith overcoming fear, explaining that Moses did not fear the wrath of the king because he maintained his future, God-based perspective (*horōn ekarterēsen*, "he kept seeing continually," a fixed idiom, as Lane explains[10]).

Forty years later, upon his return to Egypt and series of ten confrontations with Pharaoh, Moses faithfully observed the stipulations of the initial Passover, commanding the Hebrews to faithfully execute God's command concerning the application on their doorposts of the blood of a perfect lamb (Exod. 11:1–12:30). Apart from those whose profound faith led them to take such appropriate action, divine judgment on the firstborn of all Egypt was universally experienced. For the recipients of Hebrews, this was a reminder that, once announced, God's judgment is certain. As he devastated Egypt, He would judge the generation that had rejected His provision of His Son. At this hour, any attempt to temporarily wipe away or cover over the saving blood of the Lamb of God was unthinkable.

In 11:29 we transition from Moses to the Hebrews themselves. Although throughout his argument thus far the author has left not a shred of doubt concerning the nation's egregious lapse of faith once having arrived in the Sinai wilderness (see especially 3:16–19), he nevertheless draws attention to their example of faith in crossing the Red Sea (Exod. 14:15–31). Overcoming any initial fear, misgiving, or incredulity, the Exodus generation pressed forward onto the dry seabed, resulting in their salvation and the Egyptian army's doom.

Completely skipping over the disastrous absence of faith exhibited throughout the forty-year period of wilderness wandering, the writer transitions to the conquest of the Land of Promise. Led by Joshua, the Hebrews followed God's prescription to encircle the imposing and impenetrable walls of Jericho seven for seven days. By faith, the city walls came cataclysmically tumbling down (Josh. 6:12–21).

Rahab joins Abraham's wife Sarah as the only other woman mentioned in Hebrews 11 but surprisingly supersedes the matriarch in that, unlike Sarah, Rahab has the distinction of being introduced as a paragon with the specific phrase "by faith." As a native of Jericho, Rahab was not a Hebrew, yet she exercised faith in the Hebrew God, protecting Israel's spies and recognizing the supreme power of God as manifested in current local events (Josh. 2:11–12; 6:21–25). Possessing a powerful future faith perspective, Rahab did not hesitate in endangering her own life for the Lord's sake. Her faith perspective resulted in her own physical salvation in contrast to the utter destruction of her fellow citizens of Jericho. Rather than remain associated with a people under divine judgment, Rahab's faith led her to choose decisive identification with the people of God. Rahab's clarifying faith choice at a moment of profound crisis would eventually result in her listing in the rather restricted assemblage of Jesus' ancestors (Matt. 1:5).

Paragons of Faith: Israel's National History (11:32–34). At this point, the author varies his rhetorical approach, transitioning from his formula of cataloging individual "faith paragons" separated through the emphatic placement of the dative noun *pistei,* "by faith." Sensing the weighty length of his argument thus far, he segues into a rapid-fire inventory of notable names and noteworthy accomplishments from Israel's historical record.

The section is set apart from that which came previously by the author's use of the rhetorical question "And what more shall I say?" (11:32). This was "a common homiletical and literary idiom for indicating that time and space are limited."[11] Like an Egyptian mummy, the author was pressed for time and pointed out that "time will fail" him were he to relate (*diēgoumenon,* "to narrate fully") the names of any more faith paragons. However, clever rhetorician that he is, the writer then proceeds to enumerate those whom he claimed to have no time to list. This is a common rhetorical practice known as paraleipsis, a technique artfully and universally employed by politicians and orators throughout time and culture, wherein the speaker pretends to avoid mentioning the exact thing that he then proceeds to mention.[12] The use of the masculine singular participle *diēgoumenon* removes any possibility that the epistle of Hebrews could have been composed by a woman or that it was a product of dual authorship, effectively eliminating the Priscilla or Priscilla-Aquila theory of composition (see the introductory discussion on authorship, as well as Candidates for the Authorship of Hebrews beginning on pp. 8).

Six men of biblical renown are listed whose lives and careers extend from the era of the judges to that of Israel's monarchy. The names are not listed in chronological order, and while some have attempted to identify a pattern in pairs[13] or other arrangements, it is best simply to take these as an abbreviated assortment of Israel's best-loved heroes. The judge Gideon (Judg. 6–8) receives first mention. He was the hero whose lopsided victory over the Midianites was achieved by faithfully following God's counterintuitive instructions to reduce his army from 32,000 to a mere 300 fighting men armed with trumpets and clay jars.

Next on the list is Barak (Judg. 4–5), the successful commander of Israel's forces in the conflict with Sisera and his army of nine hundred manned iron chariots. It is surprising for some readers to see Barak on this list, considering his rather embarrassing reticence to go to war without the prophet Deborah "holding his hand" (see Judg. 4:8). Nonetheless, once on the field, Barak proved himself every bit the military hero and faith exemplar.

The third paragon of this section is the judge Samson who led his people through a period of Philistine oppression (Judg 13:1–16). While his moral choices were occasionally startling and even self-destructive, he is never presented in Scripture as anything less than God's chosen instrument for the hour, a man of great faith who, through the power of God and to the end of his life, struggled mightily against Israel's enemy.

The fourth paragon is the judge Jephthah (Judg 10:6–11:39). In the biblical account of Israel's victorious encounter with the Ammonites, Jephthah is presented as an extraordinarily gifted military leader and a man of great faith. It could be argued that even his unfortunate vow, that rash act for which he is most remembered in modern readers' minds, was a product of his faith.

Next on the list is David, Israel's beloved monarch and sweet psalmist. Of all the biographical accounts in Scripture, the life of David consumes the most literary real estate (1 and 2 Samuel; 1 Chronicles). More space is devoted to the story of David's life and its impact on Israel than any other figure, even Moses. As the man after God's own heart (1 Sam 13:14) and recipient of the covenant that bears his name (2 Sam. 7:8–16; 1 Chron. 17:8–14), David is unquestionably a paragon of faith whose example the readers of Hebrews would do well to remember.

The final man of biblical renown and paragon of faith to be mentioned by name on the list is Samuel (1 Sam. 1–16), the transitional figure who was

Israel's final judge prior to the establishment of the monarchy and founder of the nation's established prophetic line.[14] Samuel's citation is immediately followed by mention of the entirety of the prophets who followed him in Israel's history. Through the centuries and generations, Israel never lacked for God's prophets to serve as paragons of faith.

In 11:33–34 the author transitions from examples of faithful individuals to that of accomplishments successfully brought forth through faith. These accomplishments are listed with no parenthetical explanations as to which individuals were involved and, therefore, presume of the readers an extraordinary knowledge of Israel's history and essential familiarity with the text of Hebrew Scripture. Of course, writing as he was to a recipient community of first-century Jewish believers, the author could presume that liberty for his purposes of reminding them of faith's paragons. These two verses contain nine clauses that can thematically be clustered into three groups of three.

The first three clauses, addressing conquering kingdoms, laboring for justice (*eirgasanto dikaiosunēn*, often regrettably translated "performed acts of righteousness"), and obtaining promises, appear to be directly related to the specific accomplishments of the six figures enumerated in the previous verse. The second of the three sets of three clauses deals with celebrated deliveries from death, such as Daniel's escape from the "mouth of lions" (Dan. 6:1–27), the escape of Daniel's friends Shadrach, Meshach, and Abed-nego from the "power of fire" (Dan. 3:23–25), and any number of occasions throughout Israel's history when the nation's many heroes and prophets "escaped the edge of the sword." The third of the three sets of three clauses again centers around the specific accomplishments of the six figures enumerated in 11:32. Samson was made strong in weakness, as was Gideon against Midian and David against Goliath. Each of the six figures "became mighty on war" as well as "putting foreign armies to flight."

Paragons of Faith: Amid Trials (11:35–38). This section advances to focus on those whose exercise of faith did not result in deliverance but rather led to suffering and martyrdom. For the recipients of Hebrews, there could be no more pointed or weightier set of examples to demonstrate that the life lived by faith triumphs over all, even death.

While there are examples in the Hebrew Scripture of God raising the dead, these are the exception, never the rule. The cited women who received back their dead by resurrection were the widow of Zarephath (1 Kings 17:17–24) and the Shunammite woman (2 Kings 4:18–37), both of whom saw their sons resurrected through the power of the respective prophets Elijah and Elisha. Although it is true that God had done many stunning miracles and performed a plethora of spectacular deliverances throughout Israel's history, the exercise of faith provided no guarantee that bound God to an immediate positive response. A martyr's death was the consequence for countless members of the Hebrews community's ancestors and remained a very feasible destiny for them as well if they could but retain their courage and not lose heart. Possession of faith provided no automatic immunity.

The theological concept and practical expectation of resurrection did not truly capture the imagination of the Jewish people until the fairly recent events surrounding the origin and establishment of the holiday of Hanukkah, that is, the Maccabean revolt against Antiochus IV and the Syrian Greeks of 167–164 BC. It was at this time that numerous Jews accepted imprisonment, torture, and execution rather than renounce their faith in the God of Israel, assured that they would "obtain a better resurrection." This life was not the conclusion of existence, and death would be defeated through the exercise of faith in the eschatological future. The temptation to temporary apostasy in exchange for reduction of persecution that the Hebrews community currently faced was in no way unique to that generation. The faithful Maccabees were tortured (the chosen word *tumpanizō*, from which we derive the name of our orchestral instrument, the tympani, means to torture by beating upon like a drum.[15] The famous Jewish story retold each Hanukkah of Hannah and her seven sons, all seven of whom chose martyrdom rather than renounce their faith, would have been a prime example of those whose faith enabled them to endure in order to achieve a "better resurrection" (2 Macc. 7:1:42).

Both alternatively and occasionally in addition to eventual martyrdom, Israel's history is replete with examples of the faithful experiencing scorn and derision (*empaigmos*, "verbal abuse"), flogging (*mastigōn*, "scourges"), and imprisonment, as had the prophet Jeremiah (Jer. 20:2, 7–8; 37:15–20; 38:6–13). Members of the Hebrews community had also endured such mistreatment because of their faith (10:32–34). Tradition records that Jeremiah's life ended in martyrdom as he was stoned in Egypt by Jews who rejected his message. Stoning, this time in the courts of the temple itself, was also the fate of another prophet, Zechariah (2 Chron. 24:20–21; Matt. 23:27, 35; Luke 11:50–51; 13:34). It was also the infamous fate of the first Jewish Christian martyr, Stephen (Acts 7:58–60), and either was or soon would be (depending on the date of Hebrews' composition) the fate of James the brother of Jesus.[16] This particular fate was a very real possibility for the epistle's recipient community.

According to both Jewish and Christian tradition, another prophet who met his destiny through martyrdom was Isaiah, who was executed by King Manasseh by being "sawed in two."[17] Other faith paragons "were tempted" to renounce their faith, and others were "put to death with the sword," as was the prophet Uriah (Jer. 26:20–23). Most notable was the apostle James, the first of the

Twelve to be executed (Acts 12:2). Still others experienced economic privation, clothed "in sheepskins and goatskins" like Elijah, and were "destitute, afflicted, and ill-treated," as were many of God's other prophets, who "wandered in deserts and mountains and caves and holes in the ground." These were those whose faith qualified them, the author notes, as men of whom the world (this present age, not the one that is to come) was not worthy (11:38).

The Promised Goal of Faith (11:39–40). Chapter 11's final pair of verses serves to summarize and reiterate the chapter's preceding argument and testimonial to those whose lives operated by means of faith. The members of Hebrews' great "hall of faith" all received a testimony (*martureō*, aorist passive form as in 11:2, 4; not, contra some translations, "gained approval"; see above discussion of definitions). These paragons of faith retained a future-oriented perspective, trusting that they would eventually receive every scintilla of what God had promised them and their people. The messianic age and accompanying kingdom was awaited with patient endurance and profound anticipation.

The author explains that the delay in God's fulfillment of His promises to the Old Testament believers resulted from His awaiting church participation. Both Old and New Testament believers, being connected through our common faith, will share in the fulfillments of those promises. Together we will enter into and enjoy the unprecedented blessings of the messianic age. It took the inauguration of the new covenant though the death and resurrection of our Messiah, along with the establishment of participants in that covenant, for any of God's people to enjoy the perfection God has made possible. For all believers of every dispensation and era, Jesus is "the author and perfecter of faith" (12:2) who "has perfected for all time those who are sanctified" (10:14). Through His sacrifice, Jesus has perfected the faithful for all time and through all time (12:23, also see Use of "Perfect" in Hebrews on p. 247).

Conclusion

The provision of a substantial litany of examples of faith paragons from Israel's history in this chapter served the author's essential purpose at this point in the epistle's argument of promoting and propping up the wobbly faith commitment of the recipient community, which had already endured a considerable measure of hardship (10:32–34) and which was far from complete (12:1–4). Each listed witness in chapter 11 shares the common trait of possessing an enduring faith that powerfully sustains the confident hope that God's promises will find eventual fulfillment.

> For the person of faith, the future is no longer insecure. . . . The firm expectation of the reward is a matter of unwavering hope in God who has

disclosed the future through the word of his promise. Faith holds onto the promise, even when the evidence of harsh reality impugns its integrity, because the one who promised is himself faithful.[18]

Study Questions

1. Which of the five key words of 11:1–2 is most meaningful to Hebrews' argument? To you personally? Why?

2. Are you surprised by the inclusion of any specific individual(s) in this listing of paragons of faith? Why or why not?

3. Is there any paragon(s) of faith omitted by the author in this chapter whom you would have included had you been the author? On what basis would you include that person(s)?

4. Consider what you would be willing to endure for the sake of your faith. What will sustain you if you are forced to sustain them at some future point? How many of the listed deprivations and hardships have you already endured in your life?

5. Do you possess a future-oriented faith perspective? How can you foster that perspective and kindle it in others?

CHAPTER 15

The Enduring Lifestyle of Faith
Hebrews 12:1-29

Preview:

This chapter marks the progression of the author's argument from his historical perspective concerning those who had exhibited exemplary levels of faith to a contemporary perspective concerning the recipients' dire need to maintain a sufficient measure of endurance. The example of the faithful paragons of Israel's past should serve to mature the community's present experience of the enduring lifestyle of faith. Faith is but the first component of this lifestyle and must lead beyond short-term spiritual retrogression or stagnation and into long-term perseverance. Chapter 11's inspiring history lesson must now make way for the challenge of chapter 12's rousing exhortation. To that end, at the center of the author's challenge is the example of Jesus who, while absent from the previous chapter's explicit content, now returns as the key to the argument of chapter 12.

The Model and Measure of Endurance (12:1-4)

The chapter begins with the word "Therefore" (NASB) or "Consequently" (*toigaroun*, a word that, although commonplace in contemporary Greek literature, is only used in the New Testament here and in 1 Thess. 4:8), clearly linking the basis of this chapter's exhortation with the content of the preceding chapter. Having thus established the members of the "hall of faith," the author now refers to them as the "great cloud of witnesses" that surrounds the recipients.

This concept is often interpreted from the pulpit and Sunday school classroom through conjuring up the vivid image of Christians as participants in an athletic competition taking place in an arena or stadium. So far so good. The author unquestionably employs athletic imagery and metaphor in this section. Paul, too, speaks of the Christian life in the analogical language of popular athletic contests (see esp. 1 Cor. 9:24–27; also Gal. 2:2; 2 Tim. 4:7; et al.).

However, where the popular interpretation of this verse fails is in its appreciation of the term translated "witnesses," *marturon*. This word is related, of course, to the previous chapter's familiar verb *martureō*, "to testify," and indicates those who, through their exercise of faith, had in their lifetimes received a testimony to their faithful endurance. In short, rather than this verse suggesting the roar of robe-wearing, banner-waving stadium crowds cheering us on from their tightly packed seats from bullpen to bleachers, with perhaps Samson pumping a brawny arm in the air as he and the others root for us, the portrait presented in the text of Hebrews is of martyrs who continue their ministry through current testimony to the church's contemporary believers. "It is not so much they who look at us as we who look to them— for encouragement."[1] They are no passive audience, but rather a collection of faith VIPs whose body of accomplishments spur us on to achieve comparable greatness for the glory of God. Those who have preceded us on the path of faith continue to speak. This was true at the time of Hebrews' composition, and it remains true in the twenty-first century.

The accomplishment of the lifestyle of enduring faith requires the stripping away of every encumbrance that will impede our successful completion of the goal. To remain nimble, Greco-Roman athletes of the ancient world competed while wearing as little as possible. The phrase *ogkon apothemenoi panta* ("lay aside very encumbrance") means that anything that might handicap the race, trip us up, or weigh us down must necessarily be cast off. This goes beyond mere distractions, diversions, preoccupations, or concerns (*euperistaton*, "that which entangles"). It is sin that causes the Christian runner to stumble. The word translated "sin" possesses the definite article, which could be understood to mean sin as a general concept and as opposed to specific sins, but in the context of Hebrews, it most likely indicates the specific sin that threatened the Hebrews community, that of a return to Judaism as a system of relating to God. The Mosaic covenant was the excess weight that needed to be cut loose in order for the recipients to reach the finish line without being tripped up (10:38–39).[2]

The author's exhortation is for the faith community to keep on running the race (*agōna*, "athletic contest," from which we derive our word *agony*) set before them with *hupomonēs*, "persevering endurance." The Christian life is not a sprint, but a marathon, a lifelong, often "agonizing" pursuit of God and the lifestyle to which we have been divinely called as believers since the moment we first trusted Jesus for salvation. Awaiting us at the finish line is that same Jesus, on whom we are to fix our eyes with resolute intensity and concentrated focus (*aphorōntes*, present active participle, "keep on looking").[3]

Use of Old Testament Passages in Hebrews 12

Hebrews	Old Testament	Subject
12:2	Ps. 110:1	The divine authority of the Son
12:5–6	Prov. 3:11–12	Divine discipline
12:7–9	Deut. 8:5	Divine discipline
12:12	Isa. 35:3	Encouragement to live a sanctified life
12:13	Prov. 4:26	Encouragement to live a sanctified life
12:16–17	Gen. 25:33–34; 27:30–40	Jacob and Esau
12:18–19	Deut. 4:11–12; 5:22–27	Israel's Sinai experience
12:18–20	Exod. 19:12–23; 20:18–21	Israel's Sinai experience
12:21	Deut. 9:19	Israel's Sinai experience
12:23	Gen. 18:25	God as Judge
12:24	Gen. 4:10	Cain and Abel
12:24	Jer. 31:31	The new covenant
12:26	Exod. 19:18	Israel's Sinai experience
12:26	Hag. 2:6	Divine judgment against God's enemies
12:29	Deut. 4:24	Divine judgment against God's enemies

Jesus is described here with two complementary designations. He is the *archēgos*, "the champion," "the leader," the pioneering source and heroic author of faith. This is a rare messianic title that is used by the author of Hebrews in 2:10 (picturing Jesus as author of salvation) and 12:2 and only an additional two times in the New Testament in Acts (3:15; 5:31). He is also the *teleiōtēs* (a unique term found nowhere else in the New Testament or in Greek literature), "the perfecter," "the completer" of faith, who, through His magnificent accomplishment, now serves as the very embodiment of faith itself.

In the trials He faced as He ran His own faith race during His period of incarnation, Jesus maintained a future-oriented faith perspective. He was able to endure the cross by focusing on the joy set before Him when He would be invited to take His rightful, glorious seat at His Father's right hand (Ps. 110:1; Heb. 1:3; 2:5–9; 8:1–2; 10:12–13). The phrase *aischunēs kataphronēsas* is often translated "despising the shame" (of the cross). Rather than understanding the phrase as conveying a negative feeling of scorn or distain, it should be understood in the positive sense of "disregarding the shame" and humiliation associated with execution by crucifixion. "Any discussion of this passage must take serious note of the agony of death by crucifixion, doubtless the most despised form of death in the Roman Empire, reserved for the worst offenders"[4] and from which Roman citizens were exempt.[5] The result of Jesus' faithful endurance through the worst of circumstances was the enjoyment of the greatest of circumstances, His exaltation. The author uses the perfect tense of *kathizō* ("to sit"), indicating Jesus' continuous enthronement and position of authority.

The text of Hebrews urges its readers to "consider" (*analogisasthe*, "to calculate," "to compare and reflect," from which we derive the word *analogy*, is a word that appears only here in the New Testament, literally meaning "up with reason") Jesus' endurance of personal hostility by sinners. This calculation of the intensity of Jesus' suffering and consideration of the massive level of hostility, opposition, and scorn endured by Jesus when measured against any persecution or pressure being presently experienced in the lives of the recipient community would provide the community an indispensably corrective perspective. The profoundly simple antidote for those growing weary and losing heart is personal reflection on the experience of Jesus. He is faith's Alpha and Omega, both the source of faith and its completion.

At the point of Hebrews' composition, the recipient community had endured a veritable cornucopia of persecution (see comments on 10:32–34) but had not yet experienced martyrdom. They had not yet (!) resisted (*antikatestēte*, "to oppose," appearing only here in the New Testament) to the point of shedding blood in their striving (*antagōnizomenoi*, "to contest against," another word appearing only here and from which we derive our word antagonism) against sin.

The Relationship between Discipline and Endurance (12:5–11)

The author develops his argument by explaining that the experience of persecution, suffering, or hardship, although harsh hurdles to surmount, are often manifestations of divine discipline (*paideia*, a word that can be translated as a plain vanilla "discipline," in practical biblical usage conveys more of the idea of "instruction with robust bite") designed for the good of the believer. This provides fresh perspective on the relationship between God's discipline and our endurance, helping readers to connect the dots between divinely overseen suffering and developmental spiritual maturity.

In 12:5 the recipients are gently chided for being oblivious (*eklelēsthe*, "having altogether forgotten") to the encouragement (*paraklēseōs*, "exhortation," "comfort") of the book of Proverbs' definitive statement on the subject of divine discipline. God is characterized as *dialegetai*, "speaking" through His word to the readers, addressing them as *huie mou*, "my sons."

The author proceeds to quote Proverbs 3:11–12. The insertion of the quotation serves two purposes in contributing to the author's argument. First, it demonstrates the principle that God disciplines those whom He loves. Second, it demonstrates that the receipt of discipline is a blaring indication that the disciplined is indeed a child of God, revealing a Father's love and commitment. "God disciplines his people, collectively and individually, to draw them closer to himself."[6]

The author develops the Proverbs quotation in 12:7–11. His introductory point is that disciplinary instruction of children is universally familiar and cross-culturally understood. There were no permissive or laissez-faire fathers in the ancient milieu of the New Testament. Twentieth-century theories of progressive parenting were still millennia distant. Without a hint of irony and without placing tongue in cheek, the author could legitimately ask the rhetorical question "For what son is there whom his father fails to discipline?" Proverbs has much to say concerning the normative discipline of fathers who demonstrate their love for their children through such action (Prov. 13:24; 19:18; 22:15; 23:13–14; 29:17).

In fact, so confident was the author of societal norms that he could affirm that the absence of discipline was indication of illegitimacy. According to William Lane, the term *nothoi* ("illegitimate," "bastard," a word appearing only here in the New Testament) "must be understood in its ancient legal sense as descriptive of those who do not enjoy the privileges of the family nor the protection of the father. They are also denied by law the rights of inheritance, which belong exclusively to . . . legitimate sons."[7] Arnold Fruchtenbaum notes that traditionally, "under Jewish law, to be *mamzer* (to be illegitimate) meant three things: no right of inheritance; no right to marry into Jewish society; and no right to be buried in a Jewish cemetery."[8] In the biblical word, a household devoid of discipline was a home where the children had been formally renounced, rejected, and disinherited.

The author's second point in developing the Proverbs quotation, initiated with a transition term *eita*, "furthermore," is a *qal vachomer* ("light and heavy") argument (a rabbinical technique in which the application of truth about that with lesser significance is compared to that with greater significance). He posits that if the discipline of the believers' natural fathers had been universally respected, how much more should believers subject themselves to the loving discipline of their heavenly Father (*tō patri tōn pneumatōn*, "the Father of spirits") whose responsibility for them extends not merely into the period of physical maturity but throughout eternity.

The author contends that the discipline of the believers' natural fathers was *kata to dokoun autois*, "at their digression," and was subject to their best intentions as filtered through their human imperfection. However, God's discipline is always for the good of His children, our spiritual maturation, specifically resulting in our partaking (*metalabein*, "to share") in His holiness (Deut. 8:5).

The author makes a final point through a reintroduction of athletic imagery. He argues that no one, at any age, enjoys the process of disciplinary instruction. However, *tois di' autēs gegumnasmenois*, "to those who have been trained by exercise," belong significant advantages. As an athlete in competition benefits from the strenuous level of preceding discipline, so, too, do believers engaged in the enduring lifestyle of faith benefit from whatever level of persecution and hardship the Lord has thus far arranged for them. The eternal dividends of the Lord's instructive discipline are the fruits of both peace and righteousness.

The Obligations Regarding Faith (12:12–29)

Encouragement to Live Sanctified Lives (12:12–17). The conclusion of the previous discussion is linked to the commencement of this section through the particle *dio*, "therefore." Having just mentioned the qualities of peace and righteousness as the fruit of the divine discipline meted out to God's children, the author proceeds with some practical encouragement in achieving those goals in the community of faith.

Sustaining the athletic metaphor previously employed, the text pictures the recipient community as a fatigued contestant, drained and listless, one not only lacking a competitive edge, but perhaps in need of a wheelchair. It is as if the author perceives his readers as some droopy balloon from which air is escaping.

His encouragement derives from a combination of two Old Testament quotations, Isaiah 35:3 and Proverbs 4:26, both of which regard the strengthening of metaphorical anatomical parts. The community was to restore (*anorthōsate*, "strengthen," "straighten") their slackened (*pareimenas*, "relaxed," "weak") hands and their enfeebled (*paralelumena*, "paralyzed," "floppy") knees. Having done so, they were then to establish straight paths for their feet. The word translated "straight," *orthos* (from which we derive the root of our word *orthopedic*) appears elsewhere in the New Testament once, concerning Paul's healing of a man lame from birth (Acts 14:10). The establishment of ethically straight paths meant that the spiritually lame limb might have opportunity to properly heal and not deteriorate. Of course, the writer's metaphor speaks of the spiritual healing of which this troubled community was in such desperate need. The stronger members of the community were thus charged to look after those members who were struggling, for no chain is stronger than its weakest link, and no community is stronger than its weakest constituent.

In 12:14 the readers are exhorted to urgently pursue (*diokein*, "to press hard after") peace throughout the community. The word translated "peace" is placed in the emphatic grammatical position at the head of the sentence (i.e., "Peace pursue . . ."), indicating the significance of this quality for the successful spiritual ambiance of the readers' community. The pursuit of peace would foster the community's holiness, the quality without which no one would see God. As Jesus Himself said on the Mount of Beatitudes, it is the peacemakers who are called God's sons, and it is the pure in heart who will see God (Matt. 5:8-9). The author provides practical guidance as to how the community may realize these qualities of peace and holiness in 12:15-17.

The community is to watch out for one another, to exercise a vigorous mutual oversight (*episkopeō*, "to oversee," "to care for with authority," like a bishop over his flock, from which we derive our word *episcopal*). The concern is that no community member comes short of the grace of God. The grace of which the author speaks certainly cannot be God's saving grace, the unmerited favor bestowed on each believer that enables initial faith (Eph. 2:8-9), nor can it reference either God's potent action in designing his plan of salvation on man's behalf (2:9; 10:29; 13:9) or His sustaining grace, both of which the author has previously written about with such powerful clarity (4:16). Rather, the grace in view is that associated with "the revelation of Jesus Christ" at the second advent, as referenced by Peter (1 Peter 1:13). Paul expressed a concern parallel to the author of Hebrews regarding the avoidance of disqualification (1 Cor. 9:27) and said that each believer would receive commensurate reward or loss (Col. 3:23-25) depending on whether the quality of his work endures the assessment of divine fire (1 Cor. 3:11-15).

The danger of community defilement springs from the development within its members of a "root of bitterness." This is the spirit of rebellion and defiance previously warned of (3:7-19). As in Israel's nascent history, ten bad apples (the faithless spies) were able to spoil the whole nation. Now, if left unchecked, the failure of one community member's faith might lead to the rebellion of another, with potentially cataclysmic, exponential results. This would result in the community's defilement (*mianthōsin*, "might be defiled"), the absolute antithesis of a community characterized by the qualities of peace and holiness.

Having already exhaustively used the Exodus generation as an illustration (3:7–4:13), the writer turns to Esau, another archetypical figure from Israel's history (Gen. 25:33–34; 27:30–40), to assist in vividly punctuating his point. Esau and Jacob were Isaac's twin sons. Genesis records the story of Esau's infamous choice to exchange his birthright (*prōtotokia*, "inheritance rights of the firstborn son," a word appearing only here in the New Testament) for one supersized fast-food order of lentil stew. His shortsighted choice to exchange a permanent inheritance in order to fulfill a temporarily felt need is surely one of the single worst business transactions in human history.

However, it is not Esau's lack of business acumen to which the writer calls his readers' attention, but is rather to his stunning level of spiritual bankruptcy. According to the author, through his action of "despising his birthright" (Gen. 25:34), Esau demonstrated a classic example of the qualities of both immorality (the writer calls Esau a *pornos*, which, although it often indicates immorality of a sexual nature [as in 13:4], most likely serves here as a counterpart to the word with which it is paired, meaning "desecrator") and godlessness (*bebēlos*, "a profaner," "an unholy one, devoid of piety") whose only god was his immediately felt needs. In Jewish tradition, Esau is considered an atheistic idolater (what breadth to his profane nature!), a reprobate, a villain, and the enemy of God.[9]

The writer continues the familiar story with the phrase *iste gar*, "for you know." Not only did Esau lose out on his inheritance rights as firstborn, but he also failed to receive the father's blessing due the firstborn son. Albeit through circumstances beyond Esau's immediate control, Isaac conferred the blessings of the Abrahamic covenant to Jacob instead (Gen 27:30–40). In reality, through his earlier disposal of his birthright, Esau no longer possessed legal claim to the firstborn's blessing, either. When Esau sought the blessing of his father, Isaac explained that it was now irreparably lost to his elder son, even though Esau sought after it with tears.

The example of Esau serves the author's argument in providing an additional opportunity to reiterate his previous warnings to the readers. The phrase "he found no place for repentance" (*metanoia*, "to change the mind") is a parallel thought to the text's earlier phrase "it is impossible to renew them again to repentance" (6:6). To wit, Esau would have been avidly devoted to a "do-over." He sincerely and emotionally regretted the action he took for the consequence it bore. Yet his loss was irrevocable and the blessing irretrievable.

As with Esau's misguided decision, once the sin of falling away has been committed, there can be no turning back from its consequences. The "falling away" of the believer is an irrevocable and decisive sin that, once committed, while it can be forgiven, cannot be undone. God's impending judgment on national Israel's first-century generation for their leaders' rejection of God's messianic provision is as certain as was His judgment on the Exodus generation following their rejection of His provision at Kadesh Barnea. Deviation of the Jewish believers' allegiance from the all-sufficiency of the Messiah to the insufficiency of Judaism's Levitical system would result in their shifting themselves into a category reserved for discipline.

In addition to 6:4–6, another previous section that parallels this theme is the warning of 10:26–31 concerning the inherent hazards regarding the community's possible failure to exhibit a faithful lifestyle and to allow themselves to buckle under, giving in to external pressure and internal doubt, fear, indifference, or apathy. Esau managed to serve as the embodiment of both the traits and the fates the writer exhorted his readers to avoid.

The Superiority of the Believer's Status (12:18–24). The author advances his argument through the use of metaphor, dramatically contrasting the believing community's former position under the Mosaic covenant with their present position of superiority under the new covenant. The Mosaic covenant is likened to Israel's terrifying experience at Mount Sinai, and the new covenant is connected with a joyful, privileged experience symbolized by Mount Zion and the heavenly city of Jerusalem.

This section is linked to the previous discussion through the conjunction *gar*, "for." The theophany at Sinai as graphically recorded in Deuteronomy 4:11–12 and 5:22–27 is recalled by the author for the express purpose of explaining that the present status of the Jewish Christian believers is not analogous to that of the Exodus generation who quaked with fear at the manifest presence of the Lord in their midst. Seven elements frame the scene, listed and linked together with the connective *kai*, "and." The cumulative effect of hearing these words rhythmically read aloud, especially the rhymes of elements three, four, and six, would have conveyed an extraordinary rhetorical punch.

First, Sinai was a tangible, physical experience that *psēlaphaō*, "could be touched." Second, the mountain was ablaze, *kekaumenō puri*, "having been burned in fire." Third, it was oppressively dark (*gnophō*); and fourth, the atmosphere was that of deep gloom (*zophō*). Fifth, Sinai was enveloped in a violent storm (*thuellē*). Blasting over the whirlwind was the eerie sound of a supernaturally blown shofar, the ram's horn (*salpiggos ēchō*). Finally, and most awesome of all, was the *phōnē rhēmatōn*, "the sound of words." This was the voice of God Himself reciting the Ten Commandments (Deut. 4:12; 5:22).

So overwhelmed with dread was Israel on hearing the voice of God that they immediately begged (*paraiteomai*, "to decline," "to be excused from") that this be the final time they be subjected to direct access to God's voice (Deut. 5:25–26). They instead requested that Moses serve as God's representative spokesman from that time forward, mediating between the nation and the Lord (Deut. 5:27). Thus it was that Moses' elevated role as mediator of God's covenant arose as a result of extensive national terror.

The author of Hebrews elaborates on the terrors of Sinai, quoting a portion of Exodus 19:12–23's thrice-repeated sanction against anyone, man or animal, making physical contact with the mountain (and thereby defiling God's manifest holiness), for which the penalty was immediate execution. Under Sinai's covenant, God was untouchable. He could be perilously and cautiously approached, but only from a distance (Exod. 20:18–21).

The text of Hebrews records that so *phoberon*, "frightful" (a word also used in Heb. 10:27, 31) was the atmosphere at Sinai that even Moses himself was *ekphobos*, "full of fear" and *entromos*, "terrified." The author's quotation concerning Moses' fear does not directly derive from the encounter at Sinai as recorded in either Exodus or Deuteronomy and, therefore, has caused some bewilderment. Most commentators allay their discomfort by suggesting that the writer of Hebrews has inserted an analogous comment by Moses made at another time (Deut. 9:19) about his fear for the nation following the golden calf incident. Alternatively, the author may have simply quoted a popularly accepted contemporary Jewish tradition.

Hebrews 12:22 initiates with the welcome conjunction *alla*, "but," arriving just in time to remind us that the Christian experience was not designed to be one of manifest dread and terror, as Sinai is described. To the contrary, the Christian believer has come to the locus of the new covenant. This is Mount Zion, the heavenly Jerusalem, and the contrast could not be more pronounced. If the Sinai experience can be thought of as a horror movie, then the experience of heavenly Zion is an endless love story.

The city to which the believer in Jesus has come (*proseleluthate*, "you have approached, from which we derive our word *proselytism*, meaning "conversion"), unlike Sinai, is not presently on the earth but has been prepared by God and will be revealed in the future. This city is designated here by three names, "Mount Zion," "the city of the living God," and *Ierousalēm epouraniō*, "heavenly Jerusalem" (a phrase that appears only here in the New Testament, but a concept that emerges throughout the text of Hebrews [11:8, 10, 16; 12:28; 13:14] and elsewhere in the New Testament [John 14:2–3; Gal. 4:26;

Rev. 21:1–22:5]). Zion was originally an alternate name for Jerusalem at the time of David's conquest (2 Sam. 5:7). Over time, and as the city of Jerusalem expanded, so did the popular designation of Zion, becoming synonymous with both the city and the Temple Mount.

The city is described as home to five groups. First, the city is resplendent with an assembly of myriads of angels (reminiscent of the imagery of Dan. 7:10). Second, the city is the natural, but future, habitat of "the general assembly" (*ekklēsia*, which may alternatively be translated here as "church") "of the first-born (*prōtotokōn*) who are enrolled in heaven" (*apogegrammenōn en ouranois*). Just as Hebrews has designated Jesus as "the Firstborn" (1:6), so, too may his body, the church, be corporately considered as firstborn. Unlike Esau, who ignominiously bartered away his *prōtotokia*, the corporate assembly of the *prōtotokos* will avoid the loss of inheritance in the city of the living God.

Understandably for an eternal residence bearing this magnitude of glory, advance reservations are required. Fortunately, all those who partake of the blessings of the new covenant have had their names permanently recorded (the author uses the perfect tense with *apographō*, indicating completed action with continuing results) in God's heavenly reservation ledger. The metaphor of a heavenly scroll or series of scrolls in which the names of God's people are inscribed or, alternatively, blotted out, is replete throughout both Old Testament (Exod. 32: 33; Ps. 69:28; Isa. 4:3; Dan. 12:1) and New (Luke 10:20; Phil. 4:3; Rev. 3:5; 13:8; 17:8; 20:12), as well as in the apocryphal literature (Jubilees 2:20; Enoch 47:3–4; 104:1; 108:3).

The concept of God's ledgers is also central to the Jewish theological understanding of the two most solemn and widely observed holy days in Jewish tradition, the Feast of Trumpets (Rosh Hashanah, Jewish New Year; see comments on 6:13ff. and 11:13ff.) and the Day of Atonement, Yom Kippur (see comments on 9:6–7), when over the ten-day period that spans the two holy days (called the Days of Awe), God actively judges the world, inscribing in His ledger those whom He will for life and for death. Considering the citation of the enrollment ledgers, it is not contextually surprising to see that the third inhabitant of the heavenly Jerusalem is God Himself, portrayed as *kritē theō pantōn*, the "Judge of all" (Gen. 18:25).

The fourth group of inhabitants is "the spirits of the righteous made perfect." These are the Old Testament saints who have preceded the church, some of whom chapter 11 spoke about with such pointed eloquence, now in God's presence and awaiting the bodily resurrection to come.

The final resident is none other than the mediator (*mesitēs*, "an arbitrator," "a go-between") of the new covenant, Jesus. Hebrews 12:18–24 is not merely a tale of two mountains, Sinai and Zion, but of two mediators, Moses and Jesus, along with their respective covenants. Here, for the only time, the writer uses an alternate word for "new," *neos*, meaning "young" or "recent." In contrast to the dark gloom of Sinai, the new covenant brings fresh air and brilliant sunlight.

It is Jesus' sprinkled blood that has initiated the new covenant and accomplished our redemption. This section closes with a contrast that perhaps would have spoken somewhat more powerfully to a first-century community than a twenty-first-century one. Just as Abel's faith timelessly continues to testify throughout all generations (11:4), so, too, does this archetypical murder victim's blood still speak, crying out for justice (Gen. 4:8–12; Jubilees 4:3; Mishnah Sanhedrin 4:5). However, the personification of righteousness has now appeared. His sprinkled blood supersedes the cry of Abel's blood and definitively answers its call for justice.

Fifth Resultant Warning of Danger: Concerning Spiritual Insensitivity (12:25–29). The argument now arrives at its final warning, which arises from the immediately prior discussion of the believers' superior status under Jesus' mediation of the new covenant in contrast to the old covenant of Sinai, and the glorious city of the heavenly Jerusalem waiting to be revealed and enjoyed in the future. This fifth warning may be correctly evaluated through integration of its content with that of the previous four warnings issued thus far and then interpreting that content in the contextual framework of the author's argument. Thus far, his expressed concern has centered on first, the danger of his readers "drifting away" from their trust in Christ (2:1–4); second, their following in the rebellious doubtfulness of their ancestors (3:7–4:13); third, their stubborn refusal to trust in God's power to deliver (6:4–6); and fourth, their deliberate expression of contempt for the ministry of all three members of the Godhead by yielding to fear and publicly endorsing the Mosaic covenant over the new (10:25–31).

The fifth warning begins with the present active imperative *blepete* ("look," "see to it"), emphatically placed at the head of the sentence. Once again, as in 3:7–19, the community was to be on guard not to follow the example of their forebears in the Exodus generation. That generation had literally begged God to shut up (Deut. 5:25–27). The Christians must not be guilty of likewise refusing (*paraiteomai*, the same word used in 12:19 of the Exodus generation) to hear the Lord currently speaking to them (present active participle of *laleō*, "to talk"). The One who spoke from Sinai now speaks from heaven through His word in this epistle. The Lord has no tolerance for being "tuned out" by His children.

The rhetorician again employs a favored tactic, that of the *qal vachomer* ("light and heavy") argument, which applies truth about that with lesser significance to that with greater significance by "How much more so?" comparisons (2:1-4; 9:13-14; 10:28-29). If the Exodus generation living under the Mosaic covenant could not escape (*ekpheugō*, "to flee away from") strict divine discipline in reaction to their rejection of God (3:7-19), how could a generation living under the superior new covenant escape undergoing even greater discipline for such rebellion? To disdain the sacrifice of Jesus is certainly of greater spiritual consequence than to repudiate the leadership of Moses. It stands to reason that the punishment for violation of the superior would be much severer than for that which is inferior. As the author explained in 10:27, the consequence of the first-generation Jewish community's placing themselves in an adversarial position toward God should be "a terrifying expectation of judgment." The Lord has never been squeamish about daring to discipline. The theme of 2:3's initial warming is revisited, "How shall we escape if we neglect so great salvation?" and, as in 2:3, the author again includes himself in the equation through use of the first person plural.

The answer is found, as it was in the discussion of each previous warning passage, in defining 12:26's discipline from which there can be no escape. The recognition of the epistle's "warning passages" must be interpretively carried forward through identification of what is the content of which the readers were being warned. As previously discussed in the comments concerning 10:26-31, when the execution of the Exodus generation serves as your comparative starting point, how much qualitative room is left for an escalation in severity for the Hebrews generation? A greater sin necessarily requires a greater punishment. What is the nature of the punishment that fits this particular infidelity spoken of in Hebrews?

The text does not allow us to overvalue the *qal vachomer* ("lesser and greater") contrast and assume that the physical deaths experienced by the Exodus generation must now necessarily escalate to the spiritual deaths, the eternal damnation, of the Hebrews generation. As salvation, once divinely granted, is never ours to forfeit no matter our spiritual insensitivity and potential rebellion, the warning must therefore be that Jewish believers would forfeit their lives, not their salvation. As those who had once trusted in the Messiah, they enjoyed irrevocable spiritual benefits and therefore would never be deprived of God's eternal salvation. Yet if they turned away from the Lord Jesus in order to reidentify, even temporarily, with the generation of Israel under the impending judgment inexorably arriving within that decade, they would share in the divine discipline unleashed on the nation. The unpardonable sin of Jewish national rejection of Jesus and the consequent forthcoming judgment (Matt. 23:35-36; Luke 11:50-51; Acts 2:40) would result in unimagined devastation that would make the harsh discipline undergone by the Exodus generation seem merciful in comparison.

As the author draws the passage to a close, the text ventures beyond the forthcoming period of devastation to the final and climactic shaking of all creation immediately prior to the establishment of the messianic age. As the mountain of Sinai shook in Israel's history, in the future the entirety of heaven and earth will be shaken as well. Freely adapting a quotation from Haggai 2:6, which in context originally dealt with the prophet's encouraging announcement of Israel's glorious future at some time following the conclusion of the Babylonian exile, the writer announces God's promise (*nun de epēggeltai*, "but now he has promised," with the verb for promise in the perfect tense, indicating past action with continuing result) to *eti hapax*, "once more" shake the heavens and earth prior to the end of the age (a theme echoed as well in Isa. 13:13).

In 12:27 the author interprets the meaning of the Haggai quotation to mean that this shaking (what F. F. Bruce calls "the cosmic convulsion")[10] will remove (*metathesis*, "to remove," "to replace," "to transform"; see comments on Heb. 7:12 concerning the use of this word that appears in the New Testament only in 7:12 and here) every temporary component of creation that can be shaken apart. All that will remain for the messianic age will be that which is permanent and unshakable.

Hebrews 12:28 lays the ground for the writer's conclusion of the topic, with *dio*, "therefore." He urges his readers (and himself, as he is still writing in the first person plural) that in light of believers' promised gift of a *basileian asaleuton*, "an unshakable kingdom," the spiritually sensitive and, indeed, the only truly appropriate response is one of a worshipful attitude (*latreuōmen*, "we might worship," "we might serve") of gratitude (*echōmen charin*, an idiom meaning "to be grateful to someone").[11] This worship must be characterized by an acceptable (*euarestōs*, a word used this once in the New Testament) measure of both *eulabeias* (a word used in the New Testament only here and in 5:7) and *deous* (a word appearing only here in the New Testament), both of which are synonyms for "reverent awe."

In 12:29 the author begs off the discussion with a simple reminder of why it is in one's best interest to choose such an appropriate response to God's forthcoming gift by quoting Deuteronomy 4:24's "for our God is a consuming fire" (a parallel companion thought to the fourth warning's complementary sober conclusion that it is "a terrifying thing to fall into the hands of the living God" [10:31]). The eternal future of every believer is certain and secure. The messianic age will dawn following the cataclysmic moment when all creation is divinely shaken. However, for the Jewish believers living in first-century Jerusalem, their immediate fate was dependent on the lucidity of their faith choices.

Conclusion

By this point in the text, the author has successfully laid out every compelling argument he wished to present, every theological precept he wished to impart, and every warning he wished to issue. What remains is only the rich content of his concluding pastoral exhortations concerning their obligations to each other and to God.

Study Questions

1. What is the purpose of 12:1's assembly of witnesses that surrounds us?

2. How is Jesus the author and perfecter of faith?

3. What is the relationship, if any, between endurance and discipline? Provide a personal example of how these two elements have worked or are currently at work in your life.

4. Describe the mutual obligation possessed by believers to one another, if any.

5. Is the author's use of the Esau account helpful in illustrating the argument of Hebrews? Why or why not?

6. In which two Jewish holidays is the concept of heavenly "record books" central?

CHAPTER 16

Concluding Exhortations
Hebrews 13:1-25

Preview:

The final chapter of Hebrews contains the author's practical and pastoral summation of his preceding argument distilled into twenty-five compact pastoral verses. In light of what his readers have already read and digested, he now discusses their obligations to the believing community and to the Lord as pertains to worship. Although throughout the epistle the author's personality had briefly shimmered between the lines of exhortation, admonition, and theological instruction, it is in the letter's concluding benediction that we at last are treated to a glimpse of the man behind the epistle, a man who so earnestly hoped to sheath his quill and unleash his loving pastoral rhetoric face-to-face. While for the modern reader the ancient mystery of the author's identity remains unsolved, his heart stands clearly revealed.

Exhortation to Discharge Community Obligations (13:1-6)

Whereas thematically this chapter stands on the foundation of that which the author has previously laid, nonetheless, grammatically it seems to commence with a certain disconnected abruptness.[1] However, modern readers must restrain themselves from hyperventilating over an author's two-millennia-old stylistic choices. In this section, an assortment of five community exhortations are set forth.

The initial community obligation is to let the exercise of *philadelphia*, "brotherly love," continue to characterize their relations. The concept of a faith family whose members were derived from beyond the boundaries of immediate blood relatives was a substantially radical concept in the world of the Roman Empire, although less so among the Jews, where tribal and sectarian sentiment normally prospered.[2] The community could only thrive in an atmosphere contoured by fraternal affection.

Use of Old Testament Passages in Hebrews 13

Hebrews	Old Testament	Subject
13:2	Gen. 18:1–8; 19:1–3	Abraham, Lot, and the angels
13:5	Deut. 31:6–8	The promise of God's abiding presence
13:6	Ps. 118:6	The promise of God's abiding presence
13:11	Lev. 16:27	The Day of Atonement
13:15	Hos. 14:2	Worship
13:17	Ezek. 3:17	Community responsibilities
13:20	Isa. 55:3	The new covenant; the Davidic covenant
13:20	Jer. 32:40	The new covenant
13:20	Ezek. 37:26	The new covenant
13:20	Zech. 9:11	The new covenant
13:20	Zech. 13:7	Prophecy regarding the Messiah's death

The second community obligation derived from the first. The "love of brothers," *philadelphia*, must be accompanied by *philoxenia*, "the love of strangers." Hospitality must not be *epilanthanomai*, "neglected," for it was common practice for itinerant teachers, missionaries, messengers, merchants, refugees, and those recently released from imprisonment to seek shelter in the homes of fellow believers, perhaps even those house churches where the local community assembled. The Roman Empire was characterized by a mobility made possible by the tenacious engineering of Roman road builders. It was this mobility that enabled Paul, Peter, the apostles, and a countless assortment of unnamed believers to propagate the gospel with such stunning breadth.

So prevalent were itinerant Christian ministries by the turn of the first century that the Christian treatise the Didache sets forth a few practical (but with twenty-first-century hindsight, somewhat hilarious) ground rules that would completely undermine our modern ministry conventions of weeklong revivals, parachurch ministries, and missionary deputation:

> Let every apostle who comes to you be received as the Lord, but he must not stay more than one day, or two if it is absolutely necessary; if he stays three days, he is a false prophet. And when an apostle leaves you, let him take nothing but a loaf, until he reaches further lodging for the night; if he asks for money, he is a false prophet.[3]

The author's admonition is seasoned with a bit of incentive based on biblical precedent. Some, like Abraham and the three visitors at Mamre (Gen. 18:1–21) or his nephew Lot at Sodom (Gen. 19:1–3), had not realized that they were actually entertaining angels appearing in human form.

The third community obligation was to remember (*mimnēskesthe*, "to call to mind, "to demonstrate concern for") those who were imprisoned as though they were imprisoned alongside (*sundedemenoi*, "having been bound with," a word that appears only here in the New Testament). Some in the community had themselves experienced the hardship of imprisonment, and others had already shown passionate solidarity and sympathy with those who had been imprisoned for their faith (10:32–34). In addition, the church must demonstrate the same commitment to those who are mistreated and harassed (*kakouchoumenōn*, "those being abused," a word used in the New Testament only here and in 11:37 of the suffering paragons of faith). Since we belong to the same corporate body, believers must exhibit a highly sensitive degree of empathy toward fellow believers who undergo affliction.

The fourth community obligation relates to maintaining the fidelity of the basic sociological building block of any community, the marital relationship. Two admonitions are given concerning marriage. First, marriage is *timios*, "valuable," "precious," and therefore must be respected throughout the community (*en pasin*, "by all"). Second, the *koitē*, "the marriage bed" (related to our word *coitus*), must be *amiantos*, "undefiled." What is conveyed by the concept of defilement of the marriage bed is not the spilling of Coke on your new Sealy Posturepedic mattress, but rather marital infidelity; that is, injury to the marital relationship's sexual and emotional integrity. The faith community must foster awareness that not only does infidelity violate the basic principle of *philadelphia* (13:1) in society's basic building block, but God will judge both fornicators (*pornous*, "sexually immoral ones") and *moichous*, "adulterers" (although both words are male gender nouns, the application of this admonition applies to both sexes).

The fifth community obligation is personal in nature. The faith community must be characterized by individuals free from the love of money (*aphilarguros*, a word that appears in the New Testament only here and in Paul's instructions concerning overseer qualifications in 1 Tim. 3:3). Hebrews 13:4–5 provides a compelling combination of hot topics for any social grouping. Sex and money are, after all, the two most frequently cited catalysts for marital squabbling. These two topics have been handled sequentially in Jewish tradition ever since the initial carving of the seventh and eighth commandments on Moses' stone tablets (Exod. 20:14–15; Deut. 5:18–19).[4]

Each believer must learn the secret of contentment: to be satisfied with what finances we already possess. Money must never capture the believer's fancy, for as Jesus Himself taught, "You cannot serve God and mammon" (Matt. 6:24). In 13:5–6 the author assembles a combination of two Old Testament quotations to encourage the community to neither find their security in economic success nor fall into insecurity through economic or social duress (10:34), but rather to simply trust in the Lord. He quotes the principle of God's personal promise in Deuteronomy 31:6–8 to never desert or forsake His people in order to arrive at Psalm 118:6's confidence-building conclusion that since "the LORD is for me; I will not fear; what can man do to me?"

Exhortation to Discharge Religious Obligations (13:7–17)

In this section, an assortment of three religious obligations is presented for the faith community's attention. This section is topically bracketed at top and bottom by the subject of church leaders. Obligations to former leaders is the theme of 13:7; and obligations to current leaders is the theme of 13:17. Within those two verses, the author's topic of choice is how we relate to God.

The first obligation relates to the community's former leaders, specifically those who have since died or moved on to another community. They are to remember (this is a different word choice than that previously employed in 13:3; however, this new word, *mnēmoneuō*, carries the same definition, "to call to mind," "to make mention of," and is the source of our word *mnemonic*) "those who led you" (*hēgoumenōn*). Their leadership was characterized by their having "spoken the word of God" (*elalēsan . . . ton logon tou theou*), that is, they preached to the faith community (variations of the same expression are found in Acts 4:29, 31; 8:25; 13:46; Phil. 1:14; 1 Pet. 4:11).

In addition to honoring their former leaders' memory, the community was to consider (*anatheōrountes*, "to observe carefully," a word used only here and in reference to Paul's examination of Athenian objects of worship [Acts 17:23]) the outcome of their conduct in order to imitate (*mimeomai*, "to mimic," "to emulate," the word from which we derived our mimeograph machines) their faith.

The second religious obligation was for Jesus to be the undisputed center of the believers' faith (13:8–16). Hebrews 13:8 is quite a well-known verse, one that is often artlessly and heartlessly torn asunder from its original context to prove a particular point about why a certain church practice, spiritual gift, hymnal, Bible translation, or the like must either never change or, alternatively, must be immediately reincorporated. That common sort of textual abuse merits no mention whatsoever, and the subject is now dropped (this is an example of the rhetorical device, *paraleipsis*, the technique where the writer pretends to avoid mentioning the exact thing that he has just mentioned; see the comments on 11:32–34).

In context, the actual word order of 13:8 is "Jesus Christ, yesterday and today the same, and forever," with the author having positioned the words in the sentence to achieve the desired level of emphasis. The name "Jesus," accompanied by His title, "Christ," is employed only three times in Hebrews, two of which are in this chapter (10:10; 13:8, 21). The author's intent in commencing this section with such a unique construction is revealed by the concerns that follow in subsequent verses. Hebrews 13:8 is no declaration of the timelessness of Jesus' nature, habits, identity, role, function, or anything else to do with His person. Rather, the contrast is between the nonnegotiable integrity of the gospel message concerning salvation through Christ and the eccentric faddish teachings to which they were presently exposed.

In opposition to the solid, accurate biblical teaching they had received from their previous leaders, some members were in danger of becoming *parapheresthe*, "carried away" by teachings both *poikilais*, "varied," and *xenias*, "strange," "foreign." Apparently, an example of such teaching concerns whether the heart may be strengthened by food (in the sense that food can influence the quality of a person's character; the idea being perhaps a form of "you are what you eat," or better, "what you eat helps you to ethically improve yourself"). Now, while it is true that Psalm 104:15 teaches that God provides "food which sustains man's heart,"[5] it is absurd to consider that doctrines concerning Christian living may have developed from this verse (Rom 14:17; 1 Cor. 8:8; Col. 2:16).

As many pastors and teachers have been forced to do over the years as trendy fads regarding how to live the victorious Christian life, whether through diet or otherwise, have blown through the church, the author of Hebrews admonishes his readers to reject this nonsense outright. Instead, the community members should strengthen their hearts through the grace of God, a concept likewise supported by Paul (2 Thess 2:16–17). Jesus, our Great High Priest, is sufficient to sustain our spiritual lives.

In 13:10 the writer builds on the concepts of food and relates it both to the Jewish believing community's spiritual practice and to their standing in the contemporary religious system of Judaism. Contrasting Levitical worship in the temple with the house worship of Jewish Christians, he identifies Jesus as a superior altar to that in the Jewish sanctuary. Those who trust in the Levitical system share none of the privileges enjoyed by the followers of Jesus. The Levitical priests with their animal sacrifices had nothing on the Jewish believers and their perfect High Priest.

In 13:11 the argument expands beyond standard, daily Levitical worship to encompass the practice of the holiest day of the year, the Day of Atonement, Yom Kippur (see comments on 9:6-7). The carcasses of the two specific Day of Atonement blood sacrifices of both bull and goat, after having their blood carried into the Holy of Holies and applied by the high priest (Lev. 16:11-19), were taken from the sanctuary courts, incinerated, and disposed of "outside the camp" (Lev. 16:27-28). So powerful was the symbolic association of these animals with the nation of Israel's sin that it was prohibited for them to be eaten on Yom Kippur, although eating certain sacrifices was standard practice allowed throughout the rest of the year (Exod. 29:14).

As the Yom Kippur sacrifices were removed from the temple precincts and taken *exō tēs parembolēs* "outside the camp," *dio kai Iēsous*, "so Jesus also," who through His role as perfect Priest and sacrifice (10:12) became the complete and perfect fulfillment of the Day of Atonement, was taken and crucified *exō tēs pulēs*, "outside the gate" of the city (John 19:20). He *epathen*, "suffered," *hina hagiasē*, "that He might sanctify" *dia tou idiou haimatos*, "through His own blood" (9:18-20; 10:10, 14, 29) *ton laon*, "the people."

The author underscores the typological correspondence between the incineration of the Atonement sacrifices outside the camp and Jesus' execution outside the city gate. According to the Torah, among those who were to be executed outside the camp of Israel were the breaker of the Sabbath (Num. 15:35) and the blasphemer (Lev. 24:10-16, 23). Jesus was found guilty of blasphemy at His trial before the Sanhedrin, the council of Jewish leaders who advocated His execution by the Romans (Matt. 26:64-65; Mark 14:63-64). His rejection by the most revered, pious, and knowledgeable Jews of His day was a shameful component of the reproach He bore (Heb. 13:13; Luke 6:22)

Employing the inferential conjunction *toinun*, "accordingly," "so then," in 13:13 to draw the discussion to a rousing point of action, the author, writing in first person plural, calls his readers to join him (*exerchōmetha*, "let us go out of," "may we remove ourselves") to identify with Jesus "outside the camp" of Judaism. This entails *ton oneidismon autou pherontes*, "bearing His reproach" through identifying with and embracing the same rejection He experienced from the greater Jewish community. Since Jesus is no longer to be found in the camp of Judaism's religious system, it was urgent that His disciples join Him.

Hebrews 13:14 underscores the point. The Jewish Christian community did not possess a lasting city in Jerusalem. Judgment was at the door. Jesus Himself had warned his disciples of Jerusalem's impending destruction (Matt. 24:1–2; Luke 19:41–44; 21:20–24).[6] However, while the earthy city of Jerusalem's immediate future was bleak, the author reminded his readers of the content of their future-oriented faith. They were all seeking the city that is to come (*tēn mellousan*, "the one about to be"). This is the heavenly Jerusalem, the city of the living God, discussed previously (11:8–10, 13–16; 12:18–24).

Since the community of Jewish believers have a superior High Priest, it is through Jesus only (*di' autou*, "through Him," emphatically placed at the head of the sentence), and not through the Levitical high priesthood, that they should worship God. Through Jesus, the author called his readers to exercise their own priesthood through continually offering up *thusian aineseōs*, a "sacrifice of praise," to God. The meaning of "sacrifice of praise" is clarified by (*tout' estiv*, "that is to say") the appositional *karpon cheileōn*, "the fruit of lips" (a clause lifted from Hos. 14:2 that is employed nowhere else in the New Testament) that gratefully confess the name of Jesus. Worship must take form in both word and deed, and 13:16 exhorts believers to neither neglect doing good (*eupoiias*, the word's only usage in the New Testament) or *koinōnias* "association or fellowship," a theme that harks back to 10:25. With such sacrifices God is pleased.

The section concludes as the bottom half of the rhetorical framing device of the mention of the church's local leadership. This concerns the community's third religious obligation in this section. As they had been exhorted to honor and imitate their former leaders, they were now obligated to obey their current leadership and to *hupeikete*, "yield" (a word used only here in the New Testament), to their authority. These leaders had been divinely granted the responsibility to keep watch over the souls of the members of their local house churches (a concept reminiscent of Ezekiel's responsibility as Israel's watchman [Ezek. 3:17]). The leaders were responsible to God to provide an accounting of each congregant's spiritual maturity (James 3:1).[7] The community was to make every effort to ensure that the leaders were able to discharge their duties with joy and not grief (*stenazontes*, "inward groaning"). Indeed, sapping the joy out of church leadership is ultimately an activity with little spiritual payoff.

Exhortation to Discharge Personal Obligations (13:18–25)

In this final segment, the author exhorts his readers to discharge their personal obligations toward himself personally, his ministry colleagues, and this epistle, which he has composed on their behalf. He requests prayer for himself and his colleagues (although the request is forcefully expressed through the power of the present imperative, *proseuchesthe*). Confident of morally unobjectionable conscience, the author and companions nevertheless request prayer that they may conduct themselves with honor in all things (*kalōs thelontes anastrephesthai*, literally, "wanting to behave well").

With great emphasis (*perissoterōs*, "abundantly," "especially," "to a far greater degree") the writer urges his readers to prayer so that he may return to their midst. In his saying *hina tachion apokatastathō humin*, "that I may be restored to you the sooner," all doubt is removed as to whether the author has a previously established personal relationship with his readers. He wishes to return to this local manifestation of his faith family as soon as is feasible.

The author's request for prayer is immediately followed by his own prayer for the readers as the concluding benediction begins in 13:20–21. The substance of this theologically content-rich prayer is that the readers be sufficiently equipped *en panti agathō*, "in every good thing" to do God's will, and that He works in them that which is pleasing in His sight. The theme of his prayer is the overwhelmingly sufficient power of God to accomplish his request.

The Father is addressed as "the God of peace" and credited with the resurrection of Jesus (*anagagōn ek nekrōn*, "to lead out from the dead," a phrase also found in Rom. 10:7). Verse 20 is the sole explicit reference in the epistle to Jesus' actual resurrection. The resurrection was achieved through the agency of "the blood of the eternal covenant" (Heb. 9:20; also Isa. 55:3; Jer. 32:40; Ezek. 37:26; Zech. 9:11), that is, Christ's shed blood through which the new covenant was inaugurated.

The Son is designated as "the great Shepherd of the sheep," a phrase with roots in the imagery of both the Old Testament (Zech. 13:7) and the New (John 10:1–18; 1 Pet. 2:25; 5:4), "our Lord," equating Him with God the Father, and "Jesus Christ," his messianic title. Whether it is to the Father or to Jesus that the glory of the ages belongs is ambiguous in the prayer. Perhaps it is best to opt for both until more information is disclosed. The prayer ends with a customary Jewish "amen."

The epistle's postscript urges (*parakaleō*, "I encourage") the readers to bear with this *logou tēs paraklēseōs*, "word of exhortation." This phrase is "an idiomatic, fixed expression for a sermon in Jewish-Hellenistic and early Christian circles,"[8] and is the same phrase that was used by Pisidian Antioch's synagogue officials upon hospitably extending a customary invitation to their distinguished guests, Paul and Barnabas, to deliver a short lesson or sermon based on the contents of that Sabbath's *Torah* (five books of Moses) or *Haftorah* (the writings and the prophets) selections (Acts 13:15). When read aloud, the combination of the words *parakalō* and *paraklēseōs* would have possessed exquisite rhetorical effect. His "word of exhortation" (and what is Hebrews, if not an unbroken series of encouragements) should be easy for the readers to bear, for he notes, "I have written to you only briefly." Lane explains that this was considered a polite literary convention," with parallels in Jewish and Christian literature, including a New Testament epistle (1 Pet. 5:12).[9]

Hebrews 13:23 introduces the figure of Timothy, called "our brother." There is no reason to doubt that this is the familiar colleague of the apostle Paul and decisively links the author of Hebrews to at least the outer perimeter of the Pauline circle. The news being conveyed in the postscript is that Timothy had been recently released from an unspecified period of incarceration or some other constraining legal difficulty. Now that Timothy is again at liberty, the writer hopes to travel together with him to the readers' location. The phrasing employed, however, implies that should Timothy be detained for some reason, the writer might not wait to travel. This impatience might have at its root the writer's pressing desire to reunite with the Jerusalem believers, but as likely might have been due to the closing of the limited season when the weather permits safe crossing over Mediterranean or even the writer's reading of the political winds of war brewing across the Roman occupied Land of Promise.

Hebrews 13:24–25 contains final farewells. Through his readers, the writer sends greetings to the various leaders of the region's house churches as well as to all the believers in the region. Greetings are also transmitted from his colleagues, "those from Italy." As discussed in the introductory section on Destination, nothing can be reasonably concluded based on this ambiguous tidbit of information, and it is impossible to determine from the greeting the location of either the greeter or the greeted.

The difficulty lies in the inherent flexibility of the preposition *apo*, "from." The first interpretive option is that "those from Italy," that is, the Italians, may currently be in Italy (e.g., in Rome), and they wish to send their regards to believers abroad. This would then read, "We native Italians, who are in Rome, greet you who are elsewhere." However, while these friendly Italians may well have been sending greetings from Rome, a second interpretive option is that these are Italians living or traveling abroad, sending greetings back home to their neighbors in Rome. This would then read, "We native Italians, who are currently somewhere outside of Italy, greet our countrymen back in Rome." A third interpretive option is that while these assuredly friend-ly believers may have been an Italian contingent living or traveling abroad, they may not have been sending their greeting home to Rome, but to another community entirely. This would then read, "We native Italians, currently somewhere outside of Italy, greet our brothers who are somewhere else."

Whatever the location of the author's epistolary composition may have been, his final words comprise a traditional sign-off, quite appropriate to the letter's content, *he charis meta pantōn humōn*, "grace be with you all" (slight variations of which are used by Paul in Col. 4:18; 2 Tim. 4:22; Titus 3:15).

Conclusion

As the revolt against Rome inflamed both the cities and countryside of Judea from AD 66–67 onward, the Jewish Christians of Jerusalem and the sur-rounding regions heeded the epistle's warning and literally fled "the camp" (13:13). Jesus had also warned His disciples to flee Judea when warfare broke out against Jerusalem (Matt. 24:15–16; Luke 21:21). The outbreak of the war with Rome proved to be the event that finally separated Judea's Jewish believ-ers and their fellow Jews. In an act considered traitorous by their fellow Jews, the Jewish believers en masse followed their Master's command to leave the nation and escape the catastrophic war. Traveling east and crossing the Jordan River, they fled to safety in the city of Pella,[10] one of the region's ten major Roman metropolises (collectively known as the Decapolis). There the Jewish Christian churches found rest, having avoided partaking of God's judgment on the generation of Israel that had rejected Jesus as God's Messiah.

Study Questions

1. Name the five community obligations of 13:1–6. Is any of the five more or less important to achieve than the others? Why or why not?

2. Briefly explain one means by which Jesus has fulfilled the Day of Atonement, including typology, if any.

3. What is the motivation listed in this chapter for obeying and submitting to your church leaders?

4. In one or two paragraphs, sketch out the main argument of Hebrews. "In a nutshell," what is this book about?

5. In what way, if any, has an in-depth study of the book of Hebrews changed your spiritual life, practice, or perspective?

Use of the Old Testament in Hebrews

The author of Hebrews' entire argument rests on the Old Testament Scriptures; indeed, in a memorable phrase, "Hebrews is impregnated with the Old Testament."[1] The challenge for both the commentator and the student of the book is to recognize that the Old Testament is not the basis of the author's argument; rather, the Old Testament is his argument. Hebrews is not a book that contains Old Testament scriptural quotations to bolster and support the author's line of reasoning. On the contrary, this book actually inseparably weaves the Old Testament directly into the book's fabric from start to finish.

The biblical quotations, allusions, and references fly fast and furiously at the reader throughout the text. As the language utilized in the letter is the actual language of the Old Testament, the author's argument is accordingly strengthened (see Use of Old Testament Passages in Hebrews on pp. 230–235). According to William Lane, "it is proposed that there are thirty-one explicit quotations and four more implicit quotations, a minimum of thirty-seven allusions, nineteen instances where Old Testament material is summarized, and thirteen more where a biblical name or topic is cited without reference to a specific context."[2] My estimate of Old Testament usage is slightly higher than Lane's but not worth quibbling over. With so many quotations, allusions, and references repeated more than once, precision in this area proves challenging.

So robustly integrated is the Old Testament with the argument of Hebrews that any attempt at excision or deconstruction results in forcefully stripping the meat from the bones of this theological banquet and leaving behind a ravaged carcass of literary conjunctions and connectives and one lone personal salutation at the letter's conclusion.

Use of Old Testament Passages in Hebrews

Hebrews	Old Testament	Subject
1:2	Ps. 2:8	The Son as heir of creation
1:3	Ps. 110:1	The divine authority of the Son
1:5	Ps. 2:7	The sonship of the Messiah
1:5	2 Sam. 7:14/1 Chron. 17:13	The sonship of the Messiah
1:6	Ps. 97:7	Worship of the Son by angels
1:7	Ps. 104:4	The position of angels
1:8–9	Ps. 45:6–7	Deity of the Son
1:10–12	Ps. 102:25–27	Deity of the Son
1:13	Ps. 110:1	The divine authority of the Son
2:6–8	Ps. 8:5–7	The divine authority of the Son
2:12	Ps. 22:22	The purpose of the Son
2:13	Isa. 8:17–18	The purpose of the Son
2:13	Isa. 12:2	The purpose of the Son
2:16	Isa. 41:8–9	Messiah as Son of Abraham
3:2–5	Num. 12:7	The position of Moses
3:7–11	Ps. 95:7–11	Israel's wilderness rebellion
3:8	Exod. 17:7	Israel's wilderness rebellion
3:11	Num. 14:22–23	Israel's wilderness rebellion
3:15	Ps. 95:7–8	Admonition to faithfulness
3:16–18	Num. 14:1–35	Israel's wilderness rebellion
4:3	Ps. 95:11	God's rest denied to the faithless
4:4	Gen. 2:2	God's rest following creation
4:5	Ps. 95:11	God's rest denied to the faithless
4:7	Ps. 95:7–8	Israel's wilderness rebellion

Hebrews	Old Testament	Subject
4:8	Josh. 22:4	Israel's conquest of the Promised Land
4:10	Gen. 2:2	God's rest following creation
5:3	Lev. 9:7	The Levitical high priest's need for atonement
5:3	Lev. 16:6	The Levitical high priest's need for atonement
5:4	Exod. 28:1	The commissioning of Aaron as high priest
5:5	Ps. 2:7	The sonship of the Messiah
5:6	Ps. 110:4	The Son's Melchizedekian priesthood
5:6	Gen. 14:18–20	Melchizedek
5:9	Isa. 45:17	Eternal salvation
5:10	Ps. 110:4	The Son's Melchizedekian priesthood
6:8	Gen. 3:17–18	The divine curse of the earth
6:13	Gen. 22:16	The binding of Isaac
6:14	Gen. 22:17	The Abrahamic covenant
6:16	Exod. 22:11	The Mosaic Law concerning oaths
6:18	Num. 23:19	The unchangeable purpose of God
6:18	1 Sam. 15:29	The unchangeable purpose of God
6:19	Lev. 16:2	High priest's role on the Day of Atonement
6:20	Ps. 110:4	The Son's Melchizedekian priesthood
7:1–2	Gen. 14:17–20	Melchizedek and Abraham
7:3	Ps. 110:4	The Melchizedekian priesthood
7:5	Num. 18:21	Mosaic Law concerning Israel's Levitical tithe
7:14	Gen. 49:10	Prophecy about Messiah's descent from Judah
7:14	Isa. 11:1	Prophecy about Messiah's descent from Jesse
7:17	Ps. 110:4	The Son's Melchizedekian priesthood
7:21	Ps. 110:4	The Son's Melchizedekian priesthood

Hebrews	Old Testament	Subject
7:27	Lev. 9:7; 16:6	Levitical high priest's need for atonement
8:1	Ps. 110:1	The divine authority of the Son
8:5	Exod. 25:40	The tabernacle
8:8–12	Jer. 31:31–34	The new covenant
9:2	Exod. 25:23–26:30	The tabernacle and its components
9:3	Lev. 16:3	The Holy of Holies
9:4	Exod. 16:33	The jar of manna
9:4	Exod. 30:1–6	The altar of incense
9:4	Num. 17:8–10	The rod of Aaron
9:4	Deut. 10:3–5	The two stone tablets
9:4–5	Exod. 25:10–22	The ark of the covenant
9:6	Num. 18:2–6	The service of the Levitical priesthood
9:7	Lev. 16:2	High priest's role on the Day of Atonement
9:10	Lev. 11:2	The Mosaic Law concerning food
9:10	Lev. 11:25	The Mosaic Law concerning uncleanness
9:10	Lev. 15:18	The Mosaic Law concerning uncleanness
9:10	Num. 19:13	The Mosaic Law concerning uncleanness
9:13	Lev. 16:6–7	The Day of Atonement
9:13	Num. 19:9	The ashes of the red heifer
9:19–20	Exod. 24:3–8	The ratification of the Mosaic covenant
9:21	Lev. 8:15	The consecration of the Levitical priesthood
9:22	Lev. 17:11	The necessity of blood for atonement
9:28	Isa. 53:12	Isaiah's suffering servant
10:4	Lev. 16:6–7	The Day of Atonement
10:5–9	Ps. 40:6–8	The Levitical sacrificial system

Hebrews	Old Testament	Subject
10:11	Exod. 29:38	The Levitical priestly service
10:12	Isa. 53:10–12	Isaiah's suffering servant
10:12–13	Ps. 110:1	The divine authority of the Son
10:16–17	Jer. 31:33–34	The new covenant
10:22	Ezek. 36:25	The new covenant
10:25	Lev. 23:27; 25:9	The Day of Atonement
10:26	Num. 15:30–31	The sin of defiance
10:27	Isa. 26:11	Divine judgment against God's enemies
10:28	Deut. 17:6; 19:15	The Mosaic Law concerning testimony
10:29	Exod. 24:8	The ratification of the Mosaic covenant
10:30	Deut. 32:35–36	Divine judgment against God's enemies
10:30	Ps. 135:14	Divine justice for God's people
10:37	Isa. 26:20	Divine judgment against God's enemies
10:37–38	Hab. 2:3–4	Admonition to faithfulness
11:3	Ps. 33:6–9	Divine creation
11:4	Gen. 4:3–10	Cain and Abel
11:5	Gen. 5:24	Enoch
11:7	Gen. 6:13–7:1	Noah
11:8	Gen. 12:1–5	Abraham
11:9	Gen. 23:4; 26:3; 35:12–27	The patriarchs
11:11	Gen. 18:11–14	Sarah
11:12	Gen. 22:17	The Abrahamic covenant
11:13	Gen. 23:4	The patriarchs
11:17	Gen. 22:1–10	The binding of Isaac
11:18	Gen. 21:12	The Abrahamic covenant

Hebrews	Old Testament	Subject
11:20	Gen. 27:27–29, 39–40	Isaac's blessing of Jacob and Esau
11:21	Gen. 47:31; 48:15–16	Jacob's blessing of Joseph's sons
11:22	Gen. 50:24–25	The death of Joseph
11:23	Exod. 1:22–2:2	The birth of Moses
11:24	Exod. 2:10–15	The maturity of Moses
11:28	Exod. 12:21–30	The Passover
11:29	Exod. 14:21–31	The Exodus
11:30	Josh. 6:12–21	The conquest of Jericho
11:31	Josh. 2:11–12; 6:21–25	Rahab
11:32	Judg. 6–8	Gideon
11:32	Judg. 4–5	Barak
11:32	Judg. 13–16	Samson
11:32	Judg. 11–12	Jephthah
11:32	1–2 Samuel; 1 Chronicles	David
11:32	1 Sam. 1–16	Samuel
11:33	Dan. 6:1–27	Daniel
11:34	Dan. 3:23–25	Shadrach, Meshach, and Abed-nego
11:35	2 Kings 4:32–37	Elisha and the Shunammite's son
11:36	Jer. 20:2; 37:15	Jeremiah
11:37	2 Chron. 24:21	Zechariah the son of Jehoiada
12:2	Ps. 110:1	The divine authority of the Son
12:5–6	Prov. 3:11–12	Divine discipline
12:7–9	Deut. 8:5	Divine discipline
12:12	Isa. 35:3	Encouragement to live a sanctified life
12:13	Prov. 4:26	Encouragement to live a sanctified life

Hebrews	Old Testament	Subject
12:16–17	Gen. 25:33–34; 27:30–40	Jacob and Esau
12:18–19	Deut. 4:11–12; 5:22–27	Israel's Sinai experience
12:18–20	Exod. 19:12–23; 20:18–21	Israel's Sinai experience
12:21	Deut. 9:19	Israel's Sinai experience
12:23	Gen. 18:25	God as Judge
12:24	Gen. 4:10	Cain and Abel
12:24	Jer. 31:31	The new covenant
12:26	Exod. 19:18	Israel's Sinai experience
12:26	Hag. 2:6	Divine judgment against God's enemies
12:29	Deut. 4:24	Divine judgment against God's enemies
13:2	Gen. 18:1–8; 19:1–3	Abraham, Lot, and the angels
13:5	Deut. 31:6–8	The promise of God's abiding presence
13:6	Ps. 118:6	The promise of God's abiding presence
13:11	Lev. 16:27	The Day of Atonement
13:15	Hos. 14:2	Worship
13:17	Ezek. 3:17	Community responsibilities
13:20	Isa. 55:3	The new covenant; the Davidic covenant
13:20	Jer. 32:40	The new covenant
13:20	Ezek. 37:26	The new covenant
13:20	Zech. 9:11	The new covenant
13:20	Zech. 13:7	Prophecy regarding the Messiah's death

The motivating force behind this abundance of Old Testament citations was the author's presuppositional conviction as to the Hebrew Scriptures' nature as "sacred writings which are able to give you the wisdom that leads to salvation through faith which is in Christ Jesus. All Scripture is inspired by God and profitable for teaching, for reproof, for correction, for training in righteousness" (2 Tim. 3:15–16).

Furthermore, while the author inarguably interprets the Old Testament using both a literal and grammatical methodology (in other words, he portrays the events that are recorded in the Hebrew Scriptures as actually having happened just the way they are presented therein), he nonetheless views the Old Testament through a dominant Christological perspective. The author's major arguments all fundamentally acknowledge the great theme that flows from one extremity of the Hebrew Scriptures to the other, that of the messianic promise.

In this, the author is in good company. Throughout the New Testament, the messianic content of the Old Testament is repeatedly brought forth, most often as the razor-sharp instrument through which the gospel is both proclaimed and explained. Jesus Himself, "beginning with Moses and with all the prophets," taught His disciples "the things concerning Himself in all the Scriptures" (Luke 24:25–27), saying, "All things which are written about Me in the Law of Moses and the Prophets and the Psalms must be fulfilled" (Luke 24:44). The act of "demonstrating by the (Old Testament) Scriptures that Jesus was the Christ" was the apostle Paul's powerful strategy as well (Acts 17:2–3).

With gusto, the author of Hebrews vigorously wrings dry the ancient Scriptures, constraining them in the winepress of his exalted vision and extracting every possible ounce of intrinsic Christology contained in each text. The text of Hebrews becomes a platform on which, strata by strata, the author develops his theology about Jesus. As he builds his case, each new layer of propositional truth adheres to its neighbors through his slathering a liberal application of Old Testament mortar between every tier, without exception, creating an unassailable tower of Christological, messianic doctrine, assurance, exhortation, and encouragement that stands today as resolutely as when the tower was first constructed some two millennia ago.

The Old Testament quotations in Hebrews are exclusively drawn from the Septuagint, the second-century BC Greek translation. Throughout the text, the author conscientiously credits God as the ultimate author of Scripture, working through the agencies of both the Holy Spirit and a human individual. An individual, such as David, never receives sole attribution (4:7); it is always God speaking through means of human agency or directly through the Holy Spirit (3:7).

The Theology of Hebrews

The book of Hebrews, for all its brevity at thirteen chapters, represents an extensive contribution to the development of a comprehensive Christian theology. The book speaks to every area of systematic theology, with weight given to theology proper (the doctrinal study of God), Christology (the doctrinal study of the Messiah), and soteriology (the doctrinal study of salvation).

Theology of God the Father

The text of Hebrews provides some seventy names, titles, theological descriptions, and propositional assertions regarding God the Father (see Names, Titles, and Descriptions of God the Father in Hebrews on pp. 238–240). Not all seventy will be discussed here, but highlights will be presented. Performing this sort of systematic analysis as to how a particular New Testament text portrays God is a fascinating exercise and includes both educational and devotional aspects. We will perform such analysis on Hebrews' presentation of both the Father and, in the following section, the Son.

Naturally, the foremost focus of the author of Hebrews is God's identity as the Lord, the familiar covenant God of the Old Testament (8:2, 8, 11; 10:16, 30; 12:14; 13:6). Related to His identity as Lord, Hebrews strongly emphasizes that His activity is by no means limited to Israel's history and that He is still very much the living God (3:12; 9:14; 10:31; 12:22) who continues His involvement in the lives of His people.

The author of Hebrews places repeated stress on God's majestic nature, calling Him simply the Majesty (8:1) and the Majesty on High (1:3), the Most High God (7:1) and three times highlighting His identity as the Enthroned One (4:16; 8;1; 12:2). God is also the Ever-Present One (13:5), the All-Seeing

One (4:13) and He who is unseen (11:27). His excellence is revealed by the fact that He is the One whose purpose is unchangeable (6:17), and in His activity as the One who erected the perfect tabernacle (8:2) and His identity as the God of peace (13:20).

Names, Titles, and Descriptions of God the Father

Name/Title	Hebrews
A consuming fire	12:29
All-seeing One	4:13
Appointer of high priests	5:4, 6
Appointer of Jesus as High Priest	5:6, 10; 7:17, 21
Builder of all things	3:4
Enthroned One	4:16; 8:1; 12:2
Ever-present One	13:5
Father	2:11
Father of spirits	12:9
Father of the Son of God	1:4–5
Father who lovingly disciplines His children	12:5–10
God of the faithful	11:16
He who is unseen	11:27
He who promised	10:23
Helper	13:6
Him with whom we have to do	4:13
Initiator of the Abrahamic covenant	6:13–14
Initiator of the new covenant	8:8–12
Judge of all	12:23
Judge of fornicators and adulterers	13:4
Judge of His people	10:30

Name/Title	Hebrews
Most High God	7:1
Provider of something better for new covenant believers	11:40
The God of peace	13:20
The Living God	3:12; 9:14; 10:31; 12:22
The Lord	8:2, 8, 11; 10:16, 30; 12:14; 13:6
The Majesty	8:1
The Majesty on High	1:3
The One able to raise the dead	11:19
The One able to save Jesus from death	5:7
The One for whom and through whom are all things	2:10
The One for whom it is impossible to lie	6:18
The One in whose presence Christ appears	9:24
The One pleased with His people doing good and sharing	13:16
The One to be praised and thanked through Jesus	13:15
The One to whom church leaders will give account	13:17
The One to whom we may draw near through Jesus	7:19, 25
The One who appoints His Son	1:2; 3:2
The One who brings many sons to glory	2:10
The One who brings the Firstborn into the world	1:6
The One who called Abraham	11:8
The One who created the world through His Son	1:2
The One who designs, builds, and prepares a future city	11:10, 16
The One who desires to reveal His character to believers	6:17
The One who equips believers in every good thing to do His will	13:21
The One who gives children to His Son	2:13

Name/Title	Hebrews
The One who invites His Son to sit at His right hand	1:13
The One who is faithful	10:23; 11:11
The One who is gracious	2:9; 12:15
The One who is pleased by the faith of His people	11:5–6
The One who made the Mosaic covenant obsolete	8:13
The One who pitched the true tabernacle	8:2
The One who prepared worlds by His word	11:3
The One who raised Jesus from the dead	13:20
The One who remembers believers' actions	6:10
The One who rested from His works	4:4, 10
The One who speaks through His Son	1:2; 12:25
The One who spoke through prophets	1:1; 12:25–26
The One who subjects all things to the Son	2:8
The One who swears the disobedient will not enter His rest	3:11, 18; 4:5
The One who testified about Abel's righteousness	11:4
The One who testifies to the gospel	2:4
The One who will shake creation	12:26–27
The One who works in us that which is pleasing to Him	13:21
The One whose purpose is unchangeable	6:17
The One whose grace was operative in Jesus' death	2:9
The One whose will is known and achievable	10:36
The One whose works were finished from the world's foundation	4:3
The perfecter of the Author of salvation	2:10

Theology of God the Son

Hebrews makes its most important theological contribution in the area of Christology, the doctrine of the Messiah. As was the case with Hebrews' treatment of God the Father, the text of Hebrews also contains roughly seventy names, titles, descriptions, and propositional assertions regarding Jesus (see Names, Titles, and Descriptions of Jesus in Hebrews on pp. 243–245). Our understanding of our Messiah is invaluably enriched by the author of Hebrews' acute focus on Jesus. Of course, this focus was borne of situational necessity. Apparently the author set about compensating for the deficiency in his recipients' rudimentary understanding of Christological doctrine in apprehension that anyone in the community might take irreversibly rash and rebellious measures. According to William Lane, "His strongest encouragement was to remind the members of the house church of the character, the accomplishment, and the exalted status of their Lord."[1]

Hebrews paints a unique, delicately balanced portrait of Jesus' dual natures, both the divine and the human. It becomes apparent in deconstructing the text's complex Christology that Hebrews is literature and not visual art. Nonetheless, this Christological masterpiece has a definite color scheme that tints the letter's contents. The text of Hebrews graphically preoccupies itself with the blood of Jesus, shed for humans and offered before God, in a way that is quite unlike any other book in the New Testament collection. Consequently, the author's primary hue of choice is a deep, vivid crimson. Of course, Hebrews is in no way monochromatic, and the crimson scheme is blended and contrasted with two other colors. First is the pure white of our sinless High Priest's robe. Second is a rich, royal purple fit for adorning the exalted and returning messianic King.

By far, Jesus' exaltation receives the most attention. Following the successful accomplishment of Jesus' sacrificial mission (9:12; see also "It is finished," John 19:30), the Father raised His Son from the dead (13:20). The Son then passed through the heavens (4:14), entering the very presence of God (9:24) by the means of His own shed blood (9:12). The Son, accepting His Father's invitation to reign at His right hand, sat down, taking His rightful place (1:3; 8:1; 10:12; 12:2) as King-Priest (5:10).

Jesus' current ministry as royal High Priest includes representation before the Father to advocate on behalf of believers (6:20; 9:24). Related to His ministry of representation is His ministry of active intercession, which both assures and secures every believer's salvation (7:25) and provides requisite and sympathetic aid in time of temptation and need (2:17–18; 4:14–16). As our mediator, Jesus is the sole means through which believers may relate to the Father and through whom the Father's grace and power flow to believers (13:12–15). Jesus' high priesthood provides believers with unprecedented intimate access into the presence of God (10:19–22).

The more than seventy names, titles, descriptions, and propositional assertions concerning Jesus can be grouped into four rough, although somewhat overlapping, categorical themes, as follows. The first theme relates to His name and messianic identity. Throughout the text, the author commonly uses the personal name Jesus (2:9; 4:14; 6:20; 7:22; 10:19; 12:2, 24; 13:20), references His messianic title, Christ (3:14; 5:5; 6:1; 9:11, 14, 24, 28; 11:26), and three times uses both name and title in combination, Jesus Christ (10:10; 13:8, 21).

The second theme relates to the author's unambiguous recognition of Jesus' deity. So explicit is the presentation that even if one lacked possession of the entire remainder of the New Testament but yet had the text of Hebrews, the doctrines of the essential triunity of God's nature and Jesus' equality with God the Father could still be derived. The issue of the Messiah's deity is unavoidable to even the most casual reader of Hebrews. He is called the Lord (2:3), our Lord (7:14) and Jesus our Lord (13:20). Most critically, in the quotation from Psalm 45:6, He is called God (1:8–9).

Another theme concerns Jesus' Melchizedekian high priesthood, a concept that permeates the text of Hebrews. Although the priesthood of Jesus is implied elsewhere in the New Testament (Rom. 8:34; 1 John 2:1), Hebrews is the only New Testament book that explicitly refers to Jesus as a priest. This priesthood is distinctively based not on descent from Aaron, but on Jesus' status as a descendant of Abraham (2:16). He is the High Priest of the good things to come (9:11), a sinless High Priest (4:15), who is separated, innocent, holy, and undefiled (7:26). He is the High Priest who passed through the heavens (4:14), an exalted High Priest (7:26), a seated and exalted High Priest (8:1), and minister in the true tabernacle (8:2).

Another theme concerns Jesus' role as perfect sacrifice. He is the One who tasted death (2:14), the One who suffered outside the gate 13:12), an offering without blemish (9:14). He is the One who sanctifies us through offering His body (10:10, 14), the One who offered one final sacrifice (10:12, 14), once offered to bear sins (9:28). This sacrifice who puts away sin (9:26) gloriously became the One whose flesh is the veil before the Holy Place (10:19).

Names, Titles, and Descriptions of Jesus

Name/Title/Description	Hebrews
Aid of the tempted	2:18
Apostle of our confession	3:1
Author and perfecter of faith	12:2
Author of salvation	2:10
Christ	3:14; 5:5; 6:1; 9:11, 14, 24, 28; 11:26
Descendant of Abraham	2:16
Exact representation of God's nature	1:3
Firstborn	1:6; 12:23
Forerunner	6:20
God	1:8–9
Great Shepherd of the sheep	13:20
Guarantee of a better covenant	7:22
He who is coming	10:37
He who sanctifies	2:11
Heir of all things	1:2
Helper of Abraham's descendants	2:16
High Priest of our confession	3:1
High Priest of the good things to come	9:11
High Priest who passed through the heavens	4:14
High Priest, exalted	7:26
High Priest, holy	7:26
High Priest, innocent	7:26
High Priest, merciful and faithful	2:17
High Priest, seated and exalted	8:1

Name/Title/Description	Hebrews
High Priest, separated	7:26
High Priest, sinless	4:15
High Priest, undefiled	7:26
Instrument of creation	1:2, 10
Jesus	2:9; 4:14; 6:20; 7:22; 10:19; 12:2, 24; 13:20
Jesus Christ	10:10; 13:8, 21
Jesus our Lord	13:20
Liberator of the devil's slaves	2:15
Lord, our	7:14
Lord, the	2:3
Maker of purification of sins	1:3
Mediator of a better covenant	8:6
Mediator of a new covenant	9:15; 12:24
Minister in the true tabernacle	8:2
Obtainer of eternal redemption	9:12
Offering without blemish	9:14
Once offered to bear sins	9:28
One who learned obedience	5:8
One who returns for salvation	9:28
One worshiped by angels	1:6
Perfected One	5:9; 7:28
Priest, eternal	7:21, 24
Priest, Great, over the house of God	10:21
Priest, Melchizedekian	5:6, 10; 6:20; 7:17
Radiance of God's glory	1:3

Name/Title/Description	Hebrews
Sacrifice who puts away sin	9:26
Son	1:2, 5, 8; 3:6; 5:5, 8; 7:28
Son of God	4:14; 6:6; 10:29
Son of Man	2:6
Source of eternal salvation	5:9
The inaugurator of a new and living way	10:20
The One able to save forever	7:25
The One who appears in the presence of God	9:24
The One who has perfected the sanctified for all time	10:14
The One who is coming	10:37
The One who lives to make intercession	7:25
The One who offered one final sacrifice	10:12, 14
The One who sanctifies us through offering His body	10:10, 14
The One who sits at God's right hand	1:13; 8:1; 10:12–13; 12:2
The One who suffered outside the gate	13:12
The One who was temporarily made lower than the angels	2:7
The One who tasted death	2:14
The One whose flesh is the veil before the Holy Place	10:19
The same yesterday, today, and forever	13:8
Unchanging One whose years have no end	1:11–12
Upholder of all things	1:3
Victor over the devil	2:14

Theology of Salvation

Hebrews is a text that is thoroughly saturated with doctrine concerning salvation. These doctrines may be loosely categorized into two areas: the accomplishments of Christ and the believers' identity as a result of those accomplishments.

Christ's accomplishments concerning salvation relate to His roles as both perfect High Priest and perfect sacrifice. As the Melchizedekian High Priest, He has made purification of sins (1:3) and propitiation for sins (2:17). He is the author and source of believers' eternal salvation (2:10; 5:9). Jesus entered the Holy Place once for all, having obtained eternal redemption (9:12), and because He is an immortal intercessor, He is therefore able to save believers forever (7:25). Through His single sacrifice for sins for all believers and for all time (10:10–14), Jesus has put away sin (9:26), cleansing both flesh and conscience, the outer and inner aspects of believers, by His blood (9:13–14). As a result of the Messiah's high priesthood and sacrifice, believers are current participants in the process of sanctification ("those who are sanctified," 2:11; "holy brethren, partakers of a heavenly calling," 3:1; "we have been sanctified," 10:10). Furthermore, He has perfected those whom He has sanctified (10:10–14), something that never could have been accomplished through the Mosaic Law.

The author of Hebrews is greatly interested in the concept of perfection, applied in various ways. Perfection is mainly referenced through the contrast of Jesus' ministry with that of the Levitical system. First, Jesus Himself has been perfected through suffering (2:10), and His identity as the perfected Son was appointed through divine oath (7:28). "Having been made perfect, He became . . . the source of eternal salvation" (5:9) and serves in a "more perfect tabernacle" (9:11). For believers, Jesus is "the author and perfecter of faith" (12:2) who "has perfected for all time those who are sanctified" (10:14).

On the other hand, "the Law made nothing perfect" for perfection could not be achieved through the Levitical priesthood (7:11). Indeed, "the Law . . . can never . . . make perfect those who draw near" (10:1) because "sacrifices . . . cannot make the worshipper perfect in conscience" (9:9).

Perfection is also referenced regarding Old Testament believers, "the spirits of righteous men made perfect" (12:23) who "should not be made perfect" apart from New Testament believers (11:40).

It is an unfortunate truth that the book of Hebrews' five warning passages (2:1–4; 3:7–4:13; 5:11–6:20; 10:26–31; 12:25–29) have often been misunderstood as teaching the possibility of an apostate believer's loss of salvation. However, to interpret the warning passages in this fashion completely undercuts the author's entire argument concerning the superiority of Christ's finished sacrificial and mediatorial work. Hebrews places no limitations on the effectiveness of Jesus' once for all sacrifice (10:14). The book's position regarding this singular sacrifice, coupled together with Hebrews' categorical statements concerning the continuous function of Jesus' high priesthood (7:22–28), make it hard to imagine that a believer's transitory state of rebellion could possess the power to nullify the eternal, completed work of our

Messiah. If Christ's efforts were sufficiently powerful to initially save us from the depths of our slavery to sin and reconcile us to God (Rom. 5:10ff.; 6:6–11), it staggers the imagination to propose that somehow the potency of His work is diminished upon our redemption.

Use of "Perfect" in Hebrews

"To perfect the author of their salvation through sufferings" (2:10)

"Having been made perfect, He became . . . the source of eternal salvation" (5:9)

"If perfection was through the Levitical priesthood" (7:11)

"For the Law made nothing perfect" (7:19)

"The oath . . . appoints a Son, made perfect forever" (7:28)

"Sacrifices . . . cannot make the worshiper perfect in conscience" (9:9)

"The greater and more perfect tabernacle" (9:11)

"The Law . . . can never . . . make perfect those who draw near" (10:1)

"By one offering He has perfected *for all time those who are sanctified" (10:14)*

"Apart from us they should not be made perfect" (11:40)

"Jesus, the author and perfecter of faith" (12:2)

"The spirits of righteous men made perfect" (12:23)

Theology of End Times

The author of Hebrews considers that this present era, "these last days" (1:2), is the "consummation of the ages" (9:26), the historical moment in which God's final and decisive revelation has been realized through His Son. Even so, this preset era will eventually give way to the messianic kingdom, referred to by the author as "the age to come" (6:5), "the world to come" (2:5), and "a kingdom which cannot be shaken" (12:28), of which Christians currently experience but a foretaste (6:5). This approaching age will be characterized by the comprehensive rule of Jesus (2:5, 8). Although Jesus, as the Son of God, is presently seated at His Father's right hand (1:3, 13; 8:1; 10:12) and "crowned with glory and honor" (2:9), in this present era "we do not yet see all things subjected to Him" (2:8). "There is coming a time when all will be subject to Jesus,"[4] including every last enemy (1:13; 2:8; 10:13). Until one era yields to the next, the work of the believer is to persevere, holding fast to our confidence and our hope (3:6, 14; 6:11).

The purpose of Hebrews is not to provide a comprehensive portrait of "things to come" (10:1). Rather, the author addresses the end times strictly for exhortational purposes, communicating in a sort of "shorthand" and taking for granted that the recipients would be able to fill in the details of the broad sketches he has provided through their own common knowledge. Moreover, the eschatological presentation in Hebrews, as is the case with so many of the Old Testament prophets, conflates chronologically separated end-time events. Thankfully, we do not have the book of Hebrews in isolation, and we may correlate Hebrews teaching with that of the rest of the New Testament.

For example, the text of Hebrews references the climactic event of the messianic kingdom, the creation of new heavens and earth, and the revelation of God's city, the New Jerusalem (12:22–24). We may correlate Revelation 21:1–3, in particular, with the text of Hebrews' shaking of all the creation (12:26–29) and presentation of "the city of the living God, the heavenly Jerusalem" (12:22–24). Hebrews tells us that, in this age, believers "do not have a lasting city" (i.e., first-century Jerusalem?) and "are seeking the city which is to come" (13:14). Regarding this new Jerusalem, the author reveals that it will be inhabited by New Testament believers ("general assembly and church of the firstborn"), Old Testament believers ("the spirits of righteous men made perfect"), angels, Jesus, and God Himself (12:22–24).

Any discussion of Hebrews' eschatology must mention the author's famous definition of faith, defined as "the assurance of things hoped for, the conviction of things not seen" (11:1). In contrast to Paul, whose emphasis concerning faith is most often understood as the believer's present conviction regarding events past (i.e., the death, burial, and resurrection of Jesus), the faith emphasis of Hebrews is the believer's present conviction regarding future events ("the world to come"). These complementary emphases reveal two sides of the same coin, reminding us that faith always proceeds by looking both ways.

Theology of Israel

As befits the book's name, Hebrews makes three significant contributions to the area of Israelology. Major Jewish themes and interests are interwoven throughout and are intrinsic to the author's argument.

For example, the author develops the theological and practical relationship between the church and the four major covenants made between God and the Jewish people in the Old Testament (the Abrahamic covenant, Gen.

12:1–3, 7; 13:14–17; 15:1–21; 17:1–21; 22:15–18; the Mosaic covenant, Exod. 19:1–20:21; the Davidic covenant, 2 Sam. 7:8–16; 1 Chron. 17:7–14; and the new covenant, Jer. 31:31–34). The bulk of covenant discussion concerns the replacement of God's provisional and conditional Mosaic covenant with His permanent and unconditional new covenant. The natures of both covenants are contrasted and examined by the author, who indisputably argues for the current annulled status of the Mosaic covenant, including the Torah and the Levitical system, based on their inferior and impermanent nature (4:14–5:10; 7:11–28; 8:1–13; 9:1–10; 10:18). The sole contractual means of relationship between Jewish people and God is the new covenant, inaugurated through the superior priesthood and sacrifice of the Messiah.

Inadequacy of the Mosaic Covenant

Hebrews	Assertion Concerning Mosaic Covenant
7:18	"... its weakness and uselessness"
7:19	"The Law made nothing perfect."
8:7	"If the first covenant had been faultless, there would have been no occasion sought for a second."
8:13	"He has made the first obsolete. But whatever is becoming obsolete and growing old is ready to disappear."
9:9	"Sacrifices are offered which cannot make the worshiper perfect in conscience."
9:10	"regulations for the body imposed until a time of reformation"
10:1	"The Law ... has only a shadow of the good thing to come."
10:1	"The Law ... can never ... make perfect those who draw near."
10:3	"In those sacrifices there is a reminder of sins year by year."
10:4	"It is impossible for the blood of bulls and goats to take away sins."
10:9	"He takes away the first in order to establish the second."

A second example of Jewish themes and interests permeating Hebrews is that the text provides confirmation that the Jewish believer in Jesus can and should maintain his Jewish identity. Nowhere in the book is there the merest suggestion concerning the potential invalidation of believers' Jewish identity or a denigration concerning the continued maintenance of Jewish traditions. To the contrary, integral to the text's argument is continuity of Jewish identity. The author of Hebrews fully anticipates Jewish Christians retaining those essential Jewish distinctives that have not been abrogated through the salvific work of Jesus. Whether the examples provided from their own continued sacred Scripture are negative, concerning rebellion, or positive, concerning faith (3:7-4:13; 11:1-40), the argument assumes the recipients' historic, ethnic, and religious identification with their Jewish ancestry.

A final example of Hebrews' Jewish themes and interests is that the author makes both allusion and detailed reference to Israel's annual festivals. Passover (3:16; 9:14; 11:28-29), Pentecost (2:1; 12:18-21, 26), the Feast of Trumpets (12:22-24), and the Feast of Dedication (Hanukkah, 11:34-35) are all spotlighted in the text, with an especially prominent role reserved for the Day of Atonement (7:26-28; 9:6-10:25).

Bibliography

Bruce, F. F. *The Epistle to the Hebrews*. New International Commentary on the New Testament. Grand Rapids: Eerdmans, 1990.

Ellingworth, Paul. *The Epistle to the Hebrews: A Commentary on the Greek Text*. Grand Rapids: Eerdmans; Carlisle: Paternoster, 1993.

Fruchtenbaum, Arnold G. "Hebrews." *The Messianic Jewish Epistles: Hebrews, James, First Peter, Second Peter, Jude*. Tustin, CA: Ariel, 2005.

Hodges, Zane. "Hebrews." *The Bible Knowledge Commentary: An Exposition of the Scriptures*, edited by John F. Walvoord and Roy B. Zuck. Wheaton: Victor, 1983.

Hughes, Philip Edgcumbe. *A Commentary on the Epistle to the Hebrews*. Grand Rapids: Eerdmans, 1977.

Kent, Homer, Jr. *The Epistle to the Hebrews*. Grand Rapids: Baker, 1972.

Johnson, Luke Timothy. *Hebrews: A Commentary*. Louisville: Westminster John Knox, 2006.

Keener, Craig S. "Hebrews," *The IVP Bible Background Commentary: New Testament*. Downers Grove, IL: InterVarsity, 1993.

Lane, William L. *Hebrews 1–8* and *Hebrews 9–13*. Word Biblical Commentary. Dallas: Word, 2002.

Morris, Leon. "Hebrews." *The Expositor's Bible Commentary*. Edited by Frank E. Gaebelein. Grand Rapids: Zondervan, 1981.

Rayburn, Robert S. "Hebrews." *Evangelical Commentary on the Bible*. Vol. 3. Edited by Walter A. Elwell. Grand Rapids: Baker, 1996.

Stern, David H. "Hebrews." *Jewish New Testament Commentary: A Companion Volume to the Jewish New Testament*. Clarksville, MD: Jewish New Testament Publications, 1992.

Notes

Foreword

1. Stanley D. Toussaint, "The Eschatology of the Warning Passages in the Book of Hebrews," Grace Theological Journal 3, no. 1 (Spring 1982): PAGE.

2. William L. Lane, *Hebrews 1–8*, Word Biblical Commentary (Dallas: Word, 2002), 47A:xlvii.

Introduction—Background of Hebrews

1. Of the total of 4,942 words in Hebrews, the writer uses 1,038 different words; of that number, 169 are found only in Hebrews in the New Testament. Robert Morgenthaler, *Statistik des neutestamentlichen Wort-schatzes*, 164, cited in William L. Lane, *Hebrews 1–8*, Word Biblical Commentary (Dallas: Word, 2002), 47A:l.

2. Luke Timothy Johnson, *Hebrews: A Commentary* (Louisville: Westminster John Knox, 2006), 8.

3. There is speculation as to which translation of Hebrew Scripture was used by the early church. For example, the biblical quotations in both Hebrews and Acts are primarily from the Septuagint. There are slight discrepancies between the Hebrew text and its Greek translation, and New Testament quotations of the Old Testament generally agree with Septuagint variations.

4. Hellenistic Jews were ethnic Jews who lived outside of Israel in what is called the Jewish diaspora, the dispersion of Jewish people throughout the Roman Empire. By the first century, it is estimated that the Roman Empire consisted of some eight million Jews, an astonishing 10 percent of the empire's total population. Only about three million Jews were natives of Israel. The remaining five million were happily scattered throughout the communities of the Roman Empire. As such, Greek, not Hebrew or Aramaic was their native language.

Within Israel, Hellenistic Jews were ethnic Jews who, having lived

253

outside of Israel for decades or even generations, had now returned to live in the land of promise. The Hellenists were, to some extent, culturally distinct from native Judeans, for example, worshiping in separate Greek-speaking synagogues as opposed to synagogues that conducted their services in Hebrew. In addition, although the pervasive influence of the mainstream Greco-Roman culture would have been inescapable for either native or immigrant Jews, the lifestyles of the Jewish immigrants reflected an elevated level of Greek cultural absorption.

This assimilation included much more than which community primarily spoke Aramaic and which community primarily spoke Greek. To thrive within the Roman world, both groups would have had to demonstrate proficiency in the Greek language, although the Hellenists would be more fluent as Greek was their mother tongue. To whatever extent, the acculturation created a divergence in education, outlook, and worldview and generated for the Greek Jews heightened levels of artistic, theatric, athletic, and philosophic interests.

5. Basic college-level orientation to Aristotle's artistic proofs theory can be found in Charles U. Larson, *Persuasion: Reception and Responsibility,* 4th ed. (Belmont: Wadsworth, 1986), 29–30. For an excellent general discussion of how these Aristotelian persuasive proofs apply within Hebrews, see Johnson, *Hebrews,* 14–15, 31.

6. Johnson, *Hebrews,* 8.

7. Paul Ellingworth, *The Epistle to the Hebrews: A Commentary on the Greek Text* (Grand Rapids: Eerdmans; Carlisle: Paternoster, 1993), 2–21. Every good commentary provides a rundown of various candidates for authorship. Ellingworth's list is exhaustive.

8. Ibid., 4.

9. F. F. Bruce, *The Epistle to the Hebrews* (Grand Rapids: Eerdmans, 1990), 16.

10. William L. Lane, *Hebrews 1–8,* Word Biblical Commentary (Dallas: Word, 2002), 47A:cliv.

11. Donald Guthrie, *New Testament Introduction* (Downers Grove, IL: InterVarsity, 1970), 722.

12. Bruce, *Hebrews,* 19–20, quoting Calvin.

13. Lane, *Hebrews 1–8,* xlix.

14. Ellingworth, *Hebrews,* 12.

15. There is an ongoing debate over whether Luke was Jewish. While the overwhelming consensus has always been that Luke was a Gentile, the New Testament does not explicitly reveal Luke's nationality. However, in Paul's letter to the Colossians, Luke is listed separately (4:14) from Paul's list of Jewish coworkers (4:10–11). While this is the sole New Testament hint that Luke was a Gentile, on the surface this passage would seem to be conclusive.

There is, however, at least an adequate case to be made for Luke having been Jewish; not a native of Israel, but a Hellenistic (Greek) Jew of the Diaspora (if so, he would be the earliest recorded "Jewish doctor"). First, beneath the surface of Luke's superb mastery of Greek literary style, there are indications that, while the author wrote in Greek, he may have been thinking in Hebrew. This is indicted by the presence of Hebraisms (Hebrew word order, phrases, and terminology) scattered throughout the text of both Luke and Acts. An alternative but less satisfying way to explain the presence of such Hebraisms in Luke-Acts is that they derive from the original Jewish sources, either written or oral, which Luke translated as he compiled his account.

Second, Luke's exquisite knowledge of Jewish theological issues and sectarian parties, familiarity with the temple, acquaintance with Jewish holidays and marked concern for Jerusalem go beyond that of merely a historian's reporting of the facts. It is difficult to explain Luke's Jewish expertise and concern by simply citing the two years he spent in Israel, from AD 57–59 (Acts 21:8–27:1), or imagining the quantity of time he spent personally with his friend Paul, that noted "Hebrew of Hebrews."

Third, Luke deftly weaves quotations and allusions from the Hebrew Scripture throughout his book. His fluency and familiarity with the Law, Prophets, and Writings reveal a mind saturated in the contents of the Old Testament. Luke's facility with the Hebrew Scripture indicates comprehensive study. Such sophistication simply cannot have been developed over a limited period.

Fourth, Paul affirms in his letter to the Romans that God entrusted "the oracles of God," meaning the Holy Scriptures, to the Jewish people, in contradistinction to the Gentiles (3:2; 9:4). Paul seems to be saying that God has appointed the writing of Scripture to Jews. Therefore, since the gospel of Luke and the book of Acts are both Scripture, Luke must have necessarily been Jewish. Alternatively, Paul may have been referring only to the Hebrew Scriptures (the Old Testament).

A probable way to satisfactorily synthesize the evidence, pro and con, concerning Luke's Jewish or Gentile status, would be to posit that prior to becoming a Christian, Luke was either a God-fearer, a Gentile worshiper of the God of Israel, or a "proselyte of the gate," a near convert to Judaism. This would explain Paul having listed him separately from the Jewish Christians, Luke's familiarity with Judaism and the temple as well as his facility with the Hebrew Scripture. In addition, it would clarify the profound interest in God-fearers that Luke demonstrates throughout Luke-Acts.

16. Although for reasons left unrecorded and known only to him and those within his sphere of influence in third-century North Africa.

17. Ellingworth, *Hebrews*, 17.

18. Ibid., 21.

19. Johnson, *Hebrews*, 44.

20. Eusebius, *Ecclesiastical History*, 6.25.14, as cited in Leon Morris, "Hebrews," in Frank. E. Gaebelein, ed., *The Expositor's Bible Commentary* (Grand Rapids: Zondervan, 1981), 7.

21. There are examples of contemporary first-century, post-temple destruction writers utilizing the present tense, Josephus being the textbook example. See Josephus, *Antiquities of the Jews* 3.9.10. Therefore, the issue of tenses cannot be pushed too hard.

22. Not everyone is eager to jump aboard the pre–AD 70 compositional bandwagon, however. Lane vehemently objects, pointing out that the author of Hebrews' interest lies in the wilderness tabernacle, not the Jerusalem temple, the better to illustrate his argument concerning the covenant at Sinai, and that the tenses should be understood in a "timeless" sense, rather than an ongoing, present tense. (See above discussion in the previous note.) Lane, *Hebrews 1–8*, lxiii.

23. The biblical record indicates that a generation had a duration of forty years. This was the length of time it took for the torch of the Egyptian exodus generation to be passed to their children, the generation raised in the wilderness (Num. 32:13). Approximately forty years after John the Baptist's initial warnings and the commencement of Jesus' public ministry, the Romans decimated Jerusalem and completely demolished the temple.

24. Alfred Edersheim, *Sketches of Jewish Social Life in the Days of Christ.* (Bellingham, WA: Logos Research Systems, 2003), 23. See also D. A. Hagner's discussion in his "Jewish Christianity," in Ralph P. Martin and Peter H. Davids, *Dictionary of the Later New Testament and Its Developments*, electronic ed. (Downers Grove, IL: InterVarsity, 2000).

25. We may be confident that these "first generation" believers included at least one apostle or apostolic associate. Theirs was the ability to perform "the signs of a true apostle," that is, signs, wonders and miracles (2 Cor. 12:12). The presence of accompanying "signs and wonders" (2:4), like identifying "calling cards," provided divine validation of the credentials of those with genuine apostolic authority. For example, within Acts, it is of extreme importance to note that Luke specifies that the miracles that characterized the early church were exclusively taking place only through and by means of the apostles (Acts 2:43). Miracles, signs, and wonders were an essential component of apostleship and served as one means to authenticate their authority. Every one of the miracles recorded in Acts, without exception, was carried out by an apostle or a close apostolic associate. This fact should significantly inform the contemporary church's expectations.

26. I use the term "non-Christian Jews" and "Jewish non-Christians" here, along with "nonmessianic Jews," to avoid the clumsy and inaccurate terms "unbelieving Jews" (their rejection of Jesus does not necessitate their atheism!) and "un-Christian Jews" or the potentially offensive, however accurate, term "unsaved Jews."

27. John V. Dahms, "The First Readers of Hebrews," *Journal of the Evangelical Theological Society* 20, no. 4 (December 1977): 365.

28. Robert S. Rayburn, "Hebrews," in Walter A. Elwell, ed., *Evangelical Commentary on the Bible* vol. 3 (Grand Rapids: Baker, 1996), Heb. 1:5.

29. Bruce, *Hebrews*, 3.

30. Lane, *Hebrews 1–8*, lxix.

31. With the possible exception of the Roman Church and the approximately five(?)-year period during which the entire Jewish population had been expelled from the city of Rome by the edict of Claudius (AD 49-54?).

32. Eusebius, *Ecclesiastical History*, 4.5.

33. Bruce, *Hebrews*, 6.

34. Lane, *Hebrews 1–8*, cxiv.

35. Marvin Vincent, *Word Studies in the New Testament* (Bellingham, WA: Logos Research Systems, 2002), 4:369–70.

36. Kenneth S. Wuest, *Wuest's Word Studies from the Greek New Testament: For the English Reader* (Grand Rapids: Eerdmans, 1997), Titus 3:15.

37. Although it was illegal for Jews to proselytize Roman citizens. See Joseph A. Fitzmyer, *Acts of the Apostles*, Anchor Bible (New York: Doubleday, 1997), 31:587.

38. Claudius temporarily expelled every Jew from the city of Rome (Acts 18:2) for the cause of rioting "at the instigation of *Chrestus*" (a confused variant of *Christos*, "Christ"), as recorded in Seutonius, *Claudius* 25:4.

39. Ellingworth, *Hebrews*, 75.

40. Leaving approximately three million first-century Jewish residents in Judea. The Jewish population of Judea, however, would soon plummet precipitously, following the first and second Jewish revolts (AD 66–73 and AD 132–135 respectively), each catastrophically unsuccessful.

41. There was a large number of Hellenistic widows in Jerusalem in particular (Acts 6:1), due to the custom of many diaspora Jews returning to Jerusalem later in life so as to be buried in the holy city. There was a Jewish belief that in the last days, when the resurrection occurred, the first to rise would be those buried in the soil of Jerusalem. Those bodies buried outside of Israel, would first have to burrow underground, however, many hundreds or thousands of miles back to Israel to enjoy the resurrection. Needless to say, this immigration pattern would have left an inordinate number of widows to attend to. (This is the origin of the custom, still practiced by Jews today, of being buried together with a packet of soil from Israel.)

42. "Five individuals stated, in effect, that Matthew wrote in Aramaic and that translations followed in Greek: Papias (AD 80-155), Irenaeus (AD 130-202), Origen (AD 185-254), Eusebius (fourth century AD), and Jerome (sixth century AD)," Louis A. Barbieri Jr., "Matthew," in John F. Walvoord and Roy B. Zuck,

eds., *The Bible Knowledge Commentary: An Exposition of the Scriptures* (Wheaton: Victor, 1983–85), 2:15. This complex issue is clearly explained and accessibly examined in Craig Blomberg, *Matthew*, The New American Commentary, electronic ed., Logos Library System (Nashville: Broadman and Holman, 2001), 22:39–40.

43. It is possible that Luke may have simply adapted the apostles' original Hebrew Bible quotations to the version of the Bible used by Theophilus and a subsequent Greek audience. By the time Luke wrote Acts, the locus of the church was no longer in Israel but, rather, was in the larger, Greek-speaking, Gentile world.

44. Vincent, *Word Studies*, 4:371.

45. Arnold G. Fruchtenbaum, "Hebrews," in *The Messianic Jewish Epistles: Hebrews, James, First Peter, Second Peter, Jude* (Tustin, CA: Ariel, 2005), 5.

46. See n. 25 above.

47. Johnson, *Hebrews*, 5.

48. The biblical record indicates that a generation had a duration of forty years. This was the length of time it took for the torch of the Egyptian exodus generation to be passed to their children, the generation raised in the wilderness (Num. 32:13). Approximately forty years after John the Baptist's initial warnings and the commencement of Jesus' public ministry, the Romans decimated Jerusalem and completely demolished the temple.

49. See n. 24 above.

Chapter 1—Superiority of the Messiah as Divine Revelation

1. Josephus, *Antiquities of the Jews* 13.10.6.

2. *The Tosefta, Translated from the Hebrew, with a New Introduction*, Jacob Neusner, trans., vol. 1 (Peabody, MA: Henderson, 2002), Tosefta Sotah 13:3, p. 885.

3. Technically, the plural of *parashah* is *parashot*, but I do not expect every reader to know Hebrew (or Greek), and I will attempt to remove potentially confusing impediments along the way.

4. Kenneth S. Wuest, *Wuest's Word Studies from the Greek New Testament: For the English Reader* (Grand Rapids: Eerdmans, 1997), Heb. 1:1.

5. Arnold G. Fruchtenbaum, *Messianic Christology* (Tustin, CA: Ariel, 1998), 80. This acknowledgment is all the more noteworthy, in that Rashi always stood ready with an alternative interpretation to various pesky messianic prophecies that did not fit his theological grid.

6. Alfred Edersheim, *The Life and Times of Jesus the Messiah* (Bellingham, WA: Logos Research Systems, 1896, 2003), 2:716.

7. Babylonian Talmud, *Sukkah* 52a, as quoted in Tom Huckel, "Psalms," *The Rabbinic Messiah*, electronic ed. (Philadelphia: Hananeel House, 1998). Huckel likewise supplies a veritable laundry list of supporting quotations from ancient

Jewish sources (Babylonian Talmud, *Berakoth* 10a; *'Abodah Zarah* 3b; Midrash on Psalms, bk. 1, Psalm 2,2; 2,3; 2,8; 2,10; bk. 4, Psalm 92,10; Midrash Rabbah, *Genesis* 44, 8; 97, New Version; Pesiqta de-Reb Kahana, *Piska* 9, 11).

8. Babylonian Talmud, *Sanhedrin* 98b.

9. While the word *Shekinah* itself is not used in the Bible, the concept of God's visible, manifest presence is found throughout both testaments. The word came into vogue soon after the Second Temple era, and is used extensively thereafter and the concept considerably expanded upon within the Talmud and other rabbinical writings.

10. Wuest, *Word Studies*, Heb. 1:3.

11. Leon Morris, "Hebrews," in Frank. E. Gaebelein, ed., *The Expositor's Bible Commentary* (Grand Rapids: Zondervan, 1981), 14.

12. Within the Old Testament's Greek translation, the Septuagint.

13. William L. Lane, *Hebrews 1–8*, Word Biblical Commentary (Dallas: Word, 2002), 16.

14. Fruchtenbaum, *Messianic Christology*, 88.

15. Midrash on Psalms, bk. 1, Psalm 18, 29, as quoted in Huckel, "Psalms," *The Rabbinic Messiah*, electronic ed. (Philadelphia: Hananeel House, 1998).

16. Edersheim, *Life and Times of Jesus*, 2:721.

Chapter 2—Angels Are the Servants of God; Jesus Is the Son of God

1. See, e.g., the treatment of angels in the apocryphal books of Sirach, Tobit, and 2 Maccabees, as well as the pseudepigraphal books of Jubilees, Enoch, and 4 Maccabees.

2. Raphael Patai, *The Messiah Texts* (Detroit: Wayne State University Press, 1988), 23.

3. Josephus, *Antiquities of the Jews* 15.5.136.

4. "The Book of Jubilees," in *Pseudepigrapha of the Old Testament*, ed. Robert Henry Charles (Bellingham, WA: Logos Research Systems, 2004), 2:13.

5. Daniel J. Ebert IV, "The Chiastic Structure of the Prologue to Hebrews," *Trinity Journal* 13, no. 2 (Fall 1992): 170.

6. *Yalkut Shimoni*, a thirteenth-century compilation of earlier midrashic writings as it applies Isaiah 52:13 to the Messiah (2:571), quoted in Michael L. Brown, *Answering Jewish Objections to Jesus, Volume 3: Messianic Prophecy Objections* (Grand Rapids: Baker, 2003), 59.

7. Mark Saucy, "Exaltation Christology in Hebrews: What Kind of Reign?" *Trinity Journal* 13, no. 1 (Spring 1992): 46.

8. Specifically referred to as the Davidic covenant in 2 Sam. 23:5; 1 Kings 8:23; 2 Chron. 13:5; Ps. 89:3, 28, 34, 39; Isa. 55.

9. Joyce G. Baldwin, *1 and 2 Samuel*, Tyndale Old Testament Commentaries (Downers Grove, IL: InterVarsity, 1988), 8:213.

10. Walter Brueggemann, *First and Second Samuel* (Louisville: John Knox, 1990), 258.

11. Robert D. Bergin, *1, 2 Samuel*, New International American Commentary (Nashville: Broadman and Holman, 1996), 337.

12. See the very interesting discussion of first-century messianic expectation in Herbert W. Bateman IV, "Two First-Century Messianic Uses of the OT: Heb 1:5-13 and 4QFLOR 1.1-19," *Journal of the Evangelical Theological Society* 38, no. 1 (March 1995): 12-27.

13. The New Testament church's literal understanding of the Davidic covenant is further, and decisively, confirmed in Acts 15:15-18 through Jesus' brother James's quotation of Amos 9:11-12, a passage that speaks of God's restoration of the fallen ruins of the tabernacle of David, i.e., the house of David, the Davidic dynasty, during the future messianic kingdom. The dynasty metaphorically fell into ruin when the final Davidic king was deposed from power by Babylon (2 Kings 25:7), and Amos promised that, in fulfillment of the Davidic covenant, the dynasty of David would be restored to its former glory within the context of the messianic kingdom.

14. F. F. Bruce, *The Epistle to the Hebrews* (Grand Rapids: Eerdmans, 1990), 57, see n. 74. The Deut. 32:43 passage is missing from our standard Hebrew text. It is found only in the Greek translation, the Septuagint (the LXX), and in a Dead Sea Scrolls manuscript from Qumran Cave 4.

15. William L. Lane, *Hebrews 1-8*, Word Biblical Commentary (Dallas: Word, 2002), 26.

16. Kenneth S. Wuest, *Wuest's Word Studies from the Greek New Testament: For the English Reader* (Grand Rapids: Eerdmans, 1997), Heb. 1:6.

17. Bruce, *Hebrews*, 15.

18. Wuest, *Word Studies*, Heb. 1:6.

19. Ibid.

20. *Yalkut Shim'oni* 2.11.3, as quoted in David H. Stern, "Hebrews," *Jewish New Testament Commentary: A Companion Volume to the Jewish New Testament* (Clarksville, MD: Jewish New Testament Publications, 1992), Heb. 1:7.

21. The Aramaic paraphrase, the Targum to the Hagiographa, paraphrases 45:2 as "Your beauty, O King Messiah, surpasses that of ordinary men. The spirit of prophecy has been bestowed upon your lips; therefore the Lord has blessed you forever."

22. Herbert W. Bateman IV, "Psalm 45:6-7 and Its Christological Contributions to Hebrews," *Trinity Journal* 22, no. 1 (Spring 2001), 14.

23. Ibid., 5.

24. Ibid., 9.

25. Luke Timothy Johnson, *Hebrews: A Commentary* (Louisville: Westminster John Knox, 2006), 80.

26. Midrash Rabbah, *Genesis* 56.10, as quoted in Tom Huckel, "Psalms," *The Rabbinic Messiah*, electronic ed. (Philadelphia: Hananeel House, 1998).

27. Wuest, *Word Studies*, Heb. 1:11.

Chapter 3—Superiority of the Messiah to Angels

1. Josephus, *Antiquities of the Jews* 15.5.136.

2. "The Book of Jubilees," in *Pseudepigrapha of the Old Testament*, ed. Robert Henry Charles (Bellingham, WA: Logos Research Systems, 2004), 2:13.

3. Randall C. Gleason, "A Moderate Reformed View" in *Four Views on the Warning Passages in Hebrews*, ed. Herbert W. Bateman IV (Grand Rapids: Kregel, 2007), 336.

4. Grant R. Osborne, "A Classical Arminian View," in Herbert W. Bateman IV, gen. ed., *Four Views on the Warning Passages in Hebrews* (Grand Rapids: Kregel, 2007), 128.

5. Scot McKnight, "The Warning Passages of Hebrews: A Formal Analysis and Theological Conclusions," *Trinity Journal* 13, no. 1 (Spring 1992): 35.

6. Buist M. Fanning, "A Classical Reformed View," in Herbert W. Bateman IV, gen. ed., *Four Views on the Warning Passages in Hebrews* (Grand Rapids: Kregel, 2007), 218–19.

7. Buist M. Fanning, "A Theology of Hebrews," in Roy B. Zuck, *A Biblical Theology of the New Testament*, electronic ed. (Chicago: Moody, 1994; published in electronic form by Logos Research Systems, 1996), 407.

8. This is the position set forth in the influential and extremely popular (particularly among dispensationalists) *Ryrie Study Bible* in its note on Hebrews 6:4–6. *The Ryrie Study Bible*, Charles Caldwell Ryrie (Chicago: Moody, 1978).

9. Zane Hodges, "Hebrews," in John F. Walvoord, Roy B. Zuck, eds., *The Bible Knowledge Commentary: An Exposition of the Scriptures* (Wheaton: Victor, 1983), 2:795.

10. In the impending kingdom, their leadership responsibilities will include ruling over the twelve tribes of Israel (Matt.19:28). This foundational commission to rule Israel is why in Acts 1:15–26, at the dawn of the apostolic mission, the selection of a replacement for Judas's abandoned slot was essential. In short, it was not because the apostolic slot was empty per se that there was a need to replace Judas. Otherwise, a continuous stream of votes would eventually need to be taken upon the death of each apostle. Rather, it was necessary for the empty apostolic slot to be filled because the unimaginable had occurred: one of the twelve apostles had abandoned his present *and future* position of responsibility. As the kingdom of God was imminent, the apostles wanted to ensure that they all stood ready to fulfill their commissioned roles. This point is

demonstrated some eleven years subsequent to the events of Acts 1:15–26. Following the execution of the apostle James in AD 44 (Acts 12:1–2), the eleven surviving apostles exerted no effort to replace him. James was no Judas, and his apostolic slot remained unfilled after his death. When the kingdom of God arrives, James, unlike Judas, will not betray his future commission to rule over one of the tribes of Israel.

11. My seminary Greek professor argues this point in compelling grammatical detail in an online article. See Dan Wallace, "Hebrews 2:3–4 and the Sign Gifts," Aug. 4, 2004 @ www.Bible.org.

12. Kenneth S. Wuest, *Wuest's Word Studies from the Greek New Testament: For the English Reader* (Grand Rapids: Eerdmans, 1997), Heb 2:5.

13. An alternative view is offered by Lanier Burns, "Hermeneutical Issues and Principles in Hebrews as Exemplified in the Second Chapter," *Journal of the Evangelical Theological Society* 39, no. 4 (December 1996), 597–98.

14. See Mal Couch, "Progressive Dispensationalism: Is Christ Now on the Throne of David?—Part II," *Conservative Theological Journal* 2, no. 5 (June 1998), particularly 155ff.

15. Craig S. Keener, *The IVP Bible Background Commentary: New Testament* (Downers Grove, IL.: InterVarsity, 1993), Heb. 2:10.

16. Wuest, *Word Studies*, Heb. 2:10.

17. Fanning, "Theology of Hebrews," 383.

18. J. Julius Scott Jr. has an excellent article on this term. "*Archēgos* in the Salvation History of the Epistle to the Hebrews," *Journal of the Evangelical Theological Society* 29, no. 1 (March 1986).

19. *Pesiqta Rabbati* 161a, as quoted in Raphael Patai, *The Messiah Texts* (Detroit: Wayne State University Press, 1988), 112.

20. A helpful overview of biblical concepts concerning priesthood can be found in Alex T. M. Cheung, "The Priest as the Redeemed Man: A Biblical-Theological Study of the Priesthood," *Journal of the Evangelical Theological Society* 29, no. 3 (September 1986).

Chapter 4–Superiority of the Messiah to Moses

1. Raphael Patai, *The Messiah Texts* (Detroit: Wayne State University Press, 1988), xxxi.

2. Babylonian Talmud, *Sanhedrin* 98b.

3. Maimonides, *Epistle to Yemen*, XVI.

4. Philo of Alexandria, *The Works of Philo: Complete and Unabridged*, trans. Charles Duke Yonge (Peabody, MA: Hendrickson, 1996), 497, The Life of Moses 2.13.66ff.

5. Josephus is the textbook example. See Josephus, *Against Apion* 2.8.

6. David A. Fiensy, "The Composition of the Jerusalem Church," in Richard Bauckham, ed., *The Book of Acts in Its First Century Setting*, vol. 4: *Palestinian Setting* (Grand Rapids: Eerdmans, 1995), 221.

7. Josephus is the textbook example. See Josephus, *Antiquities of the Jews* 20.10.1.

8. There is an intriguing discussion of son versus servant patronal access in the first-century milieu in Brett R. Scott, "Jesus' Superiority over Moses in Hebrews 3:1–6," *Bibliotheca Sacra* 155, no. 618 (April 1998).

9. *Midrash Tanhuma*, quoted in Patai, *Messiah Texts*, 41.

10. David Singer, "The Rebbe, the Messiah, and the Heresy Hunter," *First Things* 133 (May 2003): 42–49.

11. Michael L. Brown, *Answering Jewish Objections to Jesus, Volume 2: Theological Objections* (Grand Rapids: Baker, 2000), 220.

12. Nacha Cattan, "Messiah Is on the Menu, and a Deli Is in a Pickle," *Forward*, May 24, 2002.

Chapter 5–Concerning Disobedience and Doubt

1. Mishnah *Sota* 9:6.

2. William L. Lane, *Hebrews 1–8*, Word Biblical Commentary (Dallas: Word, 2002), 85.

3. Randall C. Gleason, "The Old Testament Background of Rest in Hebrews 3:7–4:11," *Bibliotheca Sacra* 157, no. 627 (July 2000), esp. 288–93.

4. Ibid., 292.

5. Paul also recognized the illustrative value of the Exodus generation to his students (1 Cor. 10:6ff.), although in addressing his own specific circumstances, the author of Hebrews sees more here than mere illustration.

6. The anniversary would have concerned either His resurrection (if crucified in AD 30, as some hold) or His ministry's inauguration (if crucified in AD 33, as others hold).

7. F. F. Bruce, *The Epistle to the Hebrews* (Grand Rapids: Eerdmans, 1990), 99.

8. Babylonian Talmud, *Sanhedrin* 98a.

9. Leon Morris, "Hebrews," in Frank. E. Gaebelein, ed., *The Expositor's Bible Commentary* (Grand Rapids: Zondervan, 1981), 14.

10. Timothy Friberg, Barbara Friberg, and Neva F. Miller, *Analytical Lexicon of the Greek New Testament*, Baker's Greek New Testament Library, vol. 4 (Grand Rapids: Baker, 2000), 393.

11. Actually, the maximum scroll length on the first century is about thirty to thirty-five feet, about the length of Acts, the longest book in the New Testament.

12. Lane, *Hebrews 1–8*, 90.

13. Ibid., 97.

14. Ibid., 98.

15. Arnold G. Fruchtenbaum, "Hebrews," in *The Messianic Jewish Epistles: Hebrews, James, First Peter, Second Peter, Jude* (Tustin, CA: Ariel, 2005), 51.

16. Stanley D. Toussaint, "The Eschatology of the Warning Passages in the Book of Hebrews," *Grace Theological Journal* 3, no. 1 (Spring 1982): 71.

17. See Kaiser's interesting treatment of rest in Walter C. Kaiser, Jr., "The Promise Theme and the Theology of Rest," *Bibliotheca Sacra* 130, no. 518 (April 1973).

18. Joseph Herman Hertz, *The Authorized Daily Prayer Book* (Jacksonville, FL: Bloch, 1948; original from the University of California, digitized September 24, 2007), 977.

19. Epistle of Barnabas 15:4–9.

20. Gleason, "Old Testament Background of Rest," 296.

21. Lane, *Hebrews 1–8*, 98.

22. Ibid., 99.

23. Ibid., 100.

24. Mishnah, *Nazir 9:5*; i.e., "Has it not already been said ..."

25. Fruchtenbaum, "Hebrews," 55.

26. Ibid., 58.

27. Bruce, *Hebrews*, 111.

Chapter 6—Superiority of the Messiah to Aaron

1. The theological discussion of peccability versus impeccability (Christ's inherent ability or inability to have committed sin; whether He was able not to sin or simply not able to sin) is beyond the scope of this commentary. However, please see the excellent discussion in John F. Walvoord, "The Person and Work of Christ, Part VII: The Impeccability of Christ," *Bibliotheca Sacra* 118, no. 471 (July 1961).

2. Arnold G. Fruchtenbaum, "Hebrews," in *The Messianic Jewish Epistles: Hebrews, James, First Peter, Second Peter, Jude* (Tustin, CA: Ariel, 2005), 61.

3. Ibid., 66.

4. William L. Lane, *Hebrews 1–8*, Word Biblical Commentary (Dallas: Word, 2002), 121.

5. Buist M. Fanning, "A Theology of Hebrews," in Roy B. Zuck, *A Biblical Theology of the New Testament*, electronic ed. (Chicago: Moody, 1994; published in electronic form by Logos Research Systems, 1996), 384.

Chapter 7–Concerning Spiritual Stagnation

1. William L. Lane, *Hebrews 1–8*, Word Biblical Commentary (Dallas: Word, 2002), 136.

2. Ibid., 131.

3. Mishnah, *Sanhedrin 4:4*.

4. Scot McKnight, "The Warning Passages of Hebrews: A Formal Analysis and Theological Conclusions," *Trinity Journal* 13, no. 1 (Spring 1992): 46.

5. Randall C. Gleason, "The Old Testament Background of the Warning in Hebrews 6:4–8," *Bibliotheca Sacra* 155, no. 617 (January 1998): 78–79.

6. Ibid., 78–79.

7. Arnold G. Fruchtenbaum, "Hebrews," in *The Messianic Jewish Epistles: Hebrews, James, First Peter, Second Peter, Jude* (Tustin, CA: Ariel, 2005), 85.

8. Gleason, "Old Testament Background of the Warning," 78.

9. Ibid., 85.

10. Louis Ginzberg, Henrietta Szold, and Paul Radin, *Legends of the Jews*, 2nd ed. (Philadelphia: Jewish Publication Society, 2003), 231.

11. Lane, *Hebrews 1–8*, 153. See as an example of anchor being used alongside hope, Philo, *On Dreams That Are God Sent*, 1.277.

Chapter 8–The Priesthood of Melchizedek

1. Josephus, *Jewish Wars* 6.438.

2. Philo of Alexandria, *The Works of Philo: Complete and Unabridged*, trans. Charles Duke Yonge (Peabody, MA: Hendrickson, 1996), *Allegorical Interpretation*, 3.79.

3. Babylonian Talmud, *N'darim* 32b.

4. Louis Ginzberg, Henrietta Szold, and Paul Radin, *Legends of the Jews*, 2nd ed. (Philadelphia: Jewish Publication Society, 2003), 196.

5. Philo of Alexandria, *The Works of Philo: Complete and Unabridged*, trans. Charles Duke Yonge (Peabody, MA: Hendrickson, 1996), *On Abraham*, iii:17, 412.

6. David H. Stern, *Jewish New Testament Commentary: A Companion Volume to the Jewish New Testament* (Clarksville, MD: Jewish New Testament Publications, 1992), Heb. 7:12.

7. F. F. Bruce, *The Epistle to the Hebrews* (Grand Rapids: Eerdmans, 1990), 166.

8. Ezek. 21:27.

9. Arthur W. Kac, *The Messianic Hope* (Grand Rapids: Baker, 1975), 19.

10. Ibid., 19–20.

11. Midrash, *Genesis R.* 98:13.

12. Babylonian Talmud, *Sanhedrin* 98b.

13. Kac, *Messianic Hope*, 20.

14. William L. Lane, *Hebrews 1–8*, Word Biblical Commentary (Dallas: Word, 2002), 185.

15. Josephus, *Antiquities of the Jews* 11.196.

16. Lane, *Hebrews 1–8*, 187.

17. Ibid., 188.

18. Josephus, *Antiquities of the Jews* 20.227.

19. David J. MacLeod, "The Present Work of Christ in Hebrews," *Bibliotheca Sacra* 148, no. 590 (April 1991), 195–96.

20. Ibid., 197.

21. Josephus, *Antiquities of the Jews* 3.257. See also the apocryphal *Sirach* 45:14.

Chapter 9—Superiority of the New Covenant

1. David H. Stern, "Hebrews," *Jewish New Testament Commentary: A Companion Volume to the Jewish New Testament* (Clarksville, MD: Jewish New Testament Publications, 1992), Heb. 8:4.

2. Uniquely, Stern, the author of the influential (certainly within the messianic community) *Jewish New Testament Commentary*, understands 8:6 as a declaration that the New Testament has been given as an expansion of the Torah or perhaps a more explicit explanation of Torah. He goes so far as to claim that holding this view is "absolutely crucial for understanding the New Testament," even though he admits he has never seen this view reflected in a single translation or commentary other than his own (indicating that until his commentary came along, Christendom was deprived of an absolutely crucial interpretive element).

To be fair, the basis of his singular interpretation is not without warrant. Stern reasons that 8:6's *nenomothetetai*, a perfect passive verb that is almost universally translated within context as "enacted upon," as in "which has been enacted upon better promises," should more accurately be translated, "has been given as Torah on the basis of better promises." Indeed, the same word with the same conjugation appears in 7:11 and is usually translated "were given the Torah." Indeed, it is not unreasonable to expect consistency of translation within the same text. However, automatic application of consistency must yield way for matters of context. "Legal enactment" is the word's normative usage and makes terrific sense within the context. Slapping the label of "Torah," on the New Testament or new covenant or both (Stern uses them interchangeably) is grammatically and contextually awkward and therefore a less preferable choice.

While every commentator is entitled to publish an out of the mainstream interpretation (this commentator included!), I do find it unfortunate, particularly as a fellow messianic Jew, that Stern explicitly links failure to hold with his interpretation with conscious or unconscious anti-Semitism. I can only trust that subsequent editions to the first edition in my possession have long since been amended. See Stern, *Jewish New Testament Commentary*, comments on Heb. 8:6.

3. Stern, "Hebrews," Heb 8:7.

4. See chap. 5, n. 24.

5. Luke Timothy Johnson, *Hebrews: A Commentary* (Louisville: Westminster John Knox, 2006), 206. This commentary has an excellent survey of the discrepancies between the MT and the LXX, as well as the those between the LXX and the letter of Hebrews. However, quite extraordinarily, he fails to note any significance in the MT's singular "law" and the LXX's plural "laws."

6. Stern, "Hebrews," Heb. 8:6.

7. Ibid., Heb. 8:6.

8. *Yemenite Midrash* 349–50, as quoted by Raphael Patai, *The Messiah Texts* (Detroit: Wayne State University Press, 1988), 256–57.

9. *Genesis Rabbah* 98:9, as quoted by Patai, *Messiah Texts*, 250.

10. Patai, *Messiah Texts*, 248.

11. As quoted in ibid., 247.

Chapter 10–Superiority of the Messiah's Priestly Service

1. Depending on the uncertain weight of a talent, circa the fifteenth century BC.

2. Assuming a cubit length of eighteen inches.

3. See previous note.

4. Mishnah, *Yoma* 1:1–7.

5. Ibid., 6:4.

Chapter 11–Superiority of the Messiah's Sacrifice

1. Arnold G. Fruchtenbaum, "Hebrews," in *The Messianic Jewish Epistles: Hebrews, James, First Peter, Second Peter, Jude* (Tustin, CA: Ariel, 2005), 119.

2. For a discussion of various deficient, alternative understandings vis à vis the blood of Christ, see Philip Edgcumbe Hughes, "The Blood of Jesus and His Heavenly Priesthood in Hebrews, Part I: The Significance of the Blood of Jesus," *Bibliotheca Sacra* 130, no. 518 (April 1973).

3. Apparently the red heifer captured the imagination of some within the early church as well. Jesus is the red heifer's typological fulfillment, according to the early second century's *Epistle of Barnabas* (8:1–6).

4. Mishnah, *Parah*, 3:11.

5. Ibid., 3:6.

6. Ibid., 3:5.

7. Ibid., 3:2–3.

8. Maimonides, *Yad-HaChazakah* 1, *Halakhah* 4, as quoted in David H. Stern, "Hebrews," *Jewish New Testament Commentary: A Companion Volume to the Jewish New Testament* (Clarksville, MD: Jewish New Testament Publications, 1992), Heb. 9:13.

9. Maimonides, *Sepher Tohoroth*, as quoted by F. F. Bruce, *The Epistle to the Hebrews* (Grand Rapids: Eerdmans, 1990), 216n90.

10. William L. Lane, *Hebrews 9–13*, Word Biblical Commentary (Dallas: Word, 2002), 240.

11. Bruce, *Hebrews*, 224.

12. Johnson, 242.

13. Bruce, *Hebrews*, 228–29.

14. Philip Edgcumbe Hughes, "The Blood of Jesus and His Heavenly Priesthood in Hebrews, Part III: The Meaning of 'The True Tent' and 'The Greater and More Perfect Tent'" *Bibliotheca Sacra* 130, no. 520 (October 1973): 311.

15. Fruchtenbaum, "Hebrews," 126.

16. Lane, *Hebrews 9–13*, 249.

17. "It is wrong and inconsistent to postulate or suggest the existence of such an altar in the sanctuary above," as per Philip Edgcumbe Hughes, "The Blood of Jesus and His Heavenly Priesthood in Hebrews, Part II: The High-Priestly Sacrifice of Christ," *Bibliotheca Sacra* 130, no. 519 (July 1973): 208.

18. Fruchtenbaum, "Hebrews," 128.

Chapter 12—Sufficiency of the Messiah's Sacrifice

1. F. F. Bruce, *The Epistle to the Hebrews* (Grand Rapids: Eerdmans, 1990), 238.

2. Peruse Kaiser's careful discussion of Hebrews' argument here, in Walter C. Kaiser Jr., *The Uses of the Old Testament in the New* (Chicago: Moody, 1985), 138–41.

3. Karen H. Jobes, "The Function of Paronomasia in Hebrews 10:5–7," *Trinity Journal* 13, no. 2 (Fall 1992): 184–85.

4. Paul Ellingworth, *The Epistle to the Hebrews: A Commentary on the Greek Text* (Grand Rapids: Eerdmans; Carlisle: Paternoster, 1993), 504.

5. F. F. Bruce, *The Epistle to the Hebrews* (Grand Rapids: Eerdmans, 1990), 243.

6. Everett F. Harrison, "The Attitude of the Primitive Church toward Judaism," *Bibliotheca Sacra*, 113, no. 450 (April 1956): 130ff.

Chapter 13—Exhortation to a Lifestyle of Faith

1. Arnold G. Fruchtenbaum, "Hebrews," in *The Messianic Jewish Epistles: Hebrews, James, First Peter, Second Peter, Jude* (Tustin, CA: Ariel, 2005), 138.

2. F. F. Bruce, *The Epistle to the Hebrews* (Grand Rapids: Eerdmans, 1990), 251.

3. Rodney J. Decker, "The Exhortations of Hebrews 10:19–25," *Journal of Ministry and Theology* 6, no. 1 (Spring 2002), 59–60.

4. William L. Lane, *Hebrews 9–13*, Word Biblical Commentary (Dallas: Word, 2002), 292.

5. Thomas Kem Oberholtzer, "The Warning Passages in Hebrews Part 4: The Danger of Willful Sin in Hebrews 10:26–39," *Bibliotheca Sacra* 145, no. 580 (October 1988): 413.

6. John Niemela, "No More Sacrifice, Part 2 of 2," *Chafer Theological Seminary Journal* 5, no. 1 (January 1999): 40. I had completely missed this point in my translation work, which just demonstrates how familiar Bible verses from a preferred translation tend to lodge firmly in one's head and can present an obstacle to seeing the text in a completely fresh fashion.

7. Stanley D. Toussaint, "The Eschatology of the Warning Passages in the Book of Hebrews," *Grace Theological Journal* 3, no. 1 (Spring 1982): 77, as an example.

8. Gleason, "A Moderate Reformed View" 364.

9. Josephus is the textbook example. See Josephus, *Jewish Wars* 6.420.

10. Ibid., preface 1.6.

11. Spiros Zodhiates, *The Complete Word Study Dictionary: New Testament*, electronic ed. (Chattanooga: AMG, 2000), G5098.

12. Oberholtzer, "Warning Passages in Hebrews Part 4," 416.

13. Lane, *Hebrews 9–13*, 280.

14. See Background of Hebrews, n. 1, above, on the vocabulary of Hebrews.

15. Oberholtzer notes that Hatch and Redpath's *A Concordance to the Septuagint* (vol. 1, Grand Rapids: Baker, 1987) cites 111 uses of *apoleia* in the Septuagint, as a translation of 21 Hebrew words, including desolation (Ezek. 32:15) and physical death (Esth. 7:4). Oberholtzer, "Warning Passages in Hebrews Part 4," 418. It is therefore unnecessary to view the usage of *apoleia* as the final destruction of apostates, contra Toussaint, "Eschatology of the Warning Passages," 78.

Chapter 14—Evidence of the Lifestyle of Faith

1. William L. Lane, *Hebrews 9–13*, Word Biblical Commentary (Dallas: Word, 2002), 316.

2. Sirach 44:1.

3. 1 Maccabees 2:51ff.

4. Raphael Patai, *The Messiah Texts* (Detroit: Wayne State University Press, 1988), 23.

5. Richard N. Longenecker, "The 'Faith of Abraham' Theme in Paul, James and Hebrews: A Study in the Circumstantial Nature of New Testament Teaching," *Journal of the Evangelical Theological Society* 20, no. 3 (September 1977): 208.

6. F. F. Bruce, *The Epistle to the Hebrews* (Grand Rapids: Eerdmans, 1990), 292.

7. Longenecker, "The 'Faith of Abraham' Theme," 209–10.

8. Michael L. Brown, Answering Jewish Objections to Jesus, Volume 2: Theological Objections (Grand Rapids: Baker, 2000), 159.

9. Louis Jacobs, "Akedah," *Encyclopedia Judaica* (Jerusalem: Keter, 1992), 2:482.

10. Lane, *Hebrews 9–13*, 375.

11. Ibid., 382. Lane provides an example from Josephus, *Antiquities of the Jews* 20.256.

12. Ibid., 383.

13. Bruce, *Hebrews*, 320, is one example.

14. Lane, *Hebrews 9–13*, 384.

15. Ibid., 388.

16. Josephus, *Antiquities of the Jews* 20.200.

17. Babylonian Talmud, *Yebamoth* 49b; *Sanhedrin* 103b; also the pseudepigraphal *Ascension of Isaiah* 5:1–14 and Louis Ginzberg, Henrietta Szold, and Paul Radin, *Legends of the Jews*, 2nd ed. (Philadelphia: Jewish Publication Society, 2003), 1055.

18. Lane, *Hebrews 9–13*, 395.

Chapter 15—The Enduring Lifestyle of Faith

1. F. F. Bruce, *The Epistle to the Hebrews* (Grand Rapids: Eerdmans, 1990), 333.

2. Arnold G. Fruchtenbaum, "Hebrews," in The Messianic Jewish Epistles: Hebrews, James, First Peter, Second Peter, Jude (Tustin, CA: Ariel, 2005), 169.

3. Frederic R. Howe, "The Challenge for Spiritual Vision: An Exegesis of Hebrews 12:1-3," *Journal of the Grace Evangelical Society* 13, no. 1 (Spring 2000): 30.

4. Ibid., 33.

5. Bruce, *Hebrews*, 338.

6. William L. Lane, *Hebrews 9–13*, Word Biblical Commentary (Dallas: Word, 2002), 420.

7. Ibid., 423.

8. Fruchtenbaum, "Hebrews," 174.

9. Louis Ginzberg, Henrietta Szold, and Paul Radin, *Legends of the Jews*, 2nd ed. (Philadelphia: Jewish Publication Society, 2003), 268–70.

10. Bruce, *Hebrews*, 364.

11. Lane, *Hebrews 9–13*, 486.

Chapter 16—Concluding Exhortations

1. Some have made too much of this seeming awkwardness, theorizing that this chapter is a later addition to the remainder of the text. This sort of speculative "scholarship" is the equivalent of a group of chattering teenage girls squealing with delight as they stand in front of their lockers, avidly anticipating their snarky dissemination of the latest unsubstantiated gossip and rumor.

2. William L. Lane, *Hebrews 9–13*, Word Biblical Commentary (Dallas: Word, 2002), 510.

3. Didache 11:4–6, as related in F. F. Bruce, *The Epistle to the Hebrews* (Grand Rapids: Eerdmans, 1990), 371.

4. Lane, *Hebrews 9–13*, 518.

5. Ibid., 533.

6. Arnold G. Fruchtenbaum, "Hebrews," in The Messianic Jewish Epistles: Hebrews, James, First Peter, Second Peter, Jude (Tustin, CA: Ariel, 2005), 194.

7. As Jesus said, "For to whom much is given, much is required" (Luke 12:48), or as the great Jewish philosopher Stan Lee wrote, "With great power comes great responsibility."

8. See Background of Hebrews, n. 5, above.

9. Lane, *Hebrews 9–13*, 568.

10. See Background of Hebrews, n. 24, above.

Appendix A—Use of the Old Testament in Hebrews

1. William L. Lane, *Hebrews 1–8*, Word Biblical Commentary (Dallas: Word, 2002), cxiv.

2. Ibid., cxvi.

Appendix B—The Theology of Hebrews

1. William L. Lane, Hebrews 1–8, Word Biblical Commentary (Dallas: Word, 2002), cxxxviii.

2. Scot McKnight, "The Warning Passages of Hebrews: A Formal Analysis and Theological Conclusions," Trinity Journal 13, no. 1 (Spring 1992): 56.

About the Author

Steven Ger grew up in a Jewish family in New York and New Jersey, where he was educated in both church and synagogue due to his distinctive heritage as a Jewish Christian. He is the founder and director of Sojourner Ministries, an organization dedicated to exploring the Jewish heart of Christianity with both Jews and Gentiles. The name of the ministry is derived from the Hebrew meaning of Steven's surname. In Hebrew, the word "ger" means sojourner or wanderer. This particular "wandering" Jew's faith journey has led him to the conviction that Jesus is the Messiah who was foretold in the Hebrew Scriptures. Steven's life is dedicated to helping people see their Messiah more clearly—through Hebrew eyes.

Steven has led eleven tours to Israel, with extensions to Egypt, Greece, Jordan, Turkey and Germany. He has lectured at Dallas Theological Seminary and at Tyndale Seminary. He earned a BA in psychology and interpersonal communications from Trenton State College and a ThM from Dallas Theological Seminary. Steven is the author of *Acts: Witnesses to the World* and coauthor of *The Popular Bible Prophecy Commentary* and lives in the Dallas area with his wife, Adria, and their son, Jonathan Gabriel.

About the General Editors

Mal Couch is founder and president of Tyndale Theological Seminary and Biblical Institute in Fort Worth, Texas. He previously taught at Philadelphia College of the Bible, Moody Bible Institute, and Dallas Theological Seminary. His other publications include The Hope of Christ's Return: A Premillennial Commentary on 1 and 2 Thessalonians, A Bible Handbook to Revelation, and Dictionary of Premillennial Theology.

Edward Hindson is professor of religion, dean of the Institute of Biblical Studies, and assistant to the chancellor at Liberty University in Lynchburg, Virginia. He has authored more than twenty books, served as coeditor of several Bible projects, and was one of the translators for the New King James Version of the Bible. Dr. Hindson has served as a visiting lecturer at Oxford University and Harvard Divinity School as well as numerous evangelical seminaries. He has taught more than fifty thousand students in the past twenty-five years.

Made in the USA
Middletown, DE
21 March 2024

51343627R00166